P9-CCG-245

American Patriotism, American Protest

American Patriotism, American Protest

Social Movements Since the Sixties

Simon Hall

PENN

UNIVERSITY OF PENNSYLVANIA PRESS

PHILADELPHIA · OXFORD

Copyright © 2011 University of Pennsylvania Press

All rights reserved. Except for brief quotations used for purposes
of review or scholarly citation, none of this book may be reproduced
in any form by any means without written permission from the publisher.

Published by
University of Pennsylvania Press
Philadelphia, Pennsylvania 19104-4112
www.upenn.edu/pennpress

Printed in the United States of America on acid-free paper
10 9 8 7 6 5 4 3 2 1

Library of Congress Cataloging-in-Publication Data

Hall, Simon, 1976–
    American patriotism,, American protest : social movements since the sixties / Simon Hall.
        p.   cm.
    ISBN: 978-0-8122-4295-9 (hardcover : alk. paper)
    Includes bibliographical references and index.
    1. Subjects: Social movements—United States—History—20th century. 2. Patriotism—United
States—History—20th century. 3. Protest movements—United States—History—20th century. 4.
United States—Social conditions—1960–1980. 5. United States—Social conditions—1980– I. Title
HN59.H235   2010
303.48/4097309045—dc22   2010016971

To the memory of Tom Riley (1974–2007)

Contents

On Sunday 11 October 1987, more than 200,000 protesters gathered in Washington, D.C., for a national march for lesbian and gay rights. The day began with the unveiling on the Mall of the AIDS memorial quilt. Containing 1,920 three foot by six foot panels made by the lovers, friends, and families of those lost to the epidemic, the quilt (which by 2010 had grown to more than 40,000 panels) was a powerful and moving tribute. One newspaper report noted that as the pieces were "unfurled and hooked together" the "early morning quiet" was "punctured" by the "sound of sobs" and the reading aloud of the names of those who had died. The march itself, which began at 1 p.m., was a festive and colorful affair: scores of gay couples exchanged vows during a mass wedding and the crowd was adorned with banners, placards, flags, and balloons. Throughout the day, lesbians and gay men were urged to demand with pride their rights as American citizens. John Bush, a long-time activist, told the crowd that "All men are created equal. And we have to stand up and say, 'We're gay and we're here'," while San Francisco supervisor Harry Britt recalled his slain predecessor Harvey Milk's desire for "us to associate ourselves in a powerful way with the symbols of this country." In his keynote speech Rev. Jesse Jackson explained that the marchers had gathered to "insist on equal protection under the law for every American." With protesters singing "We Shall Overcome" and Jackson taking a high-profile role, comparisons with the civil rights movement were perhaps inevitable; certainly many demonstrators claimed inspiration from the August 1963 March on Washington.[1] Two days later more than two thousand gay men and women gathered outside the Supreme Court to protest its controversial 1986 decision to uphold a Georgia sodomy law. At about 9 a.m. activists, "moving intermittently in groups of 15 to 30," began to walk past the police barricades and toward the court, where they sat "in circles on the plaza of the building" before being handcuffed and taken away. While most walked calmly to waiting buses, some had to be "dragged across the plaza." When the demonstration ended at 2 p.m. more than 600 had been arrested, making it the "largest mass arrest at the Court since May Day in 1971, when 7,000 anti-war protesters were detained."[2] With its staging of colorful mass protest, deployment of civil disobedience, and recourse to the language of rights, the gay rights activism of October 1987 showed that the spirit of the 1960s was very much alive in Ronald Reagan's America.

Interviewed in *Newsweek* in the summer of 1970, Columbia historian Richard Hofstadter quipped that, were he to write a book chapter on the 1960s, he would entitle it "The Age of Rubbish." Looking back a half-century later at some of the less appealing features of that decade—the countercultural excess, the revolutionary posturing, and the violence—one might be tempted to agree. Certainly many commentators and former radical activists struggled at times to identify any real achievements: after all, neither participatory democracy nor leftist revolution came to America.[3] Two years after the presidential campaigns of Eugene McCarthy and Robert Kennedy, and the uprisings in Paris and on the campus of Columbia University, historian and critic Christopher Lasch cast his eye over what he called the "wreckage of the sixties" and found himself "amazed at how little has been accomplished." "Nothing," he declared, "has changed."[4] As the New Left disintegrated in a haze of marijuana smoke and internecine squabbling, former Students for a Democratic Society president Carl Oglesby voiced his own sense of despair in the pages of *Liberation* magazine; his article was entitled "Notes on a Decade Ready for the Dustbin."[5]

Forty years later, whatever one's views on the merits of the Age of Aquarius, it would be hard to argue that the Sixties were unimportant. During the last third of the twentieth century many progressives worked to preserve and extend the gains made during the 1960s, while conservatives often defined themselves in opposition to that decade's liberal politics and challenges to traditional authority.[6] When it comes to contemporary arguments around issues of minority rights and affirmative action, the desirability of welfare programs and "big government," or cultural permissiveness and gender equality, the Sixties cast a long shadow. As historian Alexander Bloom has pointed out, at the start of the third millennium Americans were "still debating issues that emerged during" the 1960s, and "still living in the conscious aftermath of its events and transformations," while, for many, political identity was shaped strongly by attitudes toward the 1960s.[7] As President Clinton explained it in 2004, "If you look back on the Sixties and think that there was more good than bad, you're probably a Democrat. If you think there was more harm than good, you're probably a Republican."[8] In short, late twentieth-century America was "a world the Sixties made."[9]

For many scholars the end of the Sixties marks a turning point in modern American political history: the moment when a resurgent conservatism put an end to an era of liberal hegemony.[10] Although Lyndon Johnson's landslide election victory of 1964 seemed to show liberalism to be in robust health, just a few years later it all looked very different, as discord at home and apparent frailty abroad served to shatter the postwar liberal consensus. In 1968 Richard Nixon had appealed to the "forgotten Americans," the "non-shouters, the non-demonstrators . . . those who do not break the law, people who pay their taxes and go to work, who send their children to school, who go to their churches," and who loved their country. Increasingly, they tired of America's inability (or seeming unwillingness) to win the war in Southeast Asia and were appalled by urban race riots, student protest, the counterculture, an activist Supreme Court, and government welfare largesse.[11] The growing mood of resentment among lower-middle- and working-class white and white ethnic Americans to what the 1960s seemed to represent is encapsulated in a letter from Curt Furr, a white North Carolinian and father of five, to Democratic senator Sam J. Ervin, on 18 June 1968:

> I'm sick of crime everywhere. I'm sick of riots. I'm sick of "poor" people demonstrations (black, white, red, yellow, purple, green or any other color!). . . . I'm sick of the U.S. Supreme Court ruling for the good of a very small part rather than the whole of our society. . . . I'm sick of the lack of law enforcemen. . . . I'm sick of Vietnam. . . . I'm sick of hippies, LSD, drugs, and all the promotion the news media give them. . . . But most of all, I'm sick of constantly being kicked in the teeth for staying home, minding my own business, working steadily, paying my bills and taxes, raising my children to be decent citizens, managing my financial affairs so I will not become a ward of the City, County, or State, and footing the bill for all the minuses mentioned herein.[12]

In part because they were able to tap into such sentiment so effectively (in the process handily blaming liberal Democrats for the nation's ills), the Republicans won five of the six presidential elections between 1968 and Bill Clinton's triumph in 1992 (the exception was the post-Watergate contest of 1976) as large numbers of blue collar ethnic and middle-class suburban white voters abandoned the Democratic Party. With the victory of Ronald Reagan *and* the Republican capture of the Senate in 1980, the political realignment begun during the second half of the 1960s seemed complete. Yet many conservatives were left unsatisfied by the Nixon and Reagan administrations. Pat Buchanan, who served as an aide in the Nixon White House, complained that "vigorously did we inveigh against the Great Society . . . enthusiastically did we fund it." He had a point: social security and welfare payments doubled during Nixon's tenure, and some have gone so far as to suggest that the 37th president was a liberal when it came to domestic policy.[13] Historians and conservative activists, meanwhile, seem to agree that in many respects there was no "Reagan Revolution." Key social welfare programs, especially those popular with middle-class voters (such as Medicare), saw their funding increase, government continued to grow, and the social agenda of the religious right remained unfulfilled. As the New Right's Ralph Reed put it, "the evangelicals were taken to the cleaners. They helped Reagan to get elected; then he took no notice of them."[14]

This book examines the dramatic changes that have taken place in American political culture since the 1960s by focusing on social protest movements: the gay rights movement, second-wave feminism, the anti-busing protests of the mid-1970s, the tax revolt, and the anti-abortion struggle. In moving away from a "top-down" focus on presidents and public policy and the well-worn terrain of malaise, stagflation, Reaganomics, and triangulation, *American Patriotism, American Protest* casts social movements and the ordinary people who created and sustained them—housewives, welfare mothers, small businessmen, evangelical Christians, students—as key political actors. Fascinating in their own right, these movements did not just voice the concerns of diverse groups of Americans—they were also of critical importance in driving policy, shaping the character of the Democratic and Republican parties, and altering the nation's political landscape.[15]

The importance of the 1960s does not lie simply in its generation of divisive new issues and shaping of subsequent political debate; the decade was also the progenitor of a host of social movements that came to prominence after Nixon's election. Just as the activists of the 1960s were shaped by their radical predecessors—illustrated, for instance, by the important influence on the civil rights, New Left, and anti-Vietnam War movements of "Old Left" luminaries (such as Anne Braden and A. J. Muste), institutions (notably the Highlander Folk School), and organizations (including the Socialist Workers Party)—so too did protesters during the 1970s and beyond draw on a complex legacy bequeathed by the New Left and its allies.[16] Indeed, for Americans of varying political persuasions the 1960s provided a model for, and justification of, protest. It is striking that conservative as well as progressive activists took inspiration and claimed legitimacy from 1960s social movements—particularly the civil rights and antiwar struggles—when deploying direct action tactics (marches, sit-ins, and boycotts), engaging in civil disobedience, adopting street theater, and invoking the language of "rights."[17]

Conservatives also followed the New Left in breaking down divisions between the "public" and "private" spheres, by organizing around issues such as schooling and birth control and arguing that the "personal was political."[18] Moreover, conservatives promoted grassroots organizing, a favored tactic of the New Left, with relish, and they used the language of participatory democracy in attacking "big government" and the power of (liberal) elites.[19] Historians have long recognized the importance of the civil rights, New Left, and anti-Vietnam War struggles to subsequent progressive movements for social change, particularly the gay rights movement and second wave feminism. More recently, scholars have begun to pay some attention to Sixties movements' influence on conservative activism during the 1970s and 1980s.[20] This book builds on this work to show how gay rights protesters, second-wave feminists, opponents of busing, property tax protesters, and anti-abortion activists can all be considered "children of the Sixties."

Focusing on this broader legacy of protest challenges the dominant school of Sixties historiography—the "rise and fall" thesis.[21] In this conceptual framework the decade began amid high hopes and idealism—symbolized by John F. Kennedy's New Frontier, Martin Luther King's dream, and the SDS Port Huron Statement. Then the radicalizing crucible of the war in Vietnam produced bitterness and disillusion: Robert Kennedy's assassination and the police riot at the Chicago convention in 1968 caused the Democratic Party to fracture; King's "dream" was replaced by urban riots and calls for Black Power; and with SDS consumed by factionalism and nihilistic rage, the terrorist Weather Underground emerged.[22]

While useful, this narrative has had a distorting effect on how the 1960s has been viewed. First, it privileges the story of national organizations, especially SDS and the Student Nonviolent Coordinating Committee (SNCC), at the expense of other organizations and movements, particularly those working at the local level.[23] Second, it associates later struggles, most notably those for women's rights and gay rights, with the "bad 1960s" story of decline and failure.[24] It also, of course, casts Sixties activism as almost entirely the preserve of the left, thereby ignoring the important story of conservative organizing.[25]

If one theme of this book is how, during the last third of the twentieth century, both progressive and conservative activists constructed social movements that drew from the wellsprings of Sixties protest, its second major focus is on the ways these movements sought to invoke the nation's founding ideals in service to their respective, if very different, causes. While John Winthrop's exhortation to his fellow pilgrims in 1630 to "be as a city upon a hill" first articulated the notion of America as an idea, it was the nation's revolutionary birth that provided it with what might be described as a national creed.[26] Rooted in the Declaration of Independence and the Bill of Rights, the ideals of self-government, liberty, equality, and justice lie at the heart of American national identity.[27] Given the ideological diversity among the founding fathers themselves, it is not surprising that the precise nature of this national creed has always been fiercely contested.[28] In some respects the long and continuing debate over just what Americanism actually is has characterized the Republic as much as the existence of the creed itself; and Americanism's malleability has enabled it to be claimed by forces from across the political spectrum. During the past 200 years it has been invoked by abolitionists, pro-slavery defenders, trades union organizers, corporate titans, champions (and opponents) of imperial expansion and crusaders for women's rights, among others.[29]

On the left, appeals rooted in Americanism have proved an effective means of generating tangible pressure for social and political change. During the mid-1930s, for example, as part of its commitment to the Popular Front strategy of forging alliances with socialists, trades unionists, and progressives, the American Communist Party (CPUSA) sought to ground itself firmly within the nation's democratic traditions. As part of this approach, which ultimately helped to boost its popularity and influence, the writings of Thomas Jefferson and Abraham Lincoln were emphasized over those of Marx and Lenin, and the American flag could often be seen on prominent display at CPUSA meetings. In 1936 the party's presidential candidate, Earl Browder, famously claimed that "Communism is 20th Century Americanism." Browder also portrayed Communists as "the most consistent fighters for . . . the enforcement of the democratic features of our Constitution, for the defense of the flag and the revival of its glorious revolutionary traditions."[30] In the early 1960s, SNCC activists pledged their "devotion to our homeland," affirmed the "tenets of American democracy as set forth in the Constitution," and sought to "revitalize the great American dream of 'liberty and justice for all'" as part of their efforts to secure first-class citizenship rights for African Americans.[31]

For some commentators, though, the 1960s stand as a watershed: a moment when many on the left, fueled largely by bitterness and despair over America's war in Vietnam, abandoned an Americanism that they viewed as inherently flawed by sexism, racism, militarism and capitalist excess. In its place they extolled ethnic and sexual difference and embraced a rhetorical anti-Americanism—symbolized by the tendency of many radicals in the late 1960s to refer to "Amerika."[32] One result, it is said, was that progressives disconnected themselves from the nation at large, and "lost the ability to pose convincing alternatives for the nation as a whole."[33] However, an examination of the gay rights movement and second-wave feminism, at both the national and the local level, challenges this thesis. As we shall see, appeals to the Declaration of Independence, the Bill of Rights, and "American" ideals of liberty, justice, and equality were made forcefully by gay rights activists and feminists during the 1970s and beyond. Patriotic protest, then, remained important to social movements on the left. Conservatives too have used the language of rights and the American Dream's emphasis on liberty and individualism to legitimize and promote their own agenda.[34] Like their activist counterparts on the left, participants in the anti-busing movement, the tax revolt, and the campaign against abortion rights have waved the American flag, invoked the words of the Declaration of Independence, and claimed the support of the nation's founders.[35]

As well as being deployed in the service of a range of very different, at times even opposing, causes since the 1960s, patriotic protest has also been constructed in a number of different ways. While the Black Panthers emphasized the Declaration of Independence's justification of the right to overthrow despotic government, anti-busing and tax protesters preferred instead to highlight the Founders' fears of a strong centralized government; and whereas gay rights activists focused on the right to the "pursuit of happiness," those opposed to abortion stressed the Declaration of Independence's guarantee of the "right to life." Generally, progressives have sought to narrow the gap between America's lofty promise of liberty and justice for all and the actual experience of oppressed or marginalized groups. Conservatives, in contrast, have tended to emphasize the nation's traditional values (rooted in Judeo-Christian morality), recall the early history of rural and small-town America, and celebrate the Republic's historic achievements.[36]

In recent years it has become a favored lament of the American historical profession that the nation's history has become "fragmented." The stunning rise of the new social history, the influence of "identity politics" (with the notion that each group is uniquely able to access and write its own, "authentic" history), and growing specialization have led many to despair that a coherent, cogent, and readable narrative could ever be assembled out of what at times seems to be an alarming amount of disparate and opaque scholarship. It has also led to concerns that, despite Americans' apparently insatiable appetite for history, the academy has become increasingly disconnected from the public. Thomas Bender, for instance, worried about the division of American history into a series of "highly cultivated" subfields, "each studied in its own terms, each with its own scholarly network and discourse."[37] How, he wondered, might one "turn a vast supply of fine studies of parts . . . into a sense of the whole?"[38]

In an August 2000 opinion piece for the *New York Times,* David Oshinsky asked whether the "Humpty Dumpty" of American historical scholarship could be put back together.[39] By bringing together a number of social movements that historians have typically studied in isolation from one another, *American Patriotism, American Protest* attempts to bridge some of the segmentations—between political and social history, histories of radicalism and conservatism, and national and local studies, for example—that have characterized recent historical writing on postwar America.[40]

In emphasizing the shared experiences, tactics, and language of groups of activists who are often seen (and who often viewed each other) as opponents, there is a danger of "soften[ing] the outlines and flatten[ing] the crises of American history."[41] Reflecting on the consensus history with which he was often associated, Richard Hofstadter wrote that "an obsessive fixation on the elements of consensus that do undoubtedly exist strips the story of the drama and the interest it has."[42] In the pages that follow I hope that the reader will find not just a convincing analysis of some of the major forces that have transformed America's political landscape since the end of the 1960s, but also plenty of entertaining historical drama: Boston housewives, with tri-cornered hats and American flags, marching in the streets to protest busing; seniors in northern California burning their tax notices and Angelenos holding candle-lit vigils to protest high property tax bills; women throwing high-heeled shoes into a "Freedom Trash Can," holding consciousness-raising sessions, and seeking a "more perfect union" through ratification of the Equal Rights Amendment; gay college students dressing up as the Statue of Liberty and demanding their rights; and anti-abortion protesters singing "We Shall Overcome." *American Patriotism, American Protest* is, in essence, the story of countless ordinary people doing extraordinary things who, inspired by the activist outpouring of the 1960s and the promise of American freedom, sought to remake their nation.

Chapter 1

Patriotism, Protest, and the 1960s

Amid the dramatic protests and social activism of the 1960s the civil rights movement stands out for its commitment to, and enthusiasm for, patriotic protest. Indeed, black leaders sought consistently to fuse respectable tactics—such as dressing smartly, behaving peacefully, and maintaining dignity even in the face of white supremacist provocation and violence—with appeals to Americanism. In short, they presented their struggle as one that was working for the fulfillment of America's own democratic promise.[1] As Marisa Chappell, Jenny Hutchinson, and Brian Ward have argued, "a careful adherence to responsible tactics like nonviolence, coupled with the promotion of eminently respectable public leaders espousing perfectly respectable American ideals in pursuit of quintessentially American democratic goals, helped to create the powerful sense of moral rectitude which was one of the early movement's most effective weapons."[2]

Within the movement the Rev. Dr. Martin Luther King, Jr., was particularly skilled at exploiting the gap between America's democratic ideal and the reality of segregation and racism to generate powerful leverage for change; indeed, from the very beginning of his career as a civil rights leader King sought to associate blacks' demands for freedom, equality and respect with the nation's founding principles. In his first major speech, delivered at a mass meeting of the Montgomery Improvement Association on 5 December 1955, King explained that the "great glory of American democracy" was the "right to protest." He went on to declare that "we are not wrong in what we are doing . . . .If we are wrong, the Constitution of the United States is wrong."[3] Of the student sit-ins that took place in spring 1960, King asserted that "in sitting down at lunch-counters, [the students] are in reality standing up for the best of the American Dream." In June, 1961, he told an audience at Lincoln University, Pennsylvania, that "in a sense, America is essentially a dream, a dream as yet unfulfilled. It is a dream of a land where men of all races, of all nationalities and creeds can live together as brothers."[4] Dr. King's most famous speech, delivered on 28 August 1963 at the March on Washington for Jobs and Freedom, was a forceful example of the civil rights movement's use of patriotic protest. Standing on the steps of the Lincoln Memorial on the National Mall—the symbolic heart of the nation—King explained that "When the architects of our republic wrote the magnificent words of the Constitution and the Declaration of Independence, they were signing a promissory note to which every American was to fall heir. This note was a promise that all men, yes, black men as well as white men, would be guaranteed the unalienable rights of life, liberty, and the pursuit of happiness." For black Americans, King declared, the time for making good that promise was long overdue. Then, in the "I have a dream' peroration, King outlined his vision of a nation free from racial discrimination and bigotry—a vision, he emphasized, that was "deeply rooted in the American dream." Supporters of black rights were simply calling on America to "rise up and live out the true meaning of its creed: We hold these truths to be self-evident that all men are created equal."[5] The civil rights movement's articulation of Americanism was made all the more compelling given the nation's leadership of the free world in the struggle against Communist totalitarianism. Civil rights activists knew that the existence of Jim Crow segregation and the systematic denial of the vote to black southerners was an international embarrassment to the United States and a source of propaganda for the Soviet Union.[6] As well as carrying American flags that summer's day in Washington, protesters also held placards that read "FREEDOM IS ON TRIAL IN AMERICA TODAY" and "AMERICAN DEMOCRACY IS ON TRIAL IN THE EYES OF THE WORLD."[7] The *New York Times* was just one of those to emphasize the march's patriotic flavour, with liberal columnist James Reston saluting the civil rights movement's ability to "invoke the principles of the founding fathers to rebuke the inequalities and hypocrisies of modern American life."[8]

King was not alone in seeking to use patriotic protest to aide the cause of black equality. In July 1960, for instance, the Student Nonviolent Coordinating Committee (SNCC) demanded that black Americans be allowed to enjoy the "full promise of our democratic heritage—first class citizenship."[9] Although SNCC chairman John Lewis's speech at the March on Washington contained some harsh words about America, he appealed to the nation's values nevertheless, calling on America to "wake up" to the problem of racial injustice and help insure that "freedom and justice" was a reality for "*all the people.*" He also accused both the Democratic and Republican parties of "betray[ing] the basic principles of the Declaration of Independence" by refusing to move quickly and decisively to eradicate institutionalized white supremacy.[10] A year later, in her eloquent testimony before the Credentials Committee at the Democratic Party national convention in Atlantic City, Mississippi sharecropper and civil rights activist Fannie Lou Hamer explained how in 1962, after attempting to register to vote, she had been thrown off the plantation where she had lived her whole life. Her commitment to the civil rights movement had also resulted in arrest by the Mississippi State Highway Patrol and a brutal beating with blackjacks in the County Jail. The forty-four-year-old Hamer was in Atlantic City to demand that the Mississippi Freedom Democratic Party, of which she was vice-chair, be recognized as the official state delegation in place of the racist lily-white state "regulars." At the end of her testimony, Hamer declared that "if the Freedom Democratic Party is not seated now, I question America, is this America, the land of the free and the home of the brave where we have to sleep with our telephones off of the hooks because our lives be threatened daily because we want to live as decent human beings, in America?"[11] The NAACP too viewed the fight for civil rights as, at least in part, a patriotic struggle. In the words of its executive secretary Roy Wilkins, the "fundamental principle" of the Association was to work for the "full participation of Negro Americans, without discrimination, in all phases of American life."[12] On the eve of his retirement after a 45-year career in the civil rights struggle, Wilkins explained that the NAACP's whole approach was rooted in the belief that "Black people want an end to discrimination and the right to be treated like any other man. It says in the Declaration of Independence, and we believe, that all men are created equal—that government is instituted among men by the consent of the governed." "This," said Wilkins, "is what we believe. It may be foolish, but . . . until somebody comes along who has a better idea, we'll stick with this."[13]

Although it featured less prominently, patriotic appeals featured in the rhetoric used by the early New Left and antiwar movements. The authors of the Port Huron Statement, for example, expressed their support for the "American values" of "Freedom and equality for each individual, government of, by, and for the people." Increasingly, however, they had begun to see "complicated and disturbing paradoxes" in the way that American society functioned—"The declaration 'all men are created equal . . .' rang hollow before the facts of Negro life in the South and the big cities of the North" while the "proclaimed peaceful intentions of the United States contradicted its economic and military investments in the Cold War status quo." Their conclusion: the nation's democratic system, intended to be "'of, by and for the people'," had been rendered "apathetic and manipulated." The activists of SDS thus pledged themselves to re-energize American democracy and work to build a more equal and more just society.[14] Americanism's influence could be seen in tactics as well as language. Seeking to mobilize the poor and dispossessed into a movement for social change, SDS's Tom Hayden drew on the example of the American revolutionaries by raising the prospect that radicals might convene a new Continental Congress as a "kind of second government, receiving taxes from its supporters, establishing contact with other nations, holding debates on American foreign and domestic policy, dramatizing the plight of all groups that suffer from the American system."[15] Hayden's idea inspired Staughton Lynd, the New Left historian and activist, to organize the Assembly of Unrepresented People, a gathering of antiwar, anti-poverty, civil rights, and New Left activists in Washington in August 1965.[16]

Early opponents of the war in Vietnam also deployed the language of Americanism in calling for an end to America's military involvement in Southeast Asia.[17] On a chilly, overcast Saturday in November 1965, for example, some 30,000 people attended an anti-war rally in Washington. With the sun setting, SDS president Carl Oglesby—an intellectual, playwright, and thirty-two-year-old father of three—delivered a rousing speech that attacked American liberals' support for what he termed imperialism.[18] Oglesby asked what Thomas Jefferson or Thomas Paine— "who first made plain our nation's unprovisional commitment to human rights"—would say if they were to sit down with two of the major architects of America's war in Vietnam, President Lyndon Johnson and his national security adviser McGeorge Bundy:

> Our dead revolutionaries would soon wonder why their country was fighting against what appeared to be a revolution. The living liberals would hotly deny that it is one: there are troops coming in from outside, the rebels get arms from other countries, most of the people are not on their side, and they practice terror against their own. Therefore: *not* a revolution.

But, Oglesby said, what would the response of "our dead revolutionaries" be to such arguments?

> They might say: "What fools and bandits, sirs, you make then of us. Outside help? Do you remember Lafayette? Or the three thousand British freighters the French navy sank for our side? Or the arms and men we got from France and Spain? And what's this about terror? Did you never hear what we did to our own Loyalists? Or about the thousand of rich Tories who fled for their lives to Canada? And as for popular support, do you not know that we had less than one-third of our people with us? That, in fact, the colony of New York recruited more troops for the British than for the revolution? Should we give it all back?

Oglesby argued that those who sought to end the war in Vietnam, and create a more just, equitable and compassionate social and political order at home, were motivated in large part by "the vision that wise and brave men saw in the time of our own Revolution."[19] Similarly in 1966 the Washington Mobilization Committee to End the War in Vietnam issued a statement extolling the "brave words and ideals" of the Declaration of Independence and arguing that the nation's military involvement in Vietnam constituted a betrayal of its founding principles. "Patrick Henry said: 'Give me liberty or give me death!'," they explained, and while "Millions of oppressed people are saying the same thing today...the U.S. is giving them death!" Moreover, the Washington Mobe sought to portray their own opposition to the Vietnam War as an act of patriotism:

> Let us revive the patriotism of our fore-fathers . . . patriotism in a democracy consists of criticism of bad policy and making of good policy by the people themselves. Help the fight for democracy! Let us aid revolutionaries in an oppressive world.[20]

Martin Luther King, who became one of the fiercest critics of the war in Vietnam, also attacked the war on patriotic (as well as moral) grounds. In a blistering speech delivered in New York City's historic Riverside Church on 4 April 1967, King denounced the United States for presuming to know what was best for the Vietnamese, argued that the Americans had mistaken a national liberation struggle for a Communist insurgency, and described his own government as the "greatest purveyor of violence in the world today." King's message was blunt: if the war continued it would be clear that the United States had "no honourable intentions in Vietnam. It will become clear that our minimal expectation is to occupy it as an American colony." The preacher from Atlanta was roundly condemned: *Life* magazine described his speech as "a demagogic slander that sounded like a script for Radio Hanoi" while presidential aide John Roche told LBJ that King had "thrown in with the commies."[21] Despite criticisms that he was engaging in anti-American behavior, King had sought to explain his condemnation of the war by means of his love of America. King's speech was, in his own words, "a passionate plea to my beloved nation." The SCLC president also reminded those who questioned why a "civil rights" leader should presume to speak on issues of foreign policy that the motto of his organization was "To save the soul of America." "It should," said King, "be incandescently clear that no one who has any concern for the integrity and life of America today can ignore the present war." In fact, King continued, "If America's soul becomes totally poisoned, part of the autopsy must read 'Vietnam.' It can never be saved so long as it destroys the deepest hopes of men the world over."[22] The Riverside speech was not the first time that King had argued that the nation's foreign policy had become de-coupled from the essential tenets of Americanism. Condemning the "Bay of Pigs' invasion, in May 1961, he had argued that "For some reason, we just don't understand the meaning of the revolution taking place in the world. There is a revolt all over the world against colonialism, reactionary dictatorship, and systems of exploitation." King speculated that "unless we as a nation...go back to the revolutionary spirit that characterized the birth of our nation, I am afraid we will be relegated to a second-class power in the world with no real moral voice to speak to the conscience of humanity."[23]

The argument that America's actions in Vietnam contradicted her commitment to freedom, equality and liberty were also advanced powerfully by liberal Democratic Senators who opposed the war policies of first Lyndon Johnson and then Richard Nixon. Alaska's Ernest Gruening, one of only two senators to vote against the 1964 Gulf of Tonkin Resolution that authorized American military escalation in Vietnam, viewed the war as violating American ideals and "commitment to the principle of national self-determination." Similarly George McGovern believed that America's policy of supporting authoritarian regimes, such as the one in Saigon, embodied "everything that is alien to our tradition of liberty and equality." In opposing the war, McGovern urged America to return to "the ideals that nourished us in the beginning."[24]

During the second half of the 1960s, as the slow pace of progress on race relations and continuing escalation of the war in Vietnam led to growing bitterness and frustration among many on the left, strategies of patriotic protest increasingly gave way to rhetorical anti-Americanism and behavior that most ordinary Americans found distasteful. Some opponents of the war in Vietnam, for example, burned the American flag, waved the flag of the National Liberation Front, chanted "Ho Ho Ho Chi Minh, NLF is Gonna Win," and lashed out at "Amerika" (the "k" was to denote fascism). Sometimes public protests had a distinct anti-American tinge: in the spring of 1966, for example, folk singer Joan Baez appeared on a platform displaying a "Shame America" sign, with red, white and blue "bombs" falling on a nude mother and two young children.[25] A minority of activists engaged in violence—destroying property, engaging in confrontations with the police, burning down buildings, and planting bombs. Some even spoke of wanting to "destroy America."[26] There was a striking change within the black freedom struggle too, as Black Power leaders and organizations emphasizing racial pride, separatism and armed struggle eclipsed established organizations that had been committed, in public at least, to nonviolence and integration. The new radicals had little time for patriotic protest: whereas Martin Luther King, Jr. had talked of his "dream," Black Power militants expressed their desire to bring "this country to its knees . . . [and] smash everything Western civilization has created."[27] Max Stanford, field chairman of the Revolutionary Action Movement (RAM), described the United States as a "Fourth Reich worse than Nazi Germany" while SNCC chairman Stokely Carmichael, in a speech before 13,000 mostly white radicals in Berkeley in October 1966, responded to suggestions that blacks simply wanted a piece of the American pie by explaining that "the American pie means *raping* South Africa, *beating* South America, *raping the Philippines, raping every country you've been in.* . . . [I] don't want to be *part* of that system!"[28] Congress of Racial Equality (CORE) leader Floyd McKissick quipped, "the greatest hypocrisy we have is the Statue of Liberty. We ought to break the young lady's legs and point her to Mississippi."[29] Little wonder, then, that in 1970 the writer Julius Lester felt able to argue that "American radicals are perhaps the first radicals anywhere who have sought to make a revolution in a country which they hate."[30]

It has been argued that during the late 1960s leftists gave up on Americanism—with the result that they disconnected themselves from the nation at large, forfeited patriotism to conservatives, and "lost the ability to pose convincing alternatives for the nation as a whole."[31] While there is much to be said for this interpretation, a few qualifications are in order. First, the portrayal of the antiwar movement in the mainstream media was not always an accurate one. Focusing on the colorful and the sensational—the burning of draft cards, the waving of enemy flags, the use of extreme rhetoric and suchlike—made for good copy, but this often came at the expense of presenting a more sober reality. The scholar Milton Katz noted that "when SANE [the National Committee for a Sane Nuclear Policy] held its overwhelmingly middle-class, middle-aged, middle-of-the-road march in Washington in November 1965, what appeared on television news and in news photos were Viet Cong flags, interruptions by the tiny American Nazi Party, and the handful of marchers, out of several thousand, who were wearing beards and sandals."[32] Two years later, journalists and commentators focused most of their attention on the March on the Pentagon—which featured witches, extravagant exorcisms and confrontations with troops—at the expense of the much larger (and presumably less exciting) rally in Washington that preceded it.[33]

Second, appeals to patriotic values continued to be made by opponents of the Vietnam War. The growing influence of liberals over the peace movement, especially disaffected Senators such as Eugene McCarthy and George McGovern, helps to explain this. But patriotic protest remained attractive to some radicals too. In advocating its policy of noncooperation with the draft and open confrontation with the military in the spring of 1967 Resistance, the first national anti-draft organization, made some trenchant criticisms of the United States. It described the "emptiness of the current equilibrium in American society" and the "violence" inherent within the "American system," and pledged to "provoke continual confrontations with the governmental institutions linked to the war." But, the group's leaders explained, in working for an end to the war abroad and radical change at home they hoped to "again see America moving in the direction of justice and democracy" and described themselves as "young Americans who still believe in the ideals our country once stood for."[34] Founded in the summer of 1967, Vietnam Veterans Against the War (VVAW) was one of the more militant antiwar groups and, according to historian Tom Wells, it "would ultimately exert a powerful impact on the American psyche."[35] VVAW and its leaders were keen to occupy patriotic terrain as they denounced America's actions in Southeast Asia and engaged in high-profile direct action protests against the conflict. In April 1971 the VVAW's John Kerry—a highly decorated veteran who had served on dangerous Swift Boat missions in the Mekong delta—testified before the Senate Foreign Relations Committee.[36] In his remarks Kerry referred to the Winter Soldier Investigation, which VVAW had held in Detroit between 31 January and 2 February.[37] He recalled how, in emotional hearings, soldiers had described committing atrocities in Southeast Asia—some had "raped, cut off ears, cut off heads, taped wires from portable telephones to human genitals and turned up the power." Kerry explained that the term "Winter Soldier" was "a play on words of Thomas Paine" who had spoken of the "Sunshine patriots and summer soldiers' who had "deserted at Valley Forge because the going was rough." VVAW believed that "they had to be winter soldiers now." "We could be quiet," said Kerry, but "we feel because of what threatens this country, not the reds, but the crimes which we are committing that threaten it, that we have to speak out."[38] The Winter Soldier hearings were just one example of VVAW use of patriotic protest. On Memorial Day 1971, for instance, veterans in Massachusetts retraced Paul Revere's famous route in reverse in order to "spread the alarm" against the war in Southeast Asia. After spending nights at the sites of the battles of Lexington and Concord, and Bunker Hill, the protest ended with a reading of the Declaration of Independence on Boston Common.[39] Then on 26 December fifteen veterans, "some clad in civilian clothes and some in military fatigues with medals on their chests," occupied the Statue of Liberty in protest against the war, hanging an American flag upside down (to signal distress) from the upper level of the statue's base. One of the veterans, Tim McCormick, explained that "The reason we chose the Statue of Liberty is that since we were children, the statue has been analogous in our minds with freedom and an America we love." But then, he explained, "we went to fight a war in the name of freedom. We saw that freedom is a selective expression allowed only to those who are white and who maintain the status quo." The twenty-four-year-old from Somerville, New Jersey, who had served as a medical corpsman, declared that "Until this symbol again takes on the meaning it was intended to have, we must continue our demonstrations all over the nation of our love of freedom and of America."[40]

Third, while it is clear that the emergence of Black Power led to a decline in the use of patriotic protest within the black freedom struggle during the late 1960s and 1970s, it was not abandoned completely. Even the militant Black Panther Party found itself drawn toward the ideas of Americanism, while other Black Power organizations sought to blend more traditional appeals to America's founding values with the newer radical style and ideology. The Panthers, founded in Oakland, California, in October 1966 by Merritt Junior College students Huey P. Newton and Bobby Seale, quickly became the most iconic Black Power organization—and it has often been viewed by its critics as anti-American.[41] It is not hard to see why. The Panthers attacked the "Amerikkkan Dream" and denounced the USA as "a barbaric organization controlled and operated by avaricious, sadistic, bloodthirsty thieves."[42] Eldridge Cleaver, the party's Minister of Information, described the U.S. flag and the American Eagle as "the true symbols of fascism" and explained that should it prove "necessary to destroy the United States of America, then let us destroy it with a smile on our faces. A smile for the freedom and liberation of our people."[43]

However, appeals to the Declaration of Independence and the Constitution actually formed an important part of the Panthers' rhetorical strategy and legitimated (in their own eyes at least) their own revolutionary struggle. As historian Bridgette Baldwin has pointed out, the Panthers "brandished both firearms and copies of the Bill of Rights" when carrying out their own patrols of the police in black ghetto neighborhoods and they quoted the Declaration of Independence at length in their ten-point platform and program.[44] Indeed the Panthers—like the radical abolitionists of a century before—understood that the Declaration of Independence justified the right to rebellion as well as proclaiming the right to "life, liberty and the pursuit of happiness," and were particularly fond of invoking the spirit of the American colonists' rebellion against the British when justifying their own calls for an overthrow of the American government. The passage in the Declaration of Independence that reads "when a long train of abuses and usurpations, pursuing invariable the same object, evinces a design to reduce them under absolute despotism, it is their right, it is their duty, to throw off such government, and to provide new guards for their future security" appeared at the end of the party's manifesto, and was referred to frequently by Panther leaders. David Hilliard cited it in a December 1969 interview with CBS's George Herman, for example, to justify Panther policy while Huey Newton drew on similar language during the Revolutionary People's Constitutional Convention of September 1970 (see below).[45]

As well as the Declaration of Independence, references to the U.S. Constitution featured prominently in Panther tracts and speeches. The Party's platform and program referred explicitly to the second and fourteenth amendments (which guaranteed the right to bear arms and the right to due process, respectively) and these, along with the right to free speech and to engage in political activism, were often cited by party members.[46] The BPP made an early name for itself by patrolling the Oakland police in an attempt to draw attention to, and reduce, the problems of police brutality that blighted black urban life, and it sought to justify these actions by pointing to the nation's founding values.[47] In "Pigs-Panthers," an article that appeared in the 22 November 1969 edition of the Party's newspaper, the author explained that the police "are in our communities to protect and serve the interests of [the] capitalist, exploitative state" and that, as such, they were part of a corrupt political structure that had distorted the promise of "Government of the people, for the people, and by the people" and replaced it with "Government of a few, for a few, and by a few." Arguing that the BPP was "working for, and in the interests of the people," the Panther slogan "All Power to the People" was linked to the nation's revolutionary founders:

> Think about the phrase, "All Power to the People." The founding fathers realized the beauty of the essence of those words and based the Constitution upon them. We must all realize their beauty, and live to make them become a reality in this country.[48]

The Panthers also sought to portray their community programs (such as free breakfasts, health clinics, and the distribution of clothes and food) as congruent with the nation's stated (though not practiced) democratic ideals. In the 10 January 1970 edition of the *Black Panther*, for instance, a report on recent activities by the Kansas City branch explained that "The Black Panther Party implements these types of [community] programs because we realize that this nation's philosophy 'Of the people, by the people, and for the people' is now a joke, a ridiculous farce. The Party, in presenting these community programs to the masses of the people, strive to make POWER TO THE PEOPLE A REALITY."[49]

The Panthers' most creative and ambitious engagement with the nation's founding ideals came in the summer of 1970 when it organized a Revolutionary People's Constitutional Convention for the purpose of rewriting the U.S. Constitution. On 19 June 1970 David Hilliard, the Panthers' chief of staff, addressed a noon rally of "around 1,000—predominantly young and about 70 per cent black" on the steps of the Lincoln Memorial in Washington. Echoing Martin Luther King's speech seven years earlier, Hilliard explained that, 107 years after the issuing of the Emancipation Proclamation, "today, black people are still not free."[50] The official statement that Hilliard read out explained, in a reference to the American colonists' justification for their own rebellion against the British, that "For 400 years now, Black people have suffered an unbroken chain of abuse at the hands of White America" and that the American Constitution "does not and never has protected our people or guaranteed to us those lofty ideals enshrined within it." The Panthers argued that, in order for black people to remain a part of the United States, it was now necessary to "have a new Constitution that will strictly guarantee our Human Rights to Life, Liberty, and the Pursuit of Happiness, which is promised but not delivered by the present Constitution." They therefore issued a call for a Revolutionary People's Convention "to write a new constitution that will guarantee and deliver to every American citizen the inviolable human right to life, liberty, and the pursuit of happiness!"[51]

The RPCC was the brainchild of the Black Panther Minister for Information, Eldridge Cleaver.[52] Born in Wabbeseka, Arkansas, on 31 August 1935 Cleaver became involved in criminal activity after his family moved to Los Angeles. In 1957 he was convicted of assault and served time in California's iconic San Quentin and Folsom jails. Cleaver was a prodigious literary talent; while in prison he penned a series of essays that in 1968 were published, to critical acclaim, in *Soul on Ice*—the book sold more than a million copies in just two years. After his release from prison in 1966 Cleaver worked as a journalist for the liberal-Catholic turned radical magazine, *Ramparts*. He decided to join the BPP in February 1967 after witnessing Huey Newton face down a cop outside the magazine's San Francisco offices, where the Panthers were due to be interviewed.[53] For Cleaver, the Constitution was "the battlefield on which the struggle of our people for their liberation is taking place." As the "ultimate source of authority, the ultimate repository of the collective sovereignty of the people" the Constitution was "supposed to represent a just and equitable organization of our collective sovereignty in a form that will guarantee us a good life and liberty in the pursuit of happiness. And we have not received this." Changing the Constitution was thus a fundamental prerequisite for a wider re-ordering and re-making of America's socioeconomic and political system. As Cleaver put it, "there's something wrong in Babylon, and the form of its organization is based upon the U.S. Constitution, and we must change this form of the system, and we must change the Constitution."[54]

During the summer of 1970 in the pages of the *Black Panther*, as well as in speeches and broadsides, party members attacked the Constitution for failing to deliver freedom and equality to black and other minority groups and oppressed peoples. Mike Ellis of the Boston chapter, for instance, compared the "sacred" Constitution to a "roll of toilet paper" and explained that "Black people were totally and completely ignored" because the Constitution had been drawn up by rich elites and slave-owners who regarded black people as property.[55] Expressing similar sentiments, Milt Zaslow proclaimed that the "time has come to declare the constitution of the United States as decadent, degenerate, obsolete, and worthy of being confined to the ash can of history."[56] Despite such sentiment, many Panthers were prepared to call upon both some of the nation's founders *and* its oft-proclaimed ideals in making their case for radical change. Afeni Shakur (the mother of the late rapper Tupac and member of the New York 21) invoked the spirit of Patrick Henry in calling for a new American Constitution and she urged her comrades to be "as firm in our desire to have liberation as the American colonialists" had been in theirs.[57] James Mott, an Oakland Panther, explained that "The Constitution is the ideological foundation of the American way of life. In simple terms it is supposed to stand for life, liberty and the pursuit of happiness." However, "somewhere through the pages of history and the passing of time, the ideals the perspectives and the goals of these words so beautifully written have become a symbol of political oppression, economic exploitation and social degradation of a people who have suffered 400 years of humility." Mott concluded that "We are all part of the American dream . . . we must create and put together some functional machinery that will guarantee and safeguard all the rights and privileges of the people who make up the backbone of this country."[58]

The RPCC took place over Labor Day weekend in Philadelphia—the "same place the pigs had theirs" as David Hilliard put it—where an estimated 6,000 black militants, members of the women's and gay liberation movements, and other assorted radicals assembled in Temple University's McGonigle Hall.[59] Outside the stars and stripes had been removed and replaced with "five flags in descending order: the Black Panther Party; the National Liberation Front of Vietnam . . . the green, black and red of black nationalism; the green marihuana leaf on the black ground of anarchy, the flag of Y.I.P.[the Yippies]; and, finally, a flag of Che Guevara."[60] A *New York Times* reporter noted that most black delegates dressed informally and that while there were "a few dashikis" the "Panthers' favorite color, black, predominated."[61] Perhaps as many as half the delegates were white.[62]

The culmination of the convention was the appearance of Panther founder and revolutionary icon, Huey P. Newton, who was the keynote speaker on the evening of Saturday 5 September. It was an eagerly awaited moment: apparently his very presence on the stage, flanked by security guards, "electrified" the crowd. What many of them did not yet realize was that Newton was far from committed to the RPCC—describing it in private at the time, and then later, as "bogus," "crazy" and "a nonsense." Indeed, he viewed the project with suspicion as an attempt by his rival Eldridge Cleaver to win control of the Panthers.[63] However, one thing that the audience came to understand only too quickly was that Newton was no charismatic speaker. Delivering his speech in a "high-pitched, almost whiney, voice," his often abstract analysis and philosophizing went down badly. Reports in the *Black Panther* spoke of the crowds rising up, "weeping like troops from hell" as the "future hove into sight."[64] But the recollection of one participant may well offer a more accurate insight into Newton's rhetorical prowess (and, for that matter, the cause of any "weeping"): "By the time he was done our disappointment in him was already palpable."[65]

While it may not have enthralled, Newton's speech did draw extensively on the tenets of Americanism. He began by telling the delegates that "we gather here in peace and friendship to claim our inalienable rights."[66] After claiming that the civil rights movement had failed to provide "life, liberty and the pursuit of happiness" Newton asserted that "Black people and oppressed people in general have lost faith in the leaders of America, in the government of America, and in the very structure of American government—that is the Constitution, its legal foundation." This "loss of faith" was, he said, "based upon the overwhelming evidence that this government will not live according to that Constitution because the Constitution is not designed for its people." Newton concluded by declaring that "The sacredness of man and of the human spirit requires that human dignity and integrity ought to be always respected by every other man. We will settle for nothing less, for at this point in history anything less is but a living death. WE WILL BE FREE and we are here to ordain a new Constitution which will ensure our freedom by enshrining (cherishing) the dignity of the human spirit."[67]

The following day the RPCC was turned over to a series of workshops held on "all aspects of the shape of a new society, its institutions, its morality and its culture."[68] Held in nearby churches and community centers, topics under consideration included "self-determination for minorities and women, the family and the rights of children, revolutionary artists, patrol and the use of military forces, land, means of production, the educational and legal system and political prisoners."[69] With the weather cool and sunny, many delegates apparently preferred to mingle outside rather than participate in these discussions.[70] Nevertheless, unlike at some previous radical gatherings, there seemed to be a genuine spirit of cooperation and the workshops proved productive; at the end of the three-day convention they agreed a series of recommendations, including "community control of the police, the courts, the educational system and the means of production," and support for South Vietnam's National Liberation Front, the Pathet Lao in Cambodia, and the Palestine liberation struggle. Loud cheers also greeted the statement that "psychedelic drugs such as grass . . . acid . . . and mescaline are instrumental in developing the revolutionary consciousness of people."[71] Plans were made to reconvene in Washington to ratify a new Constitution, but these soon ran into trouble, with the BPP claiming that it was unable to find a suitable location for the gathering. On 28 November Huey Newton told those delegates who had turned up (and stayed around while efforts were made to solve the logistical problems) that the convention would be postponed. It was never reconvened.[72]

By the early 1970s Black Student Unions had sprung up on campuses across the nation, demanding black studies curricula, the hiring of greater numbers of black faculty, an end to institutional discrimination, and a greater sense of community responsibility from higher education establishments. The influence of the Black Panther Party can be seen clearly in the "Platform and Program' that many BSUs adopted, modeled as it was on the Panthers' iconic founding statement of principles. Like the BPP, the BSU had ten key demands (including "full enrollment in the schools for our people"; an "end to the robbery by the white man of our black community"; decent educational facilities and relevant curricula; the dismissal of racist teachers; and the exclusion of "all police and special agents" from school and college campuses). While embracing militant, confrontational language—American society was, rather predictably, denounced as "racist" and "decadent"—the BSU showed a willingness to engage constructively with the nation's founding ideals and core tenets. For example, they invoked Constitutional protections in demanding that students be tried by a jury of their peers in specially created "student courts." They also demanded the creation of a student assembly "for the purpose of determining the will of the students as to the school's destiny." Like the BPP, the BSU also quoted extensively from the Declaration of Independence, albeit with one or two minor amendments:

> We hold these truths as being self-evident, that all men are created equal, that they are endowed by their creator with certain inalienable rights, that among these are life, liberty, and the pursuit of happiness. To secure these rights within the schools, governments are instituted among the students, deriving their just powers from the consent of the governed, that whenever any form of student government becomes destructive to these ends, it is the right of the students to alter or abolish it and to institute new government, laying its foundation on such principles and organizing its power in

such form as to them shall seem most likely to effect their safety and happiness.[73]

At Michigan State University the campus vehicle for Black Power was the Black Liberation Front. Founded in the summer of 1969 and led by Stan McClinton (Kimathi Mohammed), the BLF engaged in direct-action protests, organized cultural events designed to increase African Americans' appreciation of African traditions and culture, and worked with the black community of East Lansing—helping to found the "Maiden Voyage Record Shop' in the fall of 1970.[74] The BLF also worked with pupils at Lansing's Sexton High and Everett High, who sought to distribute Black Power literature and organize their fellow students. In February of 1971 McClinton was arrested and charged with trespass after he led 53 students in a sit-in at Sexton High's administration office to demand a "review committee for the policies and practices of the school system, relevant courses for blacks and a black program in observance of National Black History week." McClinton also penned an article denouncing a rule that required any outside publication to first be approved by the school principal before it could be circulated among the student body. In grounding his arguments very firmly within the Constitutional guarantees and democratic promise of the United States, McClinton illustrates the willingness of some Black Power advocates to use patriotic protest. After noting the first amendment's guarantee of freedom of speech and the press he asked, rhetorically, whether "the board of education tell[s] us that the bill of rights stops at the school steps?" The BLF chairman went on to explain that the fourth amendment "gives a person the right to be secure within their persons, houses, papers, and effects, against unreasonable searches and seizures." So how, then, "did the school board get the right to keep people from giving away private property?" McClinton concluded, "I don't know what the school board expects, but I for one will fight for my rights . . . Is liberty and justice just for the school personnel?"[75]

While the NAACP's national leadership remained resolute in its denunciation of Black Power—Roy Wilkins infamously described it as a "reverse Hitler" that could result only in "Black death" while his director of branches, Gloster Current, pledged to "take on the separatists"—the picture among the Association's grassroots membership is much more complex. In fact there seems to have been a considerable amount of support for Black Power, particularly among NAACP branches in the West and North, as well a more general desire to seek out common ground and avoid damaging splits within the freedom movement.[76] The version of Black Power that NAACP members were likely to embrace was one that blended together cultural pride with demands for tangible political influence and genuine economic leverage. This "moderate" militancy could quite easily operate in tandem with a commitment to traditional civil rights tactics, reform politics and appeals to Americanism. So while the Mid-Manhattan NAACP branch encouraged its members to attend a showing of Melvin Van Peebles' play, "Ain't Supposed to Die," and an after-party with the playwright, to promote the cause of Black culture and raise money for the Association—branch president William J. Greene could also remain committed to creating a "single society with equal opportunity and justice for all."[77] In Davenport, Iowa, William Cribbs may have expressed sympathy for Black Power—but he remained willing to invoke America's ideals in campaigning for racial justice. Writing in the branch newsletter in the spring of 1968, for example, he explained that "We know that there were Negroes at Valley Forge, at the Boston Tea Party . . . we have waited more than 350 years for our constitutional and God-given rights. We are still denied"; an editorial in the same edition of the newsletter conveyed something of the frustration that many blacks felt over the seemingly slow progress toward true equality:

> They tell us that the American way is freedom for all men—WHITE AND BLACK.
>
> They tell us that the American way is justice for all men—WHITE AND BLACK.
>
> They tell us that the American way is equality for all men—WHITE AND BLACK.
>
> TRUE????   FALSE!!!![78]

Similarly in its campaign against housing discrimination in Davenport, the Black Power Youth Council (the local NAACP youth wing) maintained a public commitment to "conduct peaceful, nonviolent demonstrations" while also pledging to "hit the streets in full Power and . . . take any action necessary." And in denouncing the city council's requirement that an individual post $500 bond in order to file a housing complaint Eugene Wyatt, the group's president, explained that they viewed the fee as a "price tag for our freedom and the Constitutional Rights, which we as Americans, are supposed to have."[79] Activists in the Oakland Branch, meanwhile, offered qualified support for Black Power. While they warned against indulging "in the very types of racism . . . that we are working so hard to overcome," they believed that Black Power provided a positive opportunity for community organizing and empowerment and that it contained within it "the determination to chart our own course to our own destiny and to participate in making America a democratic country."[80] This patriotic sentiment was also reflected in Oakland NAACP activists' desire to "work to make Oakland the leading city in the west for 'Life Liberty and the Pursuit of Happiness'."[81]

By the end of the 1960s, with some important exceptions, patriotic protest had apparently fallen out of favor among American leftists—something illustrated by the reaction to the 200th anniversary of the nation's birth. 1976 saw the July 4th Coalition—an umbrella group led by the Puerto Rican Socialist Party and the Prairie Fire Organizing Committee (an organization with links to the Weather movement)—organize an alternative to the official Bicentennial march in Philadelphia. Referring to "Amerika," the coalition demanded a "bicentennial without colonies" and sought to mobilize what it hoped would be a "massive, militant people's celebration which will place demands on the pigs' doorstep."[82] On 4 July 1976, in an "echo of the protest days of the 1960s," the Coalition mobilized a crowd of around 30,000—many "in dungarees and T-shirts, and carrying flags and banners," who heard Black Panther Elaine Brown deliver a keynote speech in which she explained that the nation's history was "one of murder and plunder."[83] But while many on the left appeared to have little time for the language of Americanism, the progressive tradition of patriotic protest would be given new life during the 1970s and beyond by the movement for gay rights and the struggle for women's equality.

Chapter 2

The Struggle for Gay Rights

I think what Gays are asking today is the same that Negroes, Mexicans, Indians, women and other minorities have said. This country claims a national basis of equality. It's about time we got it.
   —Otto H. Ulrich, Jr., treasurer, Washington Mattachine, 1971

Ours is a noble cause because we are engaged in a fight for the very promise of America.
   —Lorri L. Jean, executive director,
   Los Angeles Gay and Lesbian Center, 2000

On 30 April 2000, several hundred thousand protesters assembled on the Mall in Washington, D.C., for the Millennium March, the fourth national gay rights demonstration to be hosted in the nation's capital. "For more than six hours, under a warm spring sun" the crowd heard speeches from activists, celebrities and politicians; both President Clinton and Vice President Gore delivered videotaped remarks. The *New York Times* described the "festive" tone of the proceedings and emphasized the diversity of the marchers: "a long, ebullient parade of cops and veterans, drag queens and college students, gay parents with toddlers on their backs and heterosexual parents marching in support of gay children." One of the featured speakers was the father of Matthew Shepard, the gay Wyoming teenager who had been brutally murdered in October 1998. Dennis Shepard told the crowd to "Let people know that you are a part of America . . . and you deserve the same rights."[1] Another speaker was veteran activist Lorri L.

Jean, executive director of the Los Angeles Gay and Lesbian Center, who explained that the "gay agenda" was the "very one upon which this nation was founded."[2] In Jean's formulation the gay rights movement was a "fight for the very promise of America . . . a patriotic battle of the highest order, a battle to secure the principle that forms the bedrock of our society . . . life, liberty and the pursuit of happiness."[3]

In invoking the Declaration of Independence and associating her movement with patriotic values, Jean stood in a long tradition of gay rights activism. From its emergence in the new, urban gay subculture fashioned by World War II[4] through its mid-1960s experimentation with direct action, embrace of the revolutionary politics of the New Left, and evolution during the 1970s into a mass-based movement for equal rights, the deployment of patriotic protest was a cornerstone of the gay freedom struggle. Indeed, linking demands for gay rights with America's founding commitment to freedom, liberty, and equality typified the movement's rhetorical approach throughout the second half of the twentieth century. Moreover, the emergence of the modern gay rights movement cannot be understood fully without recognizing the importance of the broader context of 1960s activism. During the 1970s the gay movement's use of direct action (including street theater and mass marches), its commitment to local organizing and building alternative institutions (such as bookstores, newspapers, and churches), and its proud and forceful assertion that "coming out" was an empowering act with revolutionary potential (and thus that the personal was political) demonstrated the profound effect that the radical firmament of the 1960s had wrought.

The emergence of the homophile movement in the 1950s marks the beginning of the modern movement for gay rights in the United States; within that story, the work of the Mattachine Society is central. Originally founded in Los Angeles in 1951 by English immigrant, actor, and communist activist Henry "Harry" Hay, Jr., the Mattachine Foundation (as it was first called) took its name from an all-male group of masked medieval satirists. Hosting discussion sessions, fostering a sense of community, and making early forays into public relations and legal challenges, the organization grew throughout southern California and the Bay Area—perhaps 5,000 Californians had been involved in Mattachine-sponsored activities by late 1952.[5]

In May 1953, amid fears about Communist control and unease over the leadership's intention to undertake more high-profile actions, the membership ousted Hay and his cofounders and reorganized as the Mattachine Society.[6] Under the leadership of journalist Hal Call, a "raucous, aggressive and authoritarian" character, and the "reserved" Donald Lucas, a "bespectacled, balding accountant," the organization moved its headquarters to San Francisco and focused on public outreach and the provision of social services, as well as publishing a journal, the *Mattachine Review*. Local chapters, which began to spring up across the country, hosted public lectures, organized discussion groups, and provided social services to homosexuals.[7] A pioneer lesbian organization, the Daughters of Bilitis (DOB), partly modeled on Mattachine, was founded in 1955 by Del Martin, Phyllis Lyon, and six other women. It published a monthly newsletter, *The Ladder*, convened meetings, and offered valuable emotional support to women. Within Mattachine itself, tension between the local chapters and the national leadership over autonomy, money, and personality led to the dissolution of the organization's national structure in 1961, although chapters in New York, Philadelphia (renamed the Janus Society), and Washington continued to function as autonomous units.[8]

As the 1960s began, the homophile movement began to adopt a more militant orientation, a development that owed something to the prevailing *zeitgeist*. John F. Kennedy's legitimization of social activism, the direct action protests of the civil rights movement and a wider flowering of activism all affected the homophile movement. As John D'Emilio has noted, it was not surprising that the "spirit of the times infected the gay movement as well." Militants on the East Coast adopted the language and ideology of minority rights, engaged in public protest, and were unapologetic, even celebratory, about the homosexual lifestyle.[9]

The Mattachine Society of Washington, founded by Franklin Kameny and Jack Nichols in November 1961, played a key role in the emergence of this new militancy. Kameny, an army veteran and Harvard Ph.D. who had been fired from the U.S. Map Service in 1957 for being gay, emerged as "one of the most determined fighters in the East Coast homophile movement." Under his leadership, the Washington chapter became the "radical cutting edge" of the struggle as it confronted federal officials, organized public demonstrations for gay rights, and rejected inviting to speak at homophile events those "experts" who believed that homosexuality was a sickness.[10] Indeed, in March 1965 the group's membership passed an "anti-sickness" resolution. Adopted after several months of sustained and animated debate, it declared that "homosexuality is not a sickness, disturbance, or other pathology . . . but is merely a preference, orientation, or propensity, on par with, and not different in kind from, heterosexuality."[11] In a precursor of the gay liberation movement of the 1970s, Kameny coined the phrase "Gay is Good" (inspired, he later explained, by watching television footage of Stokely Carmichael exhorting a crowd to chant "Black is beautiful") and, along with DOB veteran Barbara Gittings, challenged the American Psychiatric Association's designation of homosexuality as a mental illness.[12]

Formed in December 1955 by Cuban-born Tony Segura and clinical psychologist Sam Morford, the Mattachine Society of New York was initially reluctant to embrace the radicalism that was gaining ground in Washington. Gradually, though, under pressure from Kameny's proselytizing and its own grassroots membership, the organization began to change; by May 1965 the militants were in the ascendancy.[13] They worked toward "the complete understanding and full acceptance of homosexuality as a way of life—and love" and engaged in public protest, legal challenge, cultural activities, and educational efforts in pursuit of this goal.[14] Moreover, they encouraged homosexuals to become active in Mattachine in order to experience a "new birth of freedom" and develop self-confidence, self-respect, and a "sense of dignity and self-worth as an individual."[15]

In the spring of 1965, activists in Philadelphia staged sit-ins and a series of demonstrations at a Dewey's restaurant on Seventeenth Street to protest its refusal to serve homosexuals, eventually securing an end to discriminatory treatment.[16] This was a sign of things to come: during the mid-1960s the Mattachine Societies in Washington and New York, together with the DOB and Philadelphia's Janus Society, staged a series of public demonstrations protesting discrimination against homosexuals. The influence of the civil rights movement on the homophile movement's embrace of direct action is clear. At a February 1965 meeting of New York Mattachine, for example, Julian Hodges, the group's president, urged his members to "be as militant as other minorities and force the public to face honestly our just claims to equal treatment."[17] Meanwhile a report written by Dick Leitsch and Warren D. Adkins for the Mattachine *Newsletter* explained that "other social protest movements" had shown that direct action was "a potent means both of reaching the public and effecting social change."[18]

Just as the early civil rights movement had placed great importance on projecting the "right" appearance, homophile organizations on the East Coast were conscious of public image.[19] The "rules for picketing" drawn up by the East Coast Homophile Organizations (ECHO), a loose coalition founded in 1963 that consisted of the DOB, the Janus Society, and both New York and Washington Mattachine,[20] explained that demonstrations were not an opportunity for "an individual to express his individuality, personality or ego" and that "to gain acceptance, new ideas must be clothed in familiar garb." The need for "good order, good appearance and dignity" was emphasized, and specific instructions for participants included the wearing of "conservative and conventional dress" (suits and ties for men, dresses for women), and refraining from conversing with passersby.[21]

Partly because of this emphasis on projecting a public image of respectability, the homophile protests of the mid-1960s have often been viewed as conservative by those writing from a post-Stonewall perspective. Nevertheless, at a time when there was almost no public acceptance of homosexuality, and where allies were in short supply, the homophile movement's direct action protests were courageous.[22] The tactical approach adopted by ECHO, especially given the broader context, also made a good deal of sense. As historian August Meier has argued, "American history shows that for any reform movement to succeed, it must attain respectability. It must attract moderates, even conservatives, to its ranks."[23] This was understood well by Franklin Kameny, who was keen to ensure that the homophile movement was not tainted by the countercultural style that was growing in popularity. As he explained, "It is not I who am rejecting the beatniks. I emphasize that, rightly or wrongly, it is society at large—the employers, the officials, the parents, the professionals, the great mass—who do. . . . This may be just or it may be unjust, BUT it IS. We MUST work with what IS." "All I am doing," he said, "is adopting the ONLY practical approach to getting ourselves across in a way that will get us what we want."[24]

A concern to avoid unnecessary controversy also lay behind the decision of the New York Mattachine Society to refrain from joining protests against the exclusion of homosexuals from the military that were planned for Armed Forces Day (21 May) 1966.[25] The group's president, Dick Leitsch, a "cleancut, handsome former school teacher from Kentucky," explained why his organization was unwilling to participate.[26] Believing that the day would likely see a number of protests by both supporters and opponents of the war in Vietnam, they were anxious to avoid being associated with either side—"any effort directed toward the inclusion of homosexuals in the armed forces could be seized upon by one group or the other and used against us . . . and we don't want to risk having our gains to date lost in an argument over Viet Nam." A similar position was taken by the Janus Society of Philadelphia.[27]

As part of this attempt to project a respectable image, the homophile movement sought to ground its demands in the language of Americanism. Indeed, invoking the American creed on behalf of gay rights was a central weapon in the movement's armoury. Back in 1953, West Hollywood activists associated with Los Angeles Mattachine began to publish *One*—a gay-run and edited newspaper, which quickly built up monthly sales of some 5,000 copies. *One* deployed the language of citizenship rights in the fight for gay equality, publishing editorials that declared that attempts to regulate homosexual behavior violated the "principles of American freedom."[28] Founded in 1961, Washington Mattachine's statement of purpose declared that the group was prepared to "act by any lawful means . . . to secure for homosexuals the right to life, liberty, and the pursuit of happiness, as proclaimed for all men by the Declaration of Independence; and to secure for homosexuals the basic rights and liberties established by the word and the spirit of the Constitution of the United States."[29] In July 1965, at the first open meeting of Mattachine Midwest, its president Robert Sloane linked the struggle for gay rights with the Revolutionary struggle for liberty and Abraham Lincoln's appeal, at Gettysburg, for Americans to continue the founders' "unfinished work." Sloane concluded, "We have an appointment with destiny in our generation, just as the patriots of 1776 had in theirs."[30]

Patriotism also characterized the homophile movement's direct action protests. On 17 April 1965 (the same day that Students for a Democratic Society staged its 20,000-strong protest against the war in Vietnam), ten activists demonstrated outside the White House. The following day, 29 activists marched up Fifth Avenue to 42nd Street in New York to protest Fidel Castro's discriminatory policies toward homosexuals.[31] The White House was picketed again on 29 May, when thirteen protesters carried signs reading "First Class Citizenship for Homosexuals," "Homosexuals Are American Citizens Too," and "Equal Opportunity for ALL; *ALL* Means All."[32] One newspaper report noted that the protesters were "neatly dressed" and that there were "no disturbances."[33] A final White House demonstration was held on October 23, at which about 40 "clean-cut, average American white collar citizens" participated. While there was apparently no coverage of the protest on the evening news, the 17 activists who had traveled from New York felt that the "trip had been well worth it."[34]

Other demonstrations took place that focused specifically on the federal government's discriminatory employment policies regarding homosexuals—who were automatically deemed security risks. On 26 June, 25 activists protested outside the headquarters of the Civil Service Commission,[35] while on August 28 a picket outside the State Department saw protesters carrying signs reading "The American Way: Employment based upon competence, ability, training; NOT upon private life" and "Homosexuals are American Citizens, too."[36]

The blanket policy of giving a "less than honorable" discharge to anyone within America's armed services who was discovered to be a homosexual, irrespective of his or her quality of service or performance, and the refusal to allow known homosexuals to serve in the military, were condemned by gay rights activists. An official statement by ECHO pointed out that "these policies ill-befit a nation which claims before the world to uphold the rights which this nation does and the concepts of human worth and of human dignity which our nation does; a nation which champions personal freedom, individuality, the right not to conform, as our nation does." After repeated entreaties to discuss the policy with the authorities were rebuffed or ignored, the decision to stage a picket at the

Pentagon on 31 July 1965 was made.[37] A group of 16 activists, including veterans from "various branches of the Armed Service (some with front-line combat experience)," demonstrated outside the River Entrance to the Pentagon. Signs were carried, including "U.S. claims no second class citizens; what about homosexual citizens?" and "Homosexual citizens want to serve their country too." The demonstration received extensive coverage on CBS.[38]

The Independence Day demonstrations held in Philadelphia from 1965 through 1969 demonstrate most clearly the East Coast homophile movement's dedication to using America's exalted ideals as leverage to effect meaningful change. Meeting in a coffee shop after the second White House protest, New York Mattachine's Craig Rodwell, a native of Chicago who moved to Greenwich Village in the late 1950s and became active in the homophile movement, suggested an annual July 4 protest outside Philadelphia's Independence Hall. Rodwell, who would found the Oscar Wilde Memorial Bookshop in 1967, envisaged the protest as "like a gay holiday. We can call it the Annual Reminder—the reminder that a group of Americans still don't have their basic rights to life, liberty, and the pursuit of happiness."[39] Historian Marc Stein has noted that "demonstrating on the nation's birthday in the 'birthplace of the nation' strategically identified lesbians and gay men with the highest ideals of the United States."[40]

ECHO called for a large turnout for the 1965 Reminder as a means of urging "the United States government to implement all the provisions of the Bill of Rights for all citizens, including homosexuals." They pointed out that the closing of gay bars was a denial of the right to free assembly and that the criminalization of homosexuality was a denial of the "right to the pursuit of happiness."[41] Signs carried by the forty or so demonstrators stated "Homosexual Citizens Want: Equality Before the Law," and "We Want: Equal Treatment By Our Fellow Citizens."[42] Another slogan referred explicitly to the ideals enshrined in Philadelphia in 1776—"Homosexual Americans *Still* Don't Have Our Sacred Freedoms & Rights."[43] Writing in the DOB magazine, *The Ladder*, Kay Lahusan declared that "This dignified protest, which startled many a citizen into fresh thought about the meaning of Independence Day, might well have been applauded by our Founding Fathers, who were intent on making America safe for the differences."[44] The following year, protesters outside Independence Hall sought to remind the "American people of the principles of individual freedom this country was founded upon as embodied in the Declaration of Independence and the Bill of Rights."[45] Similarly, in 1968 a flyer distributed by activists asked, "Are we guaranteeing to all of our citizens the rights, the liberties, the freedom, which took birth and first form in the Declaration of Independence?"[46]

Ultimately the homophile movement's adoption of direct action and its break with the accommodationism of the 1950s was to prove significant. As D'Emilio has argued, "the militants' rejection of the medical model, their assertion of equality, their uncompromising insistence that gays deserved recognition as a persecuted minority, and their defense of homosexuality as a viable way of living loosened the grip of prevailing norms on the self-conception of lesbians and homosexuals" and indicated the outlines of a new, positive gay identity. Partly as a result of these changes the movement grew significantly during the second half of the decade—reversing a period of decline. In the spring of 1963, New York Mattachine could count about 100 members; by the summer of 1965 it had risen to 445, and there is evidence of growth in the Janus Society and Washington Mattachine also.[47] New groups were formed, including the Society for Individual Rights, founded in California in September 1964, which became the nation's largest homophile organization, with 1,000 members in 1967 (up from 581 a year earlier), and the Phoenix Society for Individual Freedom in Kansas City. The North American Conference of Homophile Organizations (NACHO), formed in August 1966, created a national legal defense fund, challenged the closing of gay bars and the exclusion of homosexual immigrants, and organized protests against federal employment discrimination. In 1968 the Conference adopted Franklin Kameny's "Gay is Good" slogan—which symbolized a growing mood of assertiveness among gay rights activists. In short, a creative, energized, and increasingly self-confident gay rights movement was taking shape immediately prior to the Stonewall riot of June 1969. Indeed, Kameny later claimed that the homophile movement's adoption of direct action in the mid-1960s "created the mind-set which made Stonewall possible."[48]

Part "oasis and refuge," part sleazy dive, the Stonewall Inn at 53 Christopher Street was the most popular gay bar in New York's Greenwich Village. In the early hours of Saturday 28 June 1969 the Stonewall's "magical" clientele, which ranged from "tweedy East Siders to street queens," had their merriment interrupted by a police raid.[49] What followed quickly became "*the* emblematic event in modern gay and lesbian history," transforming Stonewall into the birthplace of the modern gay rights movement and inspiring gay, lesbian, bisexual, and transgender people in America and around the world.[50] As the police began to release the bar's patrons one by one, a noisy crowd assembled outside. According to a report in the *Village Voice,* as one officer attempted to guide the last of the customers, a lesbian, to a waiting patrol car, she "put up a struggle," and almost immediately the "scene became explosive"—beer cans and bottles were "heaved at the windows and a rain of coins descended on the cops."[51]

Others have questioned the specifics of this account, and it seems more likely that, in the words of activist Craig Rodwell, "there was no one thing that happened or one person, there was just . . . a flash of group—of mass—anger."[52] The crowd's reaction came as a shock to the police, who were used to being able to handle such situations with ease. They retreated into the bar on the orders of Deputy Inspector Seymour Pine, who recalled that "I had been in combat situations, [but] there was never any time that I felt more scared than then." Soon the bar itself was ablaze and reinforcements from the city's Tactical Patrol Force (TPF), a crack riot-control unit, were on the scene. The crowd—perhaps more accurately described as a mob by this point—continued to fight back. At 3:35 a.m., some two hours after the raid began, calm was restored—there were thirteen arrests and a number of serious injuries.[53]

The riot received a good deal of media coverage, which helped to bring out the crowds the following day—by early evening, "something like a carnival, an outsized block party" was taking place outside the damaged Stonewall: "handholding and kissing became endemic; cheerleaders led the crowd in shouts of 'Gay Power' and chorus lines repeatedly belted out refrains of "We are the girls from Stonewall." Police, including TPF units, watched on with grim-faced determination. As the evening progressed, more than 2,000 protesters engaged in confrontations with the police, some of which turned violent.[54]

Stonewall has become a defining event in gay history; a "year zero" that, in public consciousness and historical memory, marks the birth of the gay liberation movement. As Stein has pointed out, Stonewall is often seen "as the first act of lesbian and gay resistance *ever*." This is partly due to the efforts of gay liberation activists themselves, who sought to demonstrate that they had broken with the past by "denying that lesbian and gay politics even had a past." According to Stein, "perhaps in no movement was the denial of prior political traditions so complete."[55] But although commonly viewed as a spontaneous protest, the Stonewall Riot is more accurately understood when placed in its wider context. The funeral of gay icon Judy Garland earlier the same day helps account for the anger of the bar's patrons that night. Moreover, thanks in part to the efforts of the homophile movement, police raids on gay bars were "no longer commonplace" in New York, and the Stonewall Inn was seen by its patrons as "rightfully theirs." More important, riots and confrontational protest were not uncommon in the late 1960s, as seen in the occupation of campus buildings, antiwar demonstrations, and activities of groups like the Black Panthers and Young Lords. As D'Emilio has explained, "the Stonewall riot may very well have been the first of its kind in history, but when the patrons confronted the police they were extending to gay turf . . . modes of action" that were very familiar at the time.[56]

The weeks and months following the riot saw an explosion of gay organizing. By the end of July, activists in New York had formed the Gay Liberation Front, while other groups began to spring up in cities and on campuses across the nation.[57] The emergence of gay newspapers, speakers' bureaus, telephone helplines, churches, and bookstores signaled a flowering of gay culture and political activism. The fifty homophile organizations that had existed in 1969 became more than 800 gay rights groups just four years later, and tens of thousands of gays and lesbians became actively involved in the gay rights movement. This impressive growth was possible in part because activists were able to draw upon organizations, networks and resources that had been created and nurtured by the homophile movement during the previous two decades. If not a decisive break, Stonewall certainly marked the movement's evolution from a "thinly spread reform effort" into "a large, grassroots movement for liberation,"[58] and the riot itself was of enormous symbolic importance and rhetorical power. As the Mattachine Society of New York put it, Stonewall was the "hairpin drop heard round the world."[59]

The Gay Liberation Front, which formed in the immediate aftermath of the Stonewall riot, is indicative of the synergy between the New Left and the gay liberation movement. The organization was clearly a product of the late 1960s cultural and political milieu. Its name was modeled after South Vietnam's National Liberation Front; it embraced the revolutionary rhetoric that was then in vogue (denouncing the "dirty, vile, fucked-up capitalist conspiracy,"[60] for example), and it adopted confrontational tactics. The GLF also sought to forge meaningful alliances with other radical causes—offering support to the Black Panther Party and participating in marches against the war in Vietnam. To some extent this was done to promote the gay liberation message among potential allies, but the decision was also partly "rooted in personal experience." The GLF's founders mixed with, and held an affinity toward, New Left activists, antiwar campaigners, and Black Power advocates. A significant number of them, including John O'Brien, Jim Fouratt, and Martha Shelley, had been active in the New Left.[61] The same was true of other organizations that followed in the GLF's wake. Morris Kight, who founded Los Angeles GLF in December 1969, for example, had been head of the Dow Action Committee, which had organized protests against Dow Chemicals, the infamous napalm manufacturer.[62]

Partly because of such personal connections the GLF shared a similar political ideology to the wider New Left: it believed that gay liberation was "tied to the liberation of all peoples," and it sought to effect a radical overhaul of America's social, economic and political system.[63] The GLF's statement of purpose reveals the organization's radical political orientation as well as its embrace of militant rhetoric. "We are a revolutionary group of men and women formed with the realization that complete sexual liberation for all people cannot come about unless existing social institutions are abolished." The GLF intended to create new "social forms and relations" that would be based on "brotherhood, cooperation, human love, and uninhibited sexuality." "Babylon," the statement concluded, "has forced us to commit ourselves to one thing—revolution!"[64]

Attempts to construct multi-issue radical alliances in the 1960s, while easy enough on paper, frequently ran aground over disputes about the mechanics of coalition, arguments over tactics, and disagreement over the relative priority that should be afforded particular causes.[65] Many gay activists quickly became disillusioned with their straight radical comrades, believing that gay liberation was not taken seriously by white New Leftists and black revolutionaries—indeed, that in some cases there was a serious problem with homophobia. Jim Owles, a GLF founder who became the first president of the Gay Activists Alliance, recalled that when he was in the peace movement "they kept telling me there were greater things to work for than my own oppression and maybe I could be taken care of after the revolution."[66] The experience of Charlotte Bunch, who helped found the Furies, a radical lesbian-feminist collective, was similar—"the Left," she explained, "constantly told us that our oppression was not as great and not as important as the Vietnamese."[67] Apparent homophobia in the radical black movement also proved an obstacle to coalition building. The use of the word "faggot" by members of the Black Panther Party was especially controversial, but homophobic sentiment was not confined to them.[68] In 1971, for example, the Afro-American Society at Columbia University bluntly declared that they did not "have time to wallow in the mud with people who cannot decide if they are men or women."[69]

In addition to sharing a radical critique of the "American system," the gay liberation movement also manifested two of the defining traits of radical 1960s activism—it emphasized the politics of authenticity and embraced the notion of the "personal as political."[70] This was most notable in the way the process of "coming out" was transformed into a radical political act. Previously it had "signified the private decision to accept one's homosexual desires and to acknowledge one's sexual identity" to other homosexuals. For gay liberationists, however, "coming out" symbolized the "shedding of self-hatred," promised psychological and spiritual rebirth, and became the basis of political organizing.[71] In his 1969 tract, "A Gay Manifesto," former SDS activist and labor organizer Carl Wittman explained that "to pretend to be straight . . . is probably the most harmful pattern of behaviour. . . . If we are liberated, we are open with our sexuality. Closet queenery must end. . . . Being open is the foundation of freedom."[72]

At first glance the founding of the GLF, which symbolized the emergence of the gay liberation phase of the movement, appears to confirm the claims of those scholars who have argued forcefully that the end of the 1960s saw progressive movements and leftist activists abandon strategies rooted in appeals to Americanism. However, there are good reasons to challenge this interpretation. Even the GLF did not abandon patriotic dissent entirely, while many of the gay liberation organizations founded in its wake proved more than willing to appropriate the language of Americanism. While most activists in the early 1970s discarded the politics of respectability that had been championed by earlier gay rights leaders, they proved reluctant to abandon rhetorical and symbolic appeals to America's founding ideals.

A few weeks before the November 1969 election in New York City, thirteen members of the "Gay Commandoes," a GLF cell, infiltrated a mayoral debate sponsored by the League of Women Voters at Temple Torah in Queens. After being ignored repeatedly in the question and answer session, Marty Robinson, a twenty-six-year-old "skinny," "boyish-looking" carpenter from Brooklyn with a penchant for tight blue jeans, intervened.[73] He challenged conservative mayoral candidate Mario Procaccino to reveal his position on gay rights—"It's 1776, Mr. Procaccino. The homosexual revolution has begun."[74] It would be going too far to claim that this single incident demonstrates the centrality of patriotic dissent to GLF praxis, but it does show that appeals to Americanism and late 1960s revolutionary politics were not mutually exclusive—something that is borne out when looking at a number of other gay liberation organizations that were inspired by developments in New York.

Philadelphia's GLF, for example, was founded in the spring of 1970. One of its most influential leaders was Kiyoshi Kuromiya. A Japanese American born in 1943 in an internment camp in Wyoming and raised in California, Kuromiya was a veteran of both the civil rights and anti-Vietnam War movements.[75] Writing in the *Philadelphia Free Press* in July 1970, he claimed that "Homosexuals have burst their chains and abandoned their closets. . . . We come battle-scarred and angry to topple your sexist, racist, hateful society. We come to challenge the incredible hypocrisy of your sexual monogamy, your oppressive sexual role-playing, your nuclear family, your Protestant ethic, apple pie and Mother."[76] But Philadelphia's GLF also drew on America's historic ideals in making the case for gay rights. The group's founding statement, issued the same month as Kuromiya's attack on "apple pie and Mother," offered a radical critique of mainstream American society and culture to be sure, but it concluded with the line—"Our fight against homosexual oppression is one with the revolutionary struggle of all oppressed peoples for life, liberty and the pursuit of happiness."[77] A similar tension between the politics of revolution and the rhetoric of Americanism can be seen in an article that appeared in the 24 October 1970 edition of *Gay Flames: A Bulletin of the Homofire Movement.* Ortez Alderson, an African American activist from Chicago who was also involved with the anti-Vietnam War movement, condemned what he termed the "pigs mentality" of the American government, but also scored its hypocrisy for extolling the virtues of the Declaration of Independence while simultaneously seeking to repress homosexuals' own "pursuit of happiness."[78]

Over 27–28 June 1970 the Homophile Coordinating Council of Boston organized a series of gay pride events (including guerilla theater, seminar discussions, and a religious service) to commemorate the first anniversary of Stonewall—when "members of New York's gay community threw off the yoke of oppression." A panel discussion, sponsored by Boston's GLF and hosted at Beacon Hill's Charles Street Meeting House, made rhetorical use of the city's iconic role in the American Revolution. The session was entitled "Why Can't We Have a Dance in Boston, or Does the Cradle of Liberty Rock Only One Way?"[79]

That same month, inspired by the Stonewall rebellion and subsequent emergence of the gay liberation movement, a group of seven students at the University of Kansas founded the Lawrence Gay Liberation Front. The group's purpose was to "expose the inequities existing in this heterosexual male-dominated society and, in so doing, to dispel widespread ignorance, hostility and prejudice" against gay people. The organization also hoped to "build a sense of community and dignity among gay people at the University of Kansas, by providing an atmosphere of sympathy and understanding so as to enable them, as human beings, to develop and achieve their full potential and make their maximum contribution to society and to mankind."[80]

In August the group applied for formal university recognition. In addition to providing a degree of public legitimacy, such status would bring tangible benefits such as space on campus, available free of charge, for hosting meetings and events, and access to student activity fees for funding. On 5 September, despite support from the executive committee of the Student Senate, Chancellor Lawrence Chalmers refused the group's request on the grounds that the authorities were "not persuaded that student activity funds should be allocated either to support or oppose the sexual proclivities of students, particularly when they might lead to violation of state law." After three votes by the Student Senate in favor of recognition were vetoed by the chancellor, the GLF decided to file suit against the university.[81] With the help of renowned attorney William Kunstler and the American Civil Liberties Union, the GLF appealed the case to the Tenth Circuit Court of Appeals, but when the Supreme Court declined to hear the case the legal challenge had no place to go.[82]

In addition to its high-profile court action, the Lawrence GLF also organized a picket against a real estate agent accused of discriminating against homosexuals, and compiled voting guides that focused on candidates' positions on gay rights.[83] They also stocked a small library of gay and lesbian literature, provided counseling, and arranged talks.[84] However, the organization was probably best known for the dances it organized in the Kansas Union Ballroom.[85] Attracting people from across the region and, on one famous occasion featuring a performance by the Village People, the dances played a critical role in "creating and consolidating a gay culture and community in Lawrence."[86]

Despite using revolutionary rhetoric, such as pledging support to "all repressed and oppressed people" and condemning "uptight, authoritarian, racist, sexist Amerika," the Lawrence GLF actually displayed a striking allegiance to Americanism.[87] One of the group's official statements explained, "Paradox is the distinguishing characteristic of American society. Standing securely on the granite slats of the Bill of Rights, the Constitution, the Declaration of Independence, on the professed traditions of American liberty and justice, our society casts its eyes upon its sacred ideals while it holds those of whom it is afraid in a reality of hellish deception and oppression."[88] The Lawrence GLF believed that in a "society that professes the freedom of the individual, moral and sexual legislation has no place."[89]

In March 1972 the Front organized a dance to celebrate the First Amendment to the American Constitution. The "first annual CELEBRATION OF THE FIRST AMENDMENT DANCE" was held on 10 March in the Kansas Union Ballroom. The LGLF explained, "Why celebrate the First Amendment? If you're gay it's your amendment. If you have long hair it's your amendment. If you're Angela Davis it's your amendment. ... No matter who you are, no matter what the life style, orientation towards existence or sexuality, come celebrate one of the most important guarantees of human freedom."[90] The Lawrence GLF's allegiance to Americanism endured. A 1981 flyer produced by its successor organization, the Gay Services of Kansas, explained that its purpose was to "promote understanding of gay people among the people of Kansas and elsewhere" by "securing for gay people the rights and liberties established by the word and spirit of the Declaration of Independence and the Constitutions of the United States of America and the State of Kansas."[91] Lawrence's rich association with abolitionism and anti-slavery agitation perhaps encouraged such appeals; in recent times gay rights activists in Lawrence have portrayed their struggle as part and parcel of the town's historic commitment to liberty. Writing in the *University Daily Kansan* in October 1997, for instance, Rob McRae argued that struggling for social equality was an integral part of Lawrencian character. He pointed out that the town, founded by abolitionists and serving as the state's unofficial "Free State" Capital during the late 1850s, had "historically supported equality and justice."[92]

Gay rights activists at Stanford University also used patriotic appeals as part of their organizing efforts. The campus in Palo Alto had seen the founding of the first West Coast chapter of the Student Homophile League in February 1968. While this had proved a short-lived enterprise, the aftermath of Stonewall saw more successful and longer-lasting efforts at gay organizing at the prestigious university. The Gay Students' Union was founded in November 1970; in February 1972 it successfully won official university recognition as a Voluntary Student Organization and changed its name to the Gay People's Union. In 1974, GPU activists organized the first of what would become annual gay pride weeks on campus. Activists, one of whom was dressed as the Statue of Liberty, posed for publicity shots outside the organization's Old Firehouse headquarters carrying a "Gay Freedom" banner and a large American flag. Two years later, the gay and lesbian awareness celebrations, held over 21-29 June, were entitled "Spirit of '76: A Gay Civil Rights Event."[93]

New York's GLF had always been a highly unstable organization, and it did not take very long before, wracked by internal divisions, internecine conflicts, and increased isolation from potential allies, it went into precipitous decline. As San Francisco writer Sasha Gregory pointed out, the GLF quickly became "more an idea than an actual group of people."[94] At the end of 1969 four GLF activists—Jim Owles, Marty Robinson, Arthur Evans, and Arthur Bell—who were disillusioned with its lack of structure and its revolutionary multi-issue politics, founded the Gay Activists Alliance. The new group's constitution, approved on 21 December 1969, demanded "freedom for expression of our dignity and value as human beings through confrontation with and disarmament of all mechanisms which unjustly inhibit us: economic, social, and political." The GAA was "completely and solely dedicated" to the goals of gay rights, and it repudiated violence "except for the right of self-defense" as "unworthy of social protest." The organization rejected "all ideologies, whether political or social," and expressly forbade alliances with groups that were not dedicated to gay rights.[95] The constitution also revealed the GAA's appeal to Americanism, demanding that homosexuals "be the bearers of social and political rights which are guaranteed by the Constitution of the United States."[96] According to historians Dudley Clendinen and Adam Nagourney, the "grand sweeping language" of the GAA constitution was "deliberately, almost presumptuously, evocative of the Bill of Rights."[97]

In sharp contrast to the GLF, whose chaotic meetings have been described as "a cross between a Quaker meeting and an informal rap session," the GAA was a well-structured organization with elected officials, committees, and regular meetings run under parliamentary rules.[98] It became a single-issue interest group that, in the words of one scholar, "represented . . . a return toward the homophile movement's agenda, albeit one transformed by an infusion of countercultural style and sexual politics."[99] Indeed, the organization became famous for adopting and developing the "zap," which quickly became its trademark tactic. The "zap," a form of confrontational protest that combined political theater with direct action, revealed the influence of the countercultural activism that had emerged during the second half of the 1960s. At the major anti-Vietnam War demonstration of 21 October 1967, for instance, Abbie Hoffman and Jerry Rubin had attempted to levitate the Pentagon 300 feet in the air, claiming that the building would take on an orange glow and vibrate as the demon of war was exorcised.[100] A few months earlier, Hoffman had caused chaos at the New York Stock Exchange when he threw fistfuls of dollar bills onto the trading floor. Hoffman also testified before the House Committee on Un-American Activities wearing the uniform of a soldier from the Revolutionary War.[101]

Jim Fouratt, a founder of the GLF who went on to work with the GAA, was a close friend of Hoffman and has been credited with the idea for the Stock Exchange protest.[102] Described by one historian as looking like a "countercultural Billy the Kid" with his mustache, long blond hair, and shiny leather pants, Fouratt and his GAA cofounders helped to bring a sense of theatricality to the heart of the gay rights movement's direct action strategy.[103] By infiltrating public events and confronting public officials over their stance on gay rights, the organization forced politicians to take stands, helped shape a gay agenda, generated publicity, and empowered homosexuals.[104] By fall 1970 GAA, with its mixture of "dead earnestness and high camp," was the "most watched—and most imitated" gay rights organization in the country.[105] It lobbied for fair employment and housing legislation, pushed for the repeal of sodomy laws, and sought an end to police harassment. The organization also worked to foster a vibrant gay culture, and used its headquarters—the "Firehouse" in Greenwich Village—to host dances, cabarets, consciousness-raising sessions, film shows, and other cultural activities.[106]

The GAA's use of the zap was indicative of a "flair and sophistication that had never before been seen in gay liberation" and zaps could be humorous, colorful events. In fall 1970, GAA members occupied the offices of *Harper's Magazine*, staging an impromptu tea party, after the magazine ran a cover story that condemned homosexuality as "an affront to our rationality, living evidence of our despair of ever finding a sensible, an explainable, design to the world." In early 1971, after Vincent Gillen, president of Fidelifacts, a New York private investigative agency, boasted to a reporter that his company was efficient in alerting potential employers that applicants were homosexual—on the basis that "if one looks like a duck, walks like a duck, associates only with ducks and quacks like a duck, he is probably a duck," the GAA quickly arranged a zap. Sixty-five members of the GAA and the DOB demonstrated outside the company's headquarters. Marty Robinson dressed in an "outsized duck outfit, flapping white feathers," attracted the requisite media attention.[107]

Politicians were popular targets for the GAA—none more so than New York's mayor, John Lindsay, who endured some two years of skirmishes with the organization.[108] The first took place at a celebration in April 1970 to mark the hundredth anniversary of the founding of the Metropolitan Museum of Art, when Robinson confronted the mayor on stage, asking him when he intended "to speak out on homosexual rights."[109] A week later, on 19 April, the GAA disrupted the filming of the mayor's weekly WNEW-TV show, *With Mayor Lindsay.* Arthur Evans rushed the platform, asking "What about homosexuals. Homosexuals want an end to job discrimination." As he was escorted from the room, GAA members in the audience "clapped, stamped, and chanted." For the next 20 minutes, activists shouted "What about the laws against sodomy? We want free speech. Lindsay, you need our votes."[110] The mayor's decision to run for the Democratic presidential nomination offered the GAA an opportunity that was too good to refuse. On 25 January 1972 GAA disrupted a fund-raising event at Radio City Music Hall.[111] The following day, thirty activists occupied the headquarters of Lindsay's presidential campaign, at 415 Madison Avenue, for over two hours, to protest the Mayor's alleged "inaction" on "Intro 475," New York City's "gay civil rights bill" that had been killed off in committee.[112]

The pressure placed on politicians by the GAA to take stands on gay rights did yield some positive results. Representative Ed Koch (D.), Senator Charles Goodell (R.), and his Democratic opponent Richard Ottinger all offered support to the gay rights movement in the fall of 1970. Goodell, for instance, stated that "Constitutional principles are today clearly being abridged and denied in reference to homosexuals, and I therefore support efforts to secure their rights under the Constitution."[113] GAA president Jim Owles explained, "because [we] used public confrontation tactics when necessary, the major candidates realized that they could not ignore the demands our movement was making"—especially, he might have added, in an election year in a city with a substantial homosexual population.[114] And, on 7 February 1972 John Lindsay—by this time perhaps America's most zapped politician—issued a directive designed to protect homosexuals against discrimination in municipal hiring and promotion practices and also announced he would work for passage of a wider antidiscrimination ordinance for New York City.[115]

More widely, the GAA sought to persuade the national Democratic Party to endorse gay rights, and planned to mobilize several thousand gay rights activists at the party's Miami convention in 1972. The Alliance's demands were simple—William Bricker, president of the Washington GAA, explained that "We want our gay brothers and sisters to be able to stand up for their rights as first-class citizens."[116] To that end, they sought to have the Democratic Party adopt a gay rights plank, and even threatened that activists would stage a "kiss-in" if it refused.[117] Despite Senator George McGovern's personal support for gay rights, *realpolitik* insured that the plank went down to defeat. Nevertheless, two gay activists—Jim Foster and Madeline Davis—did get to address the convention to speak in its favor. Foster, a McGovern supporter and delegate from California's Fifth Congressional District in San Francisco, explained that "We do not come to you pleading your understanding or begging your tolerance." Rather, "We come to you affirming our pride in our lifestyle, affirming the validity to seek and maintain meaningful emotional relationships and affirming our right to participate in the life of this country on an equal basis with every citizen."[118] It would take another eight years for the national Democratic Party to endorse gay rights. The adoption of a gay rights plank at the 1980 convention was, according to Mel Boozer, a prominent gay African American delegate, a sign that "the ideals embedded in our Constitution by the founders of the Republic are alive and well in the Democratic Party."[119]

Appeals to Americanism formed a central part of the GAA's tactical approach. During November 1970, for example, Marty Robinson and Arthur Evans were invited to appear on ABC's *The Dick Cavett Show* after the GAA had threatened to disrupt the show's taping in protest at anti-gay remarks aired on a previous edition by the comedian Mort Sahl. Cavett, described by cultural commentator Clive James as "the most distinguished talk-show host in America, if sophistication and an intellectual breadth were what you wanted," interviewed Robinson and Evans, along with Dick Leitsch of New York Mattachine, for the Thanksgiving night broadcast. This provided the GAA activists with a valuable opportunity to invoke the founding principles of the nation in service to their cause. Evans, a Columbia Ph.D. student, explained that "There is no reason why we can't be full people, both economically and in terms of our feelings! . . . This is a matter of political rights, our Constitutional rights, which we have under the Declaration of Independence: 'Life, liberty, and the pursuit of happiness.'" Turning to Cavett, Evans asked "We should have that, too, don't you think?"[120]

The long campaign for a law protecting homosexuals from discrimination in New York City provides further illustration of the GAA's willingness to appeal to America's national creed. Beginning in the winter

of 1970, the GAA sought passage of a municipal bill that would prohibit discrimination on the grounds of sexual orientation in employment, public accommodation, and housing. Using zaps to put pressure
on politicians, the GAA quickly managed to win an important measure
of political support for "Intro 475," the proposed gay civil rights bill.[121]
In fall 1971, Mayor Lindsay himself endorsed it and, after it was killed
in committee, issued an executive order that a person's "private sexual
orientation" could not be used as a factor by municipal agencies in hiring and promotion decisions.[122] Defeated in 1971 and again in 1974,
the law was finally passed by the New York City Council in 1986.[123] In
their efforts to win broader public support for the bill the GAA drew on
the language of Americanism. They pointed out, for instance, that "Two
hundred years after the American Revolution," gay Americans still had
"no protection against discrimination in such essential areas as housing,
employment, and public accommodations." They also explained that,
with the "Bicentennial of the American Revolution . . . fast approaching" if the bill failed to win passage "1,000,000 New Yorkers will still have
nothing to celebrate."[124]

Sometimes appeals to Americanism took on a local flavor. In October
1972, for instance, several hundred activists attended the first Pennsylvania lesbian and gay conference in Pittsburgh—which the GAA cospon-
sored along with the Homophile Action League and Radicalesbians. In
endorsing a gay rights platform the delegates declared that "Our states
(and especially the Commonwealth of Pennsylvania) have always been a
refuge for those who have undergone persecution for their beliefs and
practices in less free environments. With the emergence of new styles of
living in our time, this Commonwealth has the opportunity to carry on
the "holy experiment" of William Penn by recognizing that any society is
enriched by diversity of opinion and action."[125]

Throughout the 1970s important gains were made and victories won
by the gay rights movement. New allies such as the American Civil Liberties Union, the National Organization for Women, and the American
Bar Association joined the cause. In 1973 the American Psychological
Association removed homosexuality from its list of mental disorders.
The Civil Service Commission ended its ban on employing homosexuals in July 1975 and a host of local antidiscrimination ordinances were
passed in municipalities across the nation. By 1976, seventeen states had
repealed their laws prohibiting sodomy.[126]

The late 1970s saw the limited but significant gains made by gay and lesbian Americans in their struggle to achieve first-class citizenship come
under sustained attack. Perhaps the most high-profile campaign took
place in Dade County, Florida. Led by Anita Bryant—a "mother, celeb-

rity singer, former Miss America, and spokeswoman for the Florida Citrus Growers"[127]—a potent coalition of conservatives and evangelical Christians succeeded in overturning a recently passed ordinance that prohibited discrimination in housing, public accommodations, and employment on the basis of "affectional or sexual preference."[128] In a special election held 7 June 1977, voters supported repeal of the ordinance by a margin of more than 2-1.[129] Between 1977 and 1980 voters overturned gay rights bills in Wichita, Kansas, St. Paul, Minnesota, and Eugene, Oregon. A particularly bitter campaign took place in California in 1978, where State Senator John Briggs attempted to ban homosexuals from teaching in the public schools. A combination of robust gay rights activism and the opposition of prominent conservative politicians, most notably former governor Ronald Reagan, saw Proposition 6 go down to defeat by more than a million votes in the November 1978 election.[130]

On 27 April 1978 the Rev. Wayne L. Dillabaugh launched his own crusade against gay rights in Madison, Wisconsin.[131] Dillabaugh, pastor of the Northport Baptist Church, sought to amend the city's equal opportunities ordinance, which afforded protection against discrimination "on the basis of sexual orientation in employment, housing, credit, city accommodations and public facilities."[132] Dillabaugh, who had spent "three stormy years" as assistant pastor at First Baptist Church in New Philadelphia, Ohio, arrived in Madison in early 1975.[133] He became a vocal critic of the Mad City's "permissive morality," campaigning against the Dangle Lounge, a downtown nude dance club owned by brothers Al and Tom Reichenberger, as well as focusing his ire on gay rights.[134] Dillabaugh intended to "clean the city up and make it a decent place for kids to grow up," and he claimed that liberalism and "some of the people and some of the politicians" were "polluted."[135] Dillabaugh was a colorful and controversial figure—once allegedly eating a live goldfish in an attempt to entice people to attend his church (why he thought this would be a crowd pleaser is not immediately clear). Described by one former associate as a "bully type" and a "real hard-nosed kind of guy," at the time he launched his crusade he was fighting charges of a misdemeanor battery for excessively spanking Timothy Fischer, a five-year-old church school pupil, with an 18-inch wooden paddle in September 1977.[136]

In spring 1978 Dillabaugh declared that Madisonians were "sick and tired of [the gay community's] liberal politics and their sexual perversion." Warning that he had a list of gay public officials that he might be prepared to make public, the pastor announced that he was "going to find out once and for all if this community is ready to stand up on its two feet to fight immorality and the destruction of our city by the activists, the homosexuals, and the liberals."[137]

In response to this challenge, Madison Gay Men and Lesbians United (The United), was formed in early May. Among its founders were Gridley Hall, member of the Madison Equal Opportunity Commission, Kathleen Nichols, coordinator of the Madison Committee for Gay Rights, and Barbara Lightner of the National Lesbian-Feminist Organization.[138] The group's general purpose was "to affirm the civil rights of gay men and lesbians and to support in its totality" the city's equal opportunities ordinance. The United planned a petition drive to demonstrate support for gay rights among Madisonians. Working in coalition with other local groups and progressive ministers, The United argued that gay rights was part of a broader civil rights/human rights agenda—and urged solidarity on the basis that "every discriminated group must realize that if we isolate ourselves from each other, we fight alone. This cannot be, for it has been said, 'United we stand; divided they pick us off—one by one.'"[139] As well as opposing attempts to repeal the equal opportunities ordinance, The United also fought to "enlarge the gay rights that we have now so that gays can live the full, dignified lives that other people can," and sought to increase understanding of gay rights among the police and local churches.[140]

For The United, supporting gay rights and opposing discriminatory practices against minorities were profoundly patriotic stances, and they grounded their demands within the framework of America's revolutionary promise of liberty:

> It has taken this country a long time to move toward fulfilling the potential of freedom for all. But we have moved in that direction through the Bill of Rights and the federal Constitution, through state laws and through city ordinances such as the one here in Madison. We will move with determination to preserve those rights—for ourselves as part of the lesbian and gay community and for all minorities and women.[141]

In an open letter published by the group in early 1979 the appeal to "Americanism" was again evident: "Madison," they said, "has always been a city of high American standards, tolerant of the diversity of belief and lifestyle of its residents. Yet today, a few dangerous demagogues threaten the tranquillity of our community."[142]

The anti-gay rights campaign was joined on June 16 by a group of 17 evangelical ministers from Dane County, including Rev. Richard "Dick" Pritchard of Heritage Congregational Church, who signed a letter to the City Council urging that it be made legal to refuse to hire homosexuals or bisexuals in the public school system and public service organizations.[143] Pritchard, a resident of Madison since 1947, was quieter and less colorful than Wayne Dillabaugh. Before rising to prominence as an untiring critic of sexual permissiveness he had been a strong supporter of African

American civil rights, joining demonstrations in Alabama and attending the August 1963 March on Washington.[144] For Pritchard, though, homosexuality was comparable with cancer or alcoholism, and he believed that gay rights encouraged "a lifestyle that is sick and wrong . . . 'Cruisers' . . . will be able to operate openly on the streets and in the schools and young people can be seduced."[145] Pritchard believed that homosexuals should be "precluded from certain sensitive occupations . . . so long as they persist in not wanting to recover."[146]

Madison, with its proud history of progressive politics and New Left activism, was perhaps one of the least hospitable locations for religious right-style campaigns against civil liberties anywhere in America during the 1970s. Indeed, the mayor in 1978 was the "cool, shrewd" Paul Soglin—an embodiment of the city's New Left radicalism.[147] Raised in a leftist household in the Hyde Park neighborhood of Chicago, Soglin studied first history and then law at the University of Wisconsin.[148] Active in both the civil rights and anti-Vietnam War movements, he was beaten by "club-swinging police officers" in October 1967 during fierce protests against Dow Chemical recruitment on the university campus and was arrested during the infamous May 1969 "Mifflin Street Block Party" protests.[149] Elected to the Madison Common Council in 1968, he won election as mayor in 1973 shortly before his twenty-eighth birthday.[150]

There appears to have been widespread support for gay rights in Madison among the city's political players—The United estimated that a large majority (15) of city council members supported the equal opportunities ordinance (in contrast to Miami (Dade County), Florida, where local ordinances could be repealed by popular referendum, in Madison the votes of 12 city councillors were required).[151] In November 1978, state representative David E. Clarenbach, who represented east and central Madison, wrote the City Council criticizing Pritchard's "crusade" as "cruel and repressive." Comparing the struggle for gay rights with the civil rights and women's rights movements, he stated that "the struggle to protect gay people from discrimination today involves an affirmation of basic human rights."[152] In February 1979, appearing at a forum organized by the Political Action Group of The United, all the major candidates for mayor (including eventual winner Joel Skornicka) pledged their support for the city's equal opportunities ordinance and "denounced" Pritchard's campaign. The United offered its support to Jim Rowen, who told the group that "to diminish the rights of any one group is to diminish the rights of all."[153] Ultimately, Dillabaugh and Pritchard's campaign failed to generate enough support among Madison's residents or political leaders, and the civil rights ordinance's protections of gay rights remained.

Some 2,000 miles west, in San Francisco, supporters of gay rights were mobilizing to defeat the Briggs Initiative and push for further policies to end discrimination against homosexuals. In 1977 Harvey Milk, who had become involved in gay rights activism shortly after moving to the city from New York in 1972, was elected to the San Francisco Board of Supervisors on his third attempt. Forming an effective alliance with liberal mayor George Moscone, Milk became a national leader of the gay rights movement. Milk was a tremendously effective neighborhood politician who, in addition to his support for gay liberation, emphasized the importance of individual rights and the need for governments that, at both national and local level, were responsive to the needs of their constituents.[154] He championed progressive measures, including a gay rights city ordinance, and helped lead the counterattack against the Briggs Initiative. On 27 November 1978, a disgruntled former city supervisor, Dan White, shot Mayor Moscone and Supervisor Milk dead in City Hall.[155]

Milk's effectiveness as a gay rights leader was rooted in his understanding of practical politics, but it also stemmed from his skill in crafting a rhetoric that inspired hope and passion among gay and lesbian Americans while simultaneously appealing to a broader, "straight," public. For Milk, much like The United in Madison, the struggle for equality for gays and lesbians was part of America's unfinished democratic promise—and Milk's rhetorical strategies compare with those used by Martin Luther King.[156] In a keynote speech outside City Hall before a crowd of 250,000 on 25 June 1978, Milk urged his "gay sisters and brothers to make the commitment to fight. For themselves, for their freedom, for their country."[157] Milk brilliantly wove demands for gay rights into a wider framework that emphasized America's historic commitment to liberty and equality and, in the dénouement, turned the rhetoric of the right firmly on its head:

Let me remind you what America is. Listen carefully.

On the Statue of Liberty it says: "Give me your tired, your poor, your huddled masses yearning to breathe free." In the Declaration of Independence it is written: "All men are created equal and they are endowed with certain inalienable rights." And in our National Anthem it says: "Oh, say does that star-spangled banner yet wave o'er the land of the free."

For Mr. Briggs and Mrs. Bryant . . . and *all* the bigots out there: That's what America is. No matter how hard you try, you cannot erase those words from the Declaration of Independence. No matter how hard you try, you cannot chip those words from off the base of the Statue of Liberty. And no matter how hard you try you cannot sing the "Star Spangled Banner" without those words.

That's what America is. Love it or leave it.[158]

Appeals to American ideals continued to occupy a central place in the struggle for gay rights during the 1980s and beyond. One of the most high-profile and moving aspects of the AIDS activism of the 1980s and 1990s, for example, was the production of the AIDS Memorial Quilt. The quilt, which contained thousands of individual panels commemorating those lost to the epidemic, was first displayed on the Mall in Washington in October 1987. The use of a quilt—that most American of icons—was part of a deliberate attempt by the NAMES Project to capture support among mainstream Americans.[159] Meanwhile a December 1987 fundraising letter for Gay and Lesbian Advocates and Defenders—a New England-based group that sought to use litigation to defend the rights of gay and lesbian Americans—declared that those who donated money to GLAD would "be contributing to an organization that stands for an old-fashioned American value: freedom."[160] In January 2010, as part of their efforts to overturn California's ban on same-sex marriage, supporters of Marriage Equality USA (MEUSA) carried placards featuring the slogan "Liberty, Justice & Marriage Equality" and a picture of the Statue of Liberty holding a bunch of flowers rather than a torch.[161]

In assessing the gay rights movement, the importance of the activist outpouring of the 1960s is clear. The homophile movement's tentative embrace of direct action protest in the mid-1960s owed much to the example set by the civil rights movement, while the move from "protest to resistance" in the antiwar movement and the growth of Black Power help explain the emergence of gay liberation at the decade's end. Organizations like the GLF used similar rhetoric, deployed similar tactics, and evinced a similar critique of the status quo to that of the New Left, and a number of SDS and antiwar movement veterans played leading roles in the post-Stonewall gay rights struggle. The New Left's conviction that the "personal" was "political" and its attempt to construct a new politics grounded in authenticity influenced the gay rights movement profoundly—most notably in the way "coming out" was championed by gay liberationists as a transformative act that promised both spiritual and political empowerment. Meanwhile, the gay movement's efforts at building alternative institutions such as bookshops, churches, and newspapers mirrored the New Left's emphasis on the importance of community structures as a basis for political action. Indeed the movement's continued strength into the 1980s and 1990s and its dedication to direct action and community organizing represent the persistence of quintessentially Sixties forms of activism and political ideology; the history of the gay rights movement provides a powerful challenge, then, to the still-common "declensionist" interpretation of the 1960s.[162]

As we have seen, appeals to America's national creed to exert political leverage and win wider public support survived the transition from the homophile movement into the era of gay liberation: patriotic protest constitutes perhaps the most important continuity between the pre and post-Stonewall movements. Some scholars have argued that the 1960s mark a turning point—a moment when many on the left, fueled by bitterness and despair over America's war in Vietnam, abandoned an Americanism that they viewed as inherently flawed and instead embraced a rhetorical anti-Americanism, thereby forfeiting the "ability to pose convincing alternatives for the nation as a whole."[163] However, the history of the gay rights movement suggests otherwise. To be sure, elements of the movement, particularly in 1969 and 1970, adopted militant rhetoric, took up radical ideological positions, and used anti-American language—the GLF denounced the Republic as "fucked up," and Carl Wittman referred to "Amerika" in his seminal "Gay Manifesto," to take two notable examples.[164] Americanism increasingly had to compete with zaps, street confrontation, occasional violence, and celebrations of gay life that many, including some in the movement, considered distasteful or counterproductive (it is hard to imagine the slogan "Suck Cock to Beat the Draft" being sanctioned by the Mattachine Society, for instance).[165] But none of this should obscure the continuing importance of patriotic protest to the gay rights movement. Numerous organizations and activists placed their demands for gay and lesbian equality within the broader tradition of America's revolutionary heritage and invoked the Republic's egalitarian rhetoric in fashioning a language of protest. From the perspective of many of its leaders as well as among the rank-and-file, the gay rights movement represented an effort to make more real the nation's democratic ideals and revolutionary promise. It was, and always had been, a profoundly patriotic struggle.

Chapter 3

Women's Rights—The Second Wave

1776 Was for Women Too
— Placard Slogan, Memphis NOW, 1974

Women's Rights: As American as Apple Pie
— Banner of Wisconsin delegation to the First National
Women's Conference, Houston, 1977

On Wednesday 26 August 1970 a crowd of more than 10,000, the vast majority of them women, marched down Fifth Avenue in New York to a rally in Bryant Park. Conceived by National Organization for Women (NOW) founder and feminist icon Betty Friedan, the march celebrated the fiftieth anniversary of the nineteenth amendment and was also part of a nationwide "Women's Strike for Equality." Five thousand gathered on Boston Common for a rally, 2,000 attended a similar event in San Francisco, in Miami protesters staged a "mock coffee-cup breaking garden party," and there were demonstrations in Washington, D.C., Philadelphia, Pittsburgh, Los Angeles, Chicago, Detroit, and Kansas City. The protests in New York began at around 10 a.m., when a dozen women gathered at Duffy Square, on Broadway, to "consecrate" a site for a statue of nineteenth-century women's rights pioneer Susan B. Anthony. Complete with cassock and surplice in her role as a "symbolic priest," Mary Orovan made the sign of the cross to the words "In the name of the Mother, the Daughter and the Holy Granddaughter. Ah-women. Ah-women." Later, at a lunchtime rally, writer Gloria Steinem, SNCC veteran Eleanor Holmes

Norton—chair of the city's Commission on Human Rights, and politician Bella Abzug all gave speeches. Abzug delivered her remarks with characteristic forcefulness, and her "finger-jabbing calls for the implementation of the strike's three principal demands"—abortion rights, establishment of 24-hour community-controlled day-care centers for the children of working mothers, and equal educational and employment opportunity—along with her statement that "we mean to have it now," were received with great enthusiasm by the crowd. Later that day the marchers inched down Fifth Avenue, overflowing the police barricades that had been designed to restrict them to just one lane, carrying placards and banners declaring "I'm a Second Class Citizen" and "Women Demand Equality." The diverse crowd included veteran suffragettes, socialists, lesbians, high school students, Black Panthers, seniors, "bra-less teenagers," nurses, young mothers, housewives, secretaries, lawyers, and opponents of the war in Vietnam. The women marched "because they wanted equality with men—and, they said, because they wanted men to think of them as human beings, not just sex objects." Despite the inevitable hecklers—who accused the women of being "traitors" and urged them "Back to the Kitchen"—the spirit of the marchers remained festive and upbeat. At the Bryant Park rally, which began at 8 p.m. in fading light, Betty Friedan declared that "This is not a bedroom war, this is a political movement," "Man is not the enemy, man is a fellow victim." Another of the speakers, feminist author Kate Millett, told the crowd that "You're beautiful; I love you," "At last we have a movement." Friedan considered the day's events to have been "beyond our wildest dreams," and she predicted that "the women's movement is going to be the biggest movement for social change in the 1970s."[1]

Friedan's prediction was a good one. During the 1970s the movement for women's rights became a national sensation. Across the country, women mobilized to demand equality and an end to discrimination—suing corporations, challenging unjust laws and writing new ones, launching insurgencies within trades unions and professional associations, founding new institutions (including day care centers, shelters, coffee shops, bookstores, newspapers, and journals), running for elective office, and championing new (and at times revolutionary) ideas. Enjoying broad public and political support, at least until the mid-1970s, second-wave feminism engaged millions of Americans in new, vibrant discussions about conceptualizations of politics and the meanings of gender, sexuality, and the family. This outpouring of creativity and organizing helped to transform the United States, and also influenced and inspired feminist movements around the world.[2] Indeed, as Sara Evans, one of feminism's leading historians, has noted, the result of second-wave feminism was "a political, legal, and cultural maelstrom that continues to this day."[3]

Of course, in many ways it is misleading to speak of "the women's movement" at all. From the beginning it was more a series of struggles and insurgencies—an extraordinary, and at times bewildering, agglomeration of national and local groups, seasoned and inexperienced activists, whites, blacks, Hispanics, Latinas, straights and lesbians, revolutionaries and reformers—with often conflicting aims and ideologies. Feminists disagreed about whether women's rights could be fought for alongside the struggle for black rights and efforts to end the war in Vietnam, or whether a separate movement was needed; they wondered whether true equality was compatible with a capitalist society; they argued over whether pursuing (or maintaining) sexual relationships with men was simply sleeping with the enemy; they debated whether America's public institutions were capable of being reformed.[4]

At one end of the ideological spectrum stood NOW. Founded in 1966 as a feminist equivalent of the National Association for the Advancement of Colored People (NAACP), it sought to eliminate discrimination against women and open up new opportunities in politics and government, the professions, education, and "every other field of importance in American society."[5] While it engaged in direct action protests, NOW was an archetypal liberal reform organization—lobbying politicians, collecting signatures on petitions, filing lawsuits, and seeking to build broad-based public support to advance its cause. Many women who joined the movement in the late 1960s and early 1970s were fiercely critical of NOW—which they viewed as both conservative (its founder, Betty Friedan, was unsympathetic toward those she viewed as seeking to launch a "bedroom war" and infamously attacked lesbians as a "lavender menace") and hierarchical (it had elected national leaders who sat atop a network of local chapters).[6]

On the opposite wing lay an assortment of radicals and revolutionaries who sought not merely equal rights but, in the words of New Haven activists Tricia Tunstall and Callie Kenady, a "total transformation of society: a restructuring of work relations, of social relations, of the family, of all social institutions . . . a revolution in every area of life."[7] The New York-based Redstockings, founded by Shulamith Firestone and Anne Koedt in February 1969, argued that "Male supremacy is the oldest, most basic form of domination" and that "All other forms of exploitation and oppression (racism, capitalism, imperialism, etc.)" were "extensions of male supremacy."[8] The Feminists, an offshoot of New York City NOW, actually restricted married women and those living with men to no more than one-third of its voting membership, on the grounds that "the identification of each woman's interests with those of a man prevents her from uniting with other women and seeing herself as a member of the class of women."[9] Some activists went even farther, taking the view that lesbianism was, in fact, the purist form of feminism. Perhaps the best-known advocates of this position were the Furies, a Washington-based collective founded in May 1971 that took its name from the goddesses of Greek mythology. One of the founders, Ginny Berson, explained that the Furies' ideology was based on the notion that "Lesbianism is not a matter of sexual preference, but rather one of political choice which every woman must make if she is to become woman-identified and thereby end male supremacy." Fellow member Charlotte Bunch argued that to "be a Lesbian is to love oneself, woman, in a culture that denigrates and despises women. . . . Lesbianism threatens male supremacy at its core. When politically conscious and organized, it is central to destroying our racist, capitalist, imperialist system."[10]

As historian Stephanie Gilmore has cautioned, however, one must be careful not to accept unquestioningly the existence of such clearly defined divisions as "radical" versus "liberal" in the women's movement. Indeed, in many places such "splits" appear to have been more rhetorical than real. Gilmore's own work has revealed that women's organizations and activists could embrace the "conservative" and the "radical" simultaneously: the Memphis chapter of NOW wrote letters, launched petition drives, lobbied politicians, and sought to work constructively with the local power structure to be sure, but it also evinced a commitment to building alternative institutions, mobilized around the issue of violence toward women (in the process embracing the maxim that the "personal" was "political"), and took part in street actions and countercultural "zaps."[11] Similarly, in Minnesota, liberal and radical streams came together in the form of the Emma Willard Task Force, founded by NOW's Gerri Helterline and Cheri Register of Twin Cities Female Liberation, which sought to combat sexism in the state school system; and in Iowa the Cedar Rapids Woman's Caucus saw "prominent, powerful women" working constructively alongside "countercultural leftists."[12]

By the mid-1970s a number of America's most iconic and influential feminists, including Eleanor Holmes Norton, Alice Walker, Maya Angelou, and bell hooks—were women of color.[13] Yet at the same time one of the most important fault lines in the feminist movement was race.[14] The rise of Black Power—both pluralists' emphasis on group solidarity and nationalists' predilection for racial separatism—made interracial coalition building, never an easy task, particularly tricky. At first glance, one might think that the renowned sexism of many (male) black militants (Black Panther Eldridge Cleaver talked of "pussy power," for example) and their tendency to blame black women for emasculating black men would have encouraged support for the women's movement. However, Sara Evans has argued that "ambivalence" best describes black women's response to the second wave.[15] Discriminated against on the grounds of race as well as gender, many black women were reluctant to be seen to criticize their menfolk and divide the race. An inspirational figure for many white women in SNCC, and an unflinching champion of equality, Mississippi sharecropper Fannie Lou Hamer explained that she was not "hung up on this about liberating myself from the black man. I'm not going to try that thing. I got a black husband, six-feet-three, 240 pounds, with a 14 shoe, that I don't *want* to be liberated from. But we are here to work side by side with this black man in trying to bring liberation to all people."[16]

Black women's experiences of exploitation and segregation in the labor market also made it difficult for them to identify with (middle-class) white women's reaction against the role of housewife, something further compounded by the intrinsic link between whiteness and femininity in the dominant culture.[17] Concerned that second-wave feminism was too middle-class in its composition and orientation, many black women remained skeptical that the movement really addressed their concerns. Former SNCC activist Frances Beal articulated many of these issues in her 1969 tract, "Double Jeopardy: To Be Black and Female":

> Another problem is that the white woman's movement is basically middle class. Very few of these women suffer the extreme economic exploitation that most black women are subjected to day by day. This is the factor that is most crucial for us . . . If the white groups do not realize that they are in fact fighting capitalism and racism, we do not have common bonds. If they do not realize that the reasons for their condition lie in the system and not simply that men get a vicarious pleasure out of "consuming their bodies for exploitive reasons" (this kind of reasoning seems to be quite prevalent in certain women's groups), then we cannot unite with them around common grievances or even discuss these groups in a serious manner because they're completely irrelevant to the black struggle.[18]

Given such concerns, many black feminists chose to organize independently. In the summer of 1973, the black caucuses of the National Women's Political Caucus and NOW formed the National Black Feminist Organization to enable black feminists to "address ourselves to the particular and specific needs of the larger, but almost cast aside, half of the Black race in Amerikka, the Black woman."[19]

During the 1970s the women's movement rattled off a string of impressive victories. In 1972 the Congress extended the Equal Pay Act to cover most white-collar employees. That same year it passed Title IX of the Higher Education Act, which cut off federal funds to educational institutions that discriminated on grounds of gender; and the Equal Rights Amendment (signed by President Nixon, it was sent to the states for ratification). Two years later, Congress passed the Equal Credit Opportunity Act, which prohibited banks and other providers of credit from discriminating against women in their lending practices. Across the nation, states modernized their divorce and rape laws and passed legislation to outlaw employment discrimination. Moreover, women began to enter professions that had traditionally been the preserve of men: during the 1970s the number of women entering law school increased 500 percent, and the proportion of female Ph.D.s increased from 11 percent to 25 percent. By the 1980s, 25 percent of new graduates of law, medical, and business schools were women—up from 5 percent in the late 1960s. In 1972, Sally Priesand became the first female rabbi and, four years later, the Episcopal Church allowed women's ordination. Litigation, too, brought about important progress: federal courts struck down a host of discriminatory practices—such as "gender differentials in state and federal pensions" and upheld the right of women to "register driver's licenses in their own names." Most famously, in 1973 the Supreme Court ruled in *Roe v. Wade* that, subject to certain ethical and medical restraints, the "right of privacy" encompassed a woman's right to an abortion.[20] During the 1970s, feminism also became institutionalized, with women establishing caucuses within existing organizations (such as trades unions and professional societies) and forming new groups—for example, the Women in Campus Ministry Caucus was founded in 1972, the National Women's Studies Association in 1977, and the National Coalition Against Domestic Violence in 1978.[21]

During the late 1970s and 1980s, however, feminism came up against an increasingly powerful conservative counter-attack. The first significant battle was over the ERA. With 30 states approving the amendment in the first year after its endorsement by Congress, and with broad bipartisan support, the ERA had seemed destined to become written into the Constitution in no time.[22] But Phyllis Schlafly and other grassroots conservatives had other ideas; STOP ERA (founded by Schlafly in 1972) helped to whip up opposition to the ERA among elected politicians and the general public—arguing that the proposed amendment would undermine the traditional family, force women to fight alongside men in the armed forces, and usher in a dangerous new world of unisex bathrooms. Although feminists and their allies were able to extend the deadline for ratification from 1979 to June 1982, the ERA ultimately fell three states short.[23] With "family" issues (sexual orientation, abortion, divorce, marriage) increasingly prominent among Republican Party activists, and with Ronald Reagan's election to the White House in November 1980, the broader political climate quickly became far less hospitable for those seeking further advances for women's equality; indeed, a good deal of effort now had to be spent in protecting existing gains, especially over abortion. But despite the efforts of some, women's rights were not rolled back. While the earlier spirit of optimism faded, the 1980s saw continued gains—in 1981, Sandra Day O'Connor became the first woman to sit on the U.S. Supreme Court; in 1983, Sally K. Ride became the first American women to travel into space; and in 1984, Geraldine Ferraro became the first female vice-presidential candidate of a major political party. By 1991, women made up 11 percent of the nation's armed forces, and over two-thirds of American universities offered women's studies courses. There was significant progress in the world of work, too. Whereas in 1960, just over a third of women had worked outside of the home, by 1990 the figure was 58 percent; the number of female lawyers and judges had increased from 7,500 to 108,200 and female doctors from 15, 672 to 174,000. And while there was still a pay gap (and in too many walks of life a "glass ceiling" and continued prejudice), women's median weekly earnings had reached 75 percent of men's (up from 62 percent in 1970).[24] Of course, the women's movement was not itself directly responsible for every gain that was made—but it had made a decisive contribution to the political debate, raised consciousness around issues of sexual and gender discrimination, and helped change public opinion, especially among women.[25] In 1983, one opinion poll suggested that 80 percent of women believed that "to get ahead a woman has to be better at what she does than a man," with only 26 percent stating that "one of the best parts of being a woman" was being a wife and mother (down from 53 percent in 1970). In 1986, the height of the conservative backlash, 56 percent of women considered themselves feminists, and 67 percent favored a strong women's movement. Even a small majority of men (51 percent) agreed with the statement that "The United States continues to need a strong women's movement to push for changes that benefit women."[26]

In the involvement of veterans from the civil rights, New Left and anti-war movements, the insistence that the "personal" was "political," the enthusiasm for local organizing and the building of alternative institutions, and the deployment of a range of direct action protests, the struggle for women's rights revealed itself to be, in the words of historian Alice Echols, "a paradigmatically sixties movement."[27] Indeed, scholars have long recognized the importance of both the reform politics and the protest movements of the 1960s to the emergence of the women's liberation movement. Set up in 1961 by John F. Kennedy, the President's Commission on the Status of Women, chaired by former first lady Eleanor Roosevelt, and the fifty state commissions that followed in its wake provided opportunities for politically engaged women to work together and forge alliances; illuminated and documented the existence of sexual discrimination and women's second-class status (in politics, the workplace, education, and law); and generated expectations that meaningful action would be taken to tackle the problems that had been highlighted.[28] The cause of women's equality was given a further boost by the addition of "sex" to Title VII of the Civil Rights Act of 1964, which covered employ-ment discrimination. Introduced by Virginia representative Howard W. Smith, a conservative segregationist and chairman of the House Rules Committee, in an attempt to wreck the Bill, the amendment was accepted after a few hours of light-hearted debate. However, the subsequent refusal of the Equal Employment Opportunities Commission (EEOC) to take sexual discrimination seriously and enforce the law led directly to the formation of the National Organization for Women (NOW) in October 1966 (indeed, EEOC offices in New York, Washington, Pittsburgh, and other cities saw some of the group's earliest direct action protests).[29]

The initial composition of NOW's leadership illustrates the links with reform liberalism perfectly: two former EEOC commissioners were NOW vice-presidents and seven of the twenty board members had been mem-bers of the State Commissions on the Status of Women.[30] NOW's state-ment of purpose declared that it was time to "take action to bring women into full participation in the mainstream of American society now, exer-cising all the privileges and responsibilities thereof in truly equal part-nership with men," and that there was a pressing need to "break through the silken curtain of prejudice and discrimination against women in government, industry, the professions, the churches, the political par-ties, the judiciary, the labor unions, in education, science, medicine, law, religion and every other field of importance in American society."[31] NOW's founders also placed their struggle for equality in the context of "the world-wide revolution of human rights now taking place within and beyond our national borders" and sought to build the equivalent of a "civil rights movement" that would "speak for women."[32]

It is clear that the broader climate of Sixties activism shaped women's liberation in critical ways.[33] Indeed, the very fact that veterans of the civil rights, New Left, and antiwar movements featured prominently among both the leadership and rank-and-file of the emerging women's move-ment provides a simple illustration of this connection. Among the more well-known figures were Naomi Weisstein (active in New Haven CORE, Chicago SNCC, and the antiwar movement at Loyola University) and Heather Booth (civil rights movement and SDS), who, in the summer of 1967, organized the first women's studies classes in the country; Jo Freeman (SCLC) and Shulamith Firestone (New Left); Robin Morgan (antiwar movement and Yippies); and Student Mobilization Committee founder Bettina Aptheker.[34]

Those active in the civil rights and New Left movements of the 1960s believed that they were engaged in a struggle to make a better and more equal world. Civil rights groups talked idealistically of building a "beloved community," with SNCC's founding statement, written in April 1960, speaking of creating "a social order of justice permeated by love."[35]

Two years later SDS released the Port Huron Statement, which declared its goal of replacing "power rooted in possession, privilege, or circumstance" with power "rooted in love, reflectiveness, reason, and creativity" and outlined the goal of establishing a "democracy of individual participation" in which political, economic and social institutions would be organized "with the well-being and dignity of man as the essential measure of success."[36]

Many women involved in these struggles experienced a dissonance between the lofty ideals of equality and participatory democracy and the reality of movement culture. SNCC chairman Stokely Carmichael's quip that the only position for women within the movement was "prone" may have been made in jest, but it reflected a wider reality nonetheless. Within Carmichael's own organization, for example, concerns about sexism were raised in a November 1964 position paper that documented various instances of bias—including the fact that women were expected, as a matter of course, to carry out clerical tasks and take the minutes at meetings. The authors, who retained anonymity out of fear of ridicule (they were later identified as Mary King and Casey Hayden), concluded that "assumptions of male superiority" were "widespread and deep rooted" and that, despite playing a critical role in running the movement, women were "not given equal say-so" when it came to decision-making.[37] That same year women in the Atlanta office, including experienced black organizers Judy Richardson and Ruby Doris Robinson, held a sit-in (in about equal parts serious and humorous) to protest the fact that women were expected to undertake almost all the clerical work—as Richardson later explained, "You know, none of the men were doing the minutes." Robinson held a sign that stated "No More Minutes Until Freedom Comes to the Atlanta Office."[38] SNCC, with its commitment to group-centered leadership and participatory democracy, was actually one of the more progressive civil rights organizations. Septima Clark, who ran the SCLC Citizenship Education Project, recalled how "Dr King didn't think too much of the way women could contribute" and that "one of the weaknesses of the civil rights movement" was the "way the men looked at the women . . . [W]hatever the man said had to be right."[39]

If anything, the situation in the New Left and anti-war movements was worse. Bettina Aptheker took a leading role in the Free Speech Movement while a student at UC-Berkeley, delivering her first public speech while standing atop the police car that had been seized in Sproul Plaza and surrounded by hundreds of students. In December 1966, she helped to found the Student Mobilization Committee (SMC)—the nation's first student anti-war coalition.[40] Looking back at the student movements of the 1960s Aptheker—whose father, Herbert, was a noted U.S. historian and Communist Party leader—claimed that "women's subordination and abuse" was "built into the everyday life of the movement itself," with the sexism prevalent in mainstream society "mirrored" in the New Left and anti-war struggles. She explained that "men made the decisions, held the press conferences and launched the mobilizations," whereas women "staffed the offices, answered the telephones, assembled the mailings, and ran the mimeograph machines, often all night. We also performed sexual favors for "important" movement leaders."[41]

Aptheker's experience of sexism was not uncommon. During the entire 1960s, for instance, only two women ever held national office within SDS and in 1964 a paltry 6 percent of executive committee places were filled by women.[42] Barbara Haber, a Brandeis graduate, recalled how in SDS she "couldn't get no respect" and "was constantly being diminished" and "treated like a secretary." In fact Haber was forced to work out an arrangement with her husband Al, an SDS founder, who would repeat her suggestions at meetings, thereby insuring that they would be taken seriously.[43] Beth Oglesby similarly complained that women were relegated to clerical and administrative tasks while "it's the men who talk, and it's the men who theorize, and it's the men who make the decisions."[44] A number of women also resented the sexual politics that surrounded the SDS leadership—whereby strong, independent women would often find themselves isolated, while those who were involved sexually with the group's male leaders were more likely to be accepted. Cindy Decker doubtless spoke for many of her SDS sisters when she explained that "here were all these sanctimonious young men going around pontificating about how the world was a bad place . . . but they treated women in totally abysmal ways."[45]

A similar story could be found within the New Left at the local level. In New Haven, Connecticut, for example, there was a vibrant radical scene, centered around the American Independent Movement (AIM). Organized initially to protest the war in Vietnam (it ran Robert Cook for Congress in 1966 in a high-profile campaign), it also sought to organize local workers, campaigned against urban renewal plans that were insensitive to the city's historic neighborhoods, and challenged Yale University's links with the military-industrial complex. Yet it appears that women activists were sidelined and treated as something of second-class citizens by some of their male counterparts. AIM veteran Nina Adams recalled that she felt "needed" and "respected," but not "central" to the organization. As she explained, "big men [were] running a show and women [were] very critical to it but somehow peripheral." The casual sexism of the organization was illustrated on the front cover of the July 1969 *AIM Newsletter*, which carried an illustration of "a barbed wire-wielding capitalist flanked by six figures who represented various oppressed groups"—all male.[46]

Among movement women, a growing awareness of the contradiction between the idealistic language of "freedom" and "equality" that they and their male counterparts espoused and their own experiences of sexist treatment, had a radicalizing effect. Many began to identify with the oppressed people whom they were attempting to organize or liberate, and raise (with increasing frequency and force) questions of sexual discrimination within the movement. In their 1965 SNCC position paper, "Sex and Caste: A Kind of Memo," Casey Hayden and Mary King explained that, "Having learned from the movement to think radically about the personal worth and abilities of people whose role in society had gone unchallenged before," a number of women in the movement had begun to try to "apply those lessons to their own relations with men."[47] A paper issued by Radical Women in April 1968 outlined the discrimination women suffered in the New Left and pointed out that the "absurdity of a movement with our goals perpetuating this kind of degradation and internal hypocrisy is becoming more apparent and more resented by women activists."[48]

When "women's issues" were raised within the movement, however, the response was often dismissive. In New Haven's radical circles, as elsewhere, many men explained that women would find themselves free after the revolution. When, in the summer of 1967, SDS adopted a women's liberation resolution at its annual convention, the story was duly carried in the July 1967 issue of *New Left Notes*. However, it appeared "alongside a cartoon of a girl—with earrings, polkadot minidress, and matching visible panties—holding a sign: 'We Want Our Rights and We Want Them Now.'"[49] New York's underground newspaper, *Rat*, referred to women as "chicks" and carried photos of naked women.[50] During the first (and only) national convention of the National Conference for New Politics (NCNP), held in Chicago's luxurious Palmer House hotel over Labor Day weekend, 1967, a women's caucus formed among the myriad civil rights, Black Power, anti-war, and other assorted radical delegates. But when some of the women, led by Jo Freeman and Shulamith Firestone, sought to present their own radical demands to the plenary session they were treated with contempt. NCNP executive director William F. Pepper patted Firestone on the head and explained, "Move on little girl; we have more important issues to talk about here than women's liberation." A week later, a group of radical women met in Chicago and wrote an influential appeal, "To the Women of the New Left," which urged women to recognize their oppression and "organize a movement for women's liberation."[51] Six months later they were publishing *voice of women's liberation*, the nation's first radical women's newspaper.[52]

Perhaps the most shocking illustration of the New Left's sexism came during the January 1969 counter-inaugural protests organized by the National Mobilization Committee. Marilyn Salzman Webb, an SDS veteran who had majored in psychology at Brandeis University before entering graduate school at Chicago, had been asked to address the counter-inaugural rally by a group of Washington feminists. Webb, who had intended to speak about "equality, abortion, child care, and treating women with respect," recalled that "I hadn't gotten three sentences out when fistfights broke out. People were yelling, 'Take her off the stage and fuck her.' 'Fuck her down a dark alley.' . . . These were supposed to be my brothers and sisters! . . . Over thirty years later, I can still feel the shock." That evening, Webb received a phone call from a woman she believed was from SDS, in which she was told that "if you or anybody like you ever gives a speech like that anywhere in the country, we'll beat the s*** out of you wherever you are." For Webb, this was the "moment I suddenly knew that we couldn't build a coalition with the left. Women's liberation was going do be an independent movement . . . we had to organize separately."[53] Given all this, it was hardly surprising that movement women increasingly opted to organize independently of men.[54]

There was, though, a more positive side to this rather sorry story. SDS's Helen Garvy recalled being encouraged by her male colleagues Paul Potter and Todd Gitlin (president and past-president of the organization respectively)—"Any time I would say 'Well, I'm not sure that I can do this,' they would say, 'Yes, you can.'" Similarly, Vivian Rothstein explained that one reason that she "liked the movement" was because she was "taken seriously."[55] While the existence of sexist and chauvinistic attitudes is indisputable, in comparison with wider American society movement women (and especially, it seems, SNCC women) found themselves in a relatively enlightened environment. Judy Richardson, an African American from Tarrytown, New York, who dropped out of Swarthmore College to work full-time in SNCC's Atlanta office, recalled that "women in the organization were respected for their capabilities—even within the context of sexism . . . and yeah, you know, there was little stuff that would happen every once in a while. . . . But most of the time, I never felt limited. Never limited about what I could do . . . as a woman, I just felt absolutely powerful, just powerful. It was amazing."[56] Indeed, complaints about sexism within SNCC often failed to resonate with black women. Cynthia Washington recalled that "[this] didn't make any particular sense to me because, at that time, I had my own project in Bolivar County, Miss. A number of black women also directed their own projects."

In fact, strong black female leaders in the civil rights movement were often a source of inspiration to white women. Jo Freeman explained that "the black women I saw and worked with provided a different model of what it meant to be a woman in our society."[57] Moreover, movement women had not simply become experienced organizers (capable of planning meetings, holding demonstrations, and organizing and participating in direct action), they had also been exposed to a rhetoric of oppression and developed an ideology that could be applied effectively to their own situation: a faith in the power of ordinary people to effect change. Bettina Aptheker recalled, "even within the secondary and at times humiliating role of enforced patriarchy which we experienced within the movement, we were part of it. . . . What we learned in the sixties, the great secret as it were, is that people have both the inherited wisdom and the collective strength to change the course of human events."[58]

Perhaps the greatest legacy of the civil rights and New Left movements for the women's liberation movement was the notion that the "personal" was "political." In 1965 Hayden and King had explained that one of the broader goals of the civil rights movement was to "build a society which would see basic human problems (which are now seen as private troubles) as public problems and would try to shape institutions to meet human needs rather than shaping people to meet the needs of those with power"; women, they said, were now seeking to apply this lesson to their own situation.[59] The idea that the traditional distinctions—between private and public, personal and political—should be broken down was a central feature of both the civil rights and New Left movements of the early 1960s. When they analyzed the kind of history that black (and white) children were taught in Mississippi's public schools, for example, or the way *in loco parentis* rules at the nation's elite universities were conceived and operated, activists came to realize that they were, in fact, opening a window onto how social, economic, cultural, and political power functioned in American society. It also became clear that personal decisions (such as challenging restrictive dormitory rules) could have political consequences.[60]

Within second-wave feminism, consciousness-raising was perhaps the single most important process by which the links between politics and personal experience could be excavated, and it was used widely throughout the movement. Writing in the women's magazine *Redbook* in November 1973, Jane Ciabattari explained how consciousness-raising was "basically a sensitizing process" whose purpose was

> to make a woman aware that as a woman she has been denied many opportunities for choice in her life. Through discussing her life on a personal level with others in her group, the reasoning goes, she will come to realize the extent to which the realities of her situation—including what has been expected of her and denied her, how she has been conditioned by

parents, teachers, and other people to fit the "feminine" mold, and how she feels about herself—are shared by other women. Such new perspectives help prepare women to recognize and cope with discrimination and to take advantage of new opportunities arising for women today.

Topics and questions covered in such discussions usually involved "your parents and their relationship to you," "your feelings about marriage, having children, pregnancy and motherhood," "have you ever lied about orgasm?" "as a child were you encouraged in certain activities and discouraged from others?" and "do you see housework as a duty only you should perform or do you see it as a favor to your family?"[61] An article on consciousness-raising that appeared in Berkeley's *It Ain't Me Babe* in January 1971 explained how the stories—about "sex, about the men in our lives, about our childhoods, our schooling, our families"—that women shared were "remarkably similar. Definite patterns of experience emerged. What we had all thought to be a personal problem, the result of our own particular situation, was common to everyone. We realized that we had all been suffering from the damage society inflicts on an oppressed group."[62] Betsy Gilbertson, who had been active in New Haven's AIM, was recruited to the women's liberation movement at the end of the 1960s. She recalled her own experience of participating in consciousness-raising:

> We would take some piece of experience, that it had never occurred, to me at least, to think about differently, and talk about it. . . . The experience that captured that best for me was one day looking at the front page of the newspaper and there was not a single woman's name on it—and I had been reading that newspaper all my life and I had never noticed that. It was like that. And this light—I mean, it was literally like someone had screwed in a light bulb. And all of a sudden I had a set of lenses for looking at the world that I hadn't had before, and the whole world looked different through them.[63]

The women's liberation movement also made extensive use of a range of direct-action tactics—occupying buildings, staging sit-ins and teach-ins, engaging in street theater—that had been pioneered by earlier Sixties movements.[64] In one of the earliest actions, NOW activists entered EEOC offices around the nation on 15 February 1967 to protest their lack of action in enforcing rules that outlawed sexual discrimination. That summer, the *New York Times* found itself picketed for maintaining a "sex-segregated want ad policy."[65] In March 1970 perhaps as many as 200 women representing a number of groups (including NOW, Redstockings, and New York Radical Feminists), and including some employees, occupied the offices of the *Ladies' Home Journal*, staging a dramatic 11-hour sit-in to protest its "demeaning" stance toward women and demanding the opportunity to edit a "liberated" issue of the magazine. They also called for the journal to end "exploitative" advertisements and to provide female employees with a free day-care center. A special supplement on women's liberation, written by supporters of the movement, was included in the August edition.[66] In April, a sit-in was held at the offices of Grove Press, a publisher of erotic literature, by women who argued that "Grove's sadomasochistic literature and pornographic films dehumanize and degrade women." The protest was sparked by the sacking of eight employees, including six women, for engaging in union organizing.[67]

Teach-ins, which had been pioneered by the anti-Vietnam War movement to good effect during 1965, were also deployed by feminists. In December 1969 activists at San Francisco State held a teach-in on women's oppression and a similar event was held at Michigan State University in March 1970.[68] At Berkeley, renowned as a centre of radical activism, women engaged in a range of protest actions lifted from the New Left playbook. In December 1969, for example, local activists "demonstrated at the Pacific Telephone Company's San Francisco office because of their refusal to accept applications from women for the position of telephone installer (a position paying twice as much as that of telephone operator)." In April the Leamington Hotel Jester's Court, a "men's-only grill," was integrated after three days of sit-ins and pickets by members of the local NOW chapter.[69] On 7 January 1970 around 60 women, including members of Berkeley NOW, gathered at UC-Berkeley's Harmon Gym to protest that karate classes were only available to men, and twenty or more of them "marched to the men's locker room (where pre-enrollment was taking place)" chanting "defense for women." A *New York Times* journalist explained that whereas "the demonstrators were preponderantly attractive young girls wearing miniskirts," the "men in the locker room they invaded . . . were preponderantly undressed." The women were denied the right to enroll, but the following day 35 women attempted to enter the class at the gym anyway, demanding "self-defense for women now." They were turned away by the police, who threatened the women with arrest. After the class finished, the activists took their protest to the office of the chancellor, Roger Heyns. The women stressed the importance of self-defense to women, both in its practical use in repelling potential attacks and its role in fostering individual and collective empowerment. Access to self-defense classes was part of a much broader list of demands, which included provision of child care for all employees and students; an end to discriminatory job placement (including segregated job advertising); an end to discrimination in admissions and hiring practices; creation of women's history courses; and an end to all housing regulations and dormitory rules.[70]

Women at Yale University similarly engaged in direct action to challenge discrimination and demand equal rights. Although women had been admitted to the Yale Graduate School since 1892, the campus had remained a decidedly male-centric place. Janet Lever and Pepper Schwartz, who began graduate studies in sociology in the fall of 1968, recalled that "the maleness of Yale was overwhelming. . . . Male eating clubs, male-populated streets, even a male-oriented health department." They explained that, simply by walking around campus, they "became acutely aware of the staring. We were conscious of ourselves as objects, common objects to be looked over and appraised."[71] While Yale's undergraduate programs were opened to women from the fall of 1969, in the short term the registration of 230 female freshman and 358 female transfer students did little to change the atmosphere. Women were outnumbered about 8-1 in 1969 (5-1 three years later); only 2 of the university's 363 full professorships were held by women (and 2 out of 785 tenured faculty in arts and sciences); and sexist attitudes were not hard to find—one male undergraduate described coeds as "like Christmas-tree decorations or something," while a senior professor conceded that women made a "fractional contribution to an undergraduate lecture. . . . They don't yawn as much."[72] Women activists engaged in a range of protests in their attempt to break down this male-centric culture. A "child-in" was held at a Yale Board meeting to demand adequate child care facilities, for example, while New Haven Green hosted a "camp-in" to protest welfare cuts.[73]

Title IX of the 1972 Education Act prohibited discrimination on the basis of sex in any education program or activity that received federal funds. Although a grace period until 1978 was provided, the slow progress toward equality prompted further protest at Yale.[74] On 3 March 1976, 19 members of the Yale women's varsity crew, disgusted with the lack of adequate shower and changing facilities at the Derby boathouse, marched into the office of Joni Barnett, director of physical education, and stripped naked to reveal the words "Title IX" "emblazoned across their chests and backs in Yale-blue paint." Chris Ernst, a senior and crew captain who went on to represent America in two Olympic games and become a world champion, read a statement accusing Yale of "exploiting" the women's bodies. For the previous two seasons the women had been forced to use "four crowded showers in a rented trailer"; during the 1975-1976 season the women had been without any facilities at all, and had simply had to stand around in the freezing cold waiting for the men to finish their showers before the bus took them back to New Haven. As junior Anne Warner explained, "For four months Barnett has ignored our request for the zoning variance necessary to get electricity and hot water into the trailer . . . we'll probably get it when Peter Pan comes back to life."[75] A few days after the protest the necessary zoning changes were approved, allowing the women to use a 50-foot trailer that provided showers and changing rooms, while the university disclosed plans to build more permanent facilities.[76]

The women's liberation movement also made innovative use of the countercultural and street theater tactics that had become increasingly prominent during the second half of the 1960s. In August 1973, in the same week that members of New York NOW held their own protest in the New York Stock Exchange (unfurling a banner from the public gallery that read "Women Power" to protest "male domination of the Wall Street empire"), a series of short skits that attacked male oppression were held in the Rockefeller Center and a "mock funeral" was held in the office of Senator James L. Buckley, an opponent of abortion rights, "in memory of the unknown women who departed this life by the horrors of illegal abortion."[77]

Counterculturalism had in fact been a prominent feature of women's liberation from the start. On 7 September 1968 around 100 women from across the nation—"mostly middle-aged careerists, and housewives with a sprinkling of 20-year-olds and grandmothers in their 60's"—picketed the Miss America Pageant in Atlantic City. They marched on the historic boardwalk outside the convention center with a giant Miss America puppet, with "chains hanging from her red, white and blue bathing suit" to demonstrate "the chains that tie us to these beauty standards against our will." Arguing that the contest was degrading to women, they placed a variety of objects—including bras, girdles, shoes, hair curlers, false eyelashes, makeup, and a copy of *Playboy* magazine, into a "freedom trash can," which they danced around singing "Liberation now!" They also crowned a sheep, adorned with yellow and blue ribbons, Miss America (a week earlier the Yippies had nominated a pig, Pigasus, for president of the United States).[78]

Street theater remained an integral part of the women's movement's armory. WITCH, founded by Robin Morgan and 12 other women in the autumn of 1968, made extensive use of countercultural zaps—its first action, on Halloween, saw the women dress as witches and "hex" the financial district; in February 1969 they released mice into Madison Square Garden to protest the Bridal Fair that was being held there.[79] In Berkeley, activists burned a diploma to protest what they viewed as the irrelevance of their studies to the reality of women's oppression in society. A Barbie doll, a novel by Norman Mailer (much criticized for his male chauvinism), birth control pills, and *Good Housekeeping*'s list of the Ten Most Admired Women (which identified the women by their husband's names only) were also incinerated in a humorous protest.[80] On 22 April 1970 members of Indiana University's women's liberation movement dressed as witches, danced in circles chanting "Free our bodies, free our minds" and, for reasons that were never particularly clear, hurled birth control pills into a crowd who were celebrating Earth Day.[81] During that summer's Women's Strike for Equality Boston activists could be found chained to a large typewriter and, in Berkeley, women took to the streets with saucepans on their backs.[82] In October a group of women staged a picket outside Mory's, New Haven's legendary eating and drinking club that was celebrated for its Welsh rarebit and Whippenpoofs.[83] While it was not officially a part of the university, Mory's served as a de facto faculty club and symbol of Yale's traditions and, despite the admission of female undergraduates it maintained a ban on women members.[84] Along with their placards (one read "I always eat at Mory's with all the other sexist pigs," another "I'm so glad I'm an elite so I can eat at Mory's"), some women also waved skulls in an apparent allusion to Yale's secret, elitist (and until 1991 all-male) society Skull and Bones.[85] After losing its liquor license in 1972 as the result of a legal challenge brought by women, in March 1974 Mory's agreed to admit women as members.[86]

In September 1974, six years after their iconic protest, women's liberation activists returned to the Miss America contest in Atlantic City, staging a three-day "Wonder Women" conference and a parade down the historic boardwalk. On Saturday 7 September a number of the 2,000 feminists who joined the march, which stretched for eight blocks, wore costumes. Members of the Essex County, New Jersey, chapter of NOW—who had filed the successful lawsuit that opened up Little League to girls—wore baseball uniforms and carried signs that read "Diamonds are a girl's best friend." Women from Maine dressed as suffragettes, and women from Ocean City, New Jersey, "wore old-fashioned bathing suits and carried signs reading, 'Ocean City NOW makes waves'." Featured speakers included Democratic Representative Bella Abzug, former NOW president and Wellesley faculty member Wilma Scott Heide, and Barbara Love, lesbian author of *Sappho Was a Right On Woman*, and workshops were held on a wide range of topics—including feminist humor, bellydancing, herstory, sexuality, abortion, rape, and women in prison.[87]

The legacy of the 1960s was not limited to the use of sit-ins, street theater, and other forms of direct action. The women's movement's embrace of participatory democracy, grassroots organizing, and the building of parallel structures is illustrative of the profound influence of the civil rights, New Left, and anti-war movements. Formed in 1971, the Greater New Haven Women's Political Caucus (GNHWPC) was a "feminist organization designed to advance the rights and freedoms of women in and through politics and government." Drawing supporters from New Haven, East Haven, West Haven, Branford, Woodbridge, and other local communities, the organization embraced the pre-figurative politics (the idea that the means of protest should align with the ultimate goals) that had characterized the early civil rights movement, arguing that "the way power is distributed is related to the way in which it is used and the objectives for which it is used." It therefore sought to fashion an organizational structure that reflected its aims (freedom, equality, justice). Traditional hierarchies, majority voting, and Robert's Rules of Order were rejected in favor of "new organizational forms which distribute power, responsibility and decision making equally among all members. We presently work without officers, through task forces, through a steering committee open to all members and by consensus decision making."[88] Similarly, the Chicago NOW chapter had been experimenting with its committee structure, dispensing with fixed chairs and seeking to "bring everybody closer to each other and to the workings of NOW."[89]

In their efforts to foster participatory democracy and effect radical change, civil rights and New Left activists had pioneered the creation of parallel structures, or counter-institutions—with the Mississippi Freedom Schools, Mississippi Freedom Democratic Party, and Assembly of Unrepresented People among the more prominent examples. Staughton Lynd, the historian and activist who had directed the Freedom Schools, talked of building "the new society within the shell of the old." Like Lynd, Tom Hayden viewed parallel structures as a vital part of the movement's armory; the architect of the Port Huron Statement explained that "free institutions" might serve as the "building blocks of a new society." As Alice Echols has pointed out, the women's movement embraced such ideas with enthusiasm, "creating an amazing panoply of counterinstitutions," including health clinics, telephone helplines, and book stores in numerous American cities. In 1970 women founded the Feminist Federal Credit Union of Detroit; activists in New Haven followed suit in August 1974, opening the Connecticut Feminist Federal Credit Union to combat alleged discriminatory lending practices by some banks. Susan Osborne, a co-manager of the Union, explained that they had created the institution so that "we can save money together and . . . lend our money to each other."[90] The Atlanta Lesbian Feminist Alliance, founded in 1972, maintained a meeting house and a library, and published a monthly newsletter, *Atalanta*.[91] In New Haven, women produced a weekly radio show, established a speakers' bureau, and even formed a women's liberation rock band.[92]

In the struggle for women's equality in the United States there has been a long tradition of seeking to invoke the nation's founding values as a means to bring about change. Indeed, the use of patriotic protest can be traced back to the birth of the nation itself. As the leaders of the colonial rebellion were preparing for their final, definitive break with the British Crown, Abigail Adams wrote to her husband in Philadelphia. While she "long[ed] to hear that you have declared an independency" she also urged that "in the new Code of Laws which I suppose it will be necessary for you to make I desire you would Remember the Ladies, and be more generous and favorable to them than your ancestors."[93] Seventy years later, at the Seneca Falls Convention, the founders of modern American feminism drew extensively on the Declaration of Independence in articulating their demands for equal treatment. Not only did the "Declaration of Sentiments" state that "We hold these truths to be self-evident; that all men and women are created equal," but it also drew up an extensive list of the "repeated injuries and usurpations on the part of man toward woman" for submission "to a candid world."[94] In the early years of the twentieth century suffragists marched behind huge American flags, laid claim to the nation's founding ideals and Constitutional protections, and demanded "equal representation for equal taxation."[95]

Among second-wave feminists one could find skepticism and hostility toward the United States. Some activists referred to "Amerikka" to emphasize what they viewed as the racist, militaristic, and imperialistic aspects of the nation's character.[96] Writing to *off our backs* in March 1972 Norma Ojeman, president of a NOW branch, explained that "We have made a start in SPRINGFIELD, ILL.—the heart of "LINCOLN" land and all that bull shit."[97] Nevertheless, strategies of patriotic protest endured during the era of women's liberation. When Denise Ryan challenged the restrictive dormitory rules at Michigan State University, for instance, students organized supportive rallies under the slogan "No nation can long exist half slave and half free."[98] Iowa feminist Bev Mitchell recalled attending a 1971 rally in Chicago's Grant Park and encountering "one woman dressed in nothing but the American flag" and a "sparkly top hat."[99] On Tuesday 24 February 1970, members of the Yale Women's Alliance marched from the Hall of Graduate Studies to the dining room of Berkeley College to publicize a series of women's liberation workshops to be held over the coming weekend.[100] Two leafleters entered the dining hall, "followed by a trombonist who played a suitable fanfare." Then, "a girl dressed as the Statue of Liberty entered with two supporters of women's freedom who chanted, 'Out of the houses, up from the desks! Out from under, women unite!'" Several girls representing "male chauvinists" proceeded to attack "Miss Liberty" with cries of "Take away her book and give her a typewriter!" and "Take her torch and give her a mop! Take her crown and give her some curlers!" She was then "crowned Miss America" by someone claiming to be Bert Parks, the longtime television host of the Miss America pageant. The performance-cum-protest ended with the entire troupe shouting "All of this has got to stop! Take off your curlers; Throw down the mop! Come and join us Thursday night. Up from under, women unite!"[101] Women's Liberation stickers bearing the slogan "Only men are created equal" also appeared on storefronts and in some university buildings to publicize the cause.[102]

In March 1972 Patricia H. Durgin of Syracuse, New York, wrote to the feminist magazine *off our backs* pointing out that there was no woman judge on the Supreme Court and no female state governor—that, "In short, we are governed without representation and it is *our* money, *our* taxes which support this sexist government now in power. This has happened to us since the founding of this country two centuries ago and it is time to put an end to it." Durgin urged women to sign a petition indicating their refusal to pay taxes, or to withhold a portion of what they owed, until equal representation at all levels of government had been achieved. She declared that it was "time for another American Revolution when all the Sisters in this country who are without identity, without equal citizenship, without a voice in the decisions which affect their own lives, will together declare in the words of the founders of this country— 'No taxation without representation.'"[103] The revolutionary analogy was reprised in September 1974 when women from the Trenton, New Jersey, branch of NOW dressed as Revolutionary War soldiers during a protest in Atlantic City against the Miss America contest.[104]

NOW, which sought to "bring women into full participation in the mainstream of American society now," pledged to "confront . . . the conditions" that prevented women from "enjoying the equality of opportunity and freedom of choice"—an equality they were entitled to "as individual Americans, and as human beings."[105] Meanwhile the organization's Legal Defense Fund, founded in 1969, stated clearly its belief that "Sexism has no place in a nation devoted to 'justice for all.'"[106] In the fall of 1979 Kathe Rauch, president of New York NOW, attacked those who sought to overturn *Roe v. Wade* and the legalization of abortion rights. Drawing on the Declaration of Independence, she claimed that "Freed— for a time—from our physiological servitude to motherhood, we become threatening, too whole, for those who want to conserve the old order. The way it used to be is much more important to them than our lives, let alone our pursuit of happiness."[107]

Women for Racial and Economic Equality (WREE), founded in New York in 1974, sought to "address the broad economic and racial inequalities confronting all women and their families."[108] In 1976 it campaigned for a "Women's Bill of Rights" that would guarantee equal pay, equal economic opportunity, and access to housing, healthcare, childcare and education. WREE explained that "As a result of the people's pressure to guarantee the basic freedoms for which they had just fought, the Founders of our Republic included a Bill of Rights as part of our nation's

Constitution." Yet while the "women of our Republic [had] struggled for freedom with fervor and dedication," "only in this century did we win the right to vote [and] still our rights as human beings are denied, ignored or scorned." WREE pointed out that women were "not equal before the law; nor does society at large recognize our equality. Our numbers in political office remain pitifully small. There can be no real equality of freedom while any section of our people is denied its rights." WREE called for a bill of rights for women, arguing that "In this, the United Nations International Women's Decade, and the Bi-Centennial of the American Revolution, the need is desperate for a WOMEN'S BILL OF RIGHTS— for legislation to specifically guarantee the equality of all women in our country."[109] By the early 1980s WREE was supporting efforts to secure a Constitutional Amendment that would guarantee the right to employment opportunity, arguing that "any democratic government today must provide its citizens with jobs, so that all of us can enjoy our right to 'life, liberty and the pursuit of happiness'."[110]

Perhaps the most prominent use of patriotic protest by the women's liberation movement came during the campaign for the Equal Rights Amendment.[111] On 10 August 1970, for example, a coalition of women's groups "seized" the Statue of Liberty, hanging a giant banner from the tenth floor balcony that proclaimed "Women of the World Unite!" They also demonstrated on Liberty Island for several hours in support of the ERA, which was being debated by the House of Representatives; featured speakers at the demonstration included former suffragist Judge Dorothy Kenyon and Kate Millett. NOW's Cindy Cisler explained that the statue had been chosen because "it is ironic that a woman symbolizes the abstract idea of liberty, but in reality we are not free."[112] The Statue of Liberty also appeared prominently in publicity materials produced by ERAmerica, a national coalition that campaigned for ratification; while the American Association of University Women produced red, white, and blue pamphlets that described the ERA as a matter of "simple justice, the American way to equality of opportunity."[113] During a public debate in Memphis about the possibility of Tennessee repealing its ratification of the ERA, members of the NOW chapter protested with placards that stated "1776 Was for Women Too."[114] In May 1980 Chicagoan Lois Anne Rosen sought to persuade her state representative, Robert Krska, to vote for ratification, asking "How can you be an American and be against equality?"[115] In the Empire State during the fall of 1975, the New York Coalition for Equal Rights (NYCER) was pushing for an amendment to the State Constitution that would ensure that "Equality of rights under the law shall not be denied or abridged by the state of New York or any subdivision thereof on account of sex."

The broad coalition (it counted the NAACP, NOW, Women Strike for

Peace, the United Auto Workers, New York State Americans for Democratic Action, the National Council of Negro Women, the National Gay Task Force, and Lesbian Feminist Liberation among its supporters) appealed directly to patriotic values, just as Martin Luther King, Jr., had a decade before.[116] They explained that "In 1776, we promised that America would be a place where individuals counted for what they are. Not where they came from or what their ancestors did." While America had "tried to make good on that promise," inequalities remained, with women often receiving "lower pay for the same work, or fewer chances to advance than men." With the nation's Bicentennial fast approaching, the NYCER argued that the proposed amendment would not "change the world" but simply enable "us to deliver on our 200-year-old promise. By its adoption New Yorkers can remind the nation that America was founded on principles of individual worth and dignity."[117] Indeed, the Bicentennial appears to have encouraged the use of patriotic protest. In an editorial in the *New York Times* in March 1976, for example, Letty Cottin Pogrebin, an editor of *Ms.* magazine, called on women to "use 1976 to challenge the American dream, not celebrate it"; to "celebrate the Bicentennial in the only way that makes sense: by using our vote, our voice and our rage to plot the next and deepest American Revolution— the one that frees the real silent majority: womankind."[118]

Much of the energy, creativity, and diversity of the women's movement came into sharp relief during the autumn of 1977, when 2,000 delegates and thousands of observers assembled in Houston for the National Women's Conference.[119] The gathering is also indicative of the enduring appeal of Americanism for advocates of women's rights. The conference itself was conceived in part as a way for America to commemorate "International Women's Year" (which the United Nations had designated as 1975), thereby illustrating the American movement's transnational connections. But the upcoming celebration of the Bicentennial of the American Revolution had also been a factor. In 1975 Representative Bella Abzug had introduced legislation proposing that a conference be held to coincide with the nation's 200th birthday celebrations. At the end of 1975 a revised law was passed, which stated that the Bicentennial was a "particularly appropriate time" to explore issues of gender discrimination and set up a National Commission to organize the conference, to be preceded by a series of state meetings. In June 1976 Congress approved a $5 million appropriation.[120]

In the build-up to the conference, 56 state and territorial meetings were held across the nation for the purpose of selecting delegates and drawing up a "National Plan of Action" that would "identify the barriers that prevent women from participating in all aspects of national life." The process of selecting delegates has been described by historian Ruth Rosen as a "competitive, brutal, but invigorating experiment in American democracy."[121] The state and local meetings were often passionate and colorful affairs, with conservative opponents of feminism (outraged, in part, by the federal funding) mobilized against progressives. In Utah, for instance, 14,000 women, "mostly conservative, with the avid encouragement of the Mormon Church, packed a meeting that chose 14 conference delegates."[122] In Albany, New York, more than 8,000 women attended the final session of the state conference—with voting lines stretching through the "long corridors and lobbies" of the Empire State Plaza, some waiting up to seven hours to vote amid rumors that "conservative factions" were engaging in "slowdown tactics."[123] In New Jersey, 3,000 women attended the state convention, held at Princeton University.[124] Overall, some 150,000 women—"from Eskimo villages to the Florida Keys," "from metropolitan suburbs and inner city ghettos and midwest farms"—met "on State fair grounds, college campuses, in hotels, civic centers, veterans' auditoriums, and under Hawaiian palm trees" to select delegates and shape the agenda.[125]

In the weeks before the conference a high-profile torch relay was held across a 2,600-mile route from Seneca Falls, New York, to Houston. Although conservatives took the opportunity to assail the entire event—Clint Fuller, an aide to North Carolina's Senator Jesse Helms, claimed that it was controlled by supporters of "abortion, lesbianism, or some other feminist position," while Phyllis Schlafly denounced it as "antifamily"—the relay generated largely positive headlines.[126] On November 18, during the last mile of the relay, three young athletes carried the torch, accompanied by Bella Abzug, Billie Jean King, Betty Friedan, and hundreds of cheering supporters carrying large American flags.[127] Maya Angelou then opened the conference by reading "a stirring rendition of a new 'Declaration of Sentiments' which she entitled, '. . . To Form a More Perfect Union'."[128]

For "three hectic, fractious, exhilarating days" the Sam Houston Memorial Coliseum was the site for the "largest political conference of women ever assembled" in America.[129] It was an extraordinarily diverse gathering; Patricia Benavidez, a 34-year-old delegate from Washington State, described it as a "kaleidoscope of American womanhood . . . I see women here from all walks of life, this is a reflection of what the women's movement is supposed to be."[130] The official report of the conference described how those in attendance were "of all colors, cultures and heritages," "all occupations," "single and married, divorced or widowed" with a "small number of lesbians,"[131] and, as an article in *Time Magazine* explained, there "were rich, poor, radical, conservative, Democratic, Republican and politically noninvolved." Perhaps 20 percent of the delegates were pro-family conservatives (some were men sent from conservative states). In short, "No previous women's gathering could begin to match its diversity of age, income, race, occupation or opinion."[132] A wide range of topics were debated and by the end of the conference delegates had approved a revised National Plan of Action that called for passage of the ERA, offered strong support for abortion rights, urged an end to discrimination based on sexual orientation and sought to address the concerns of "battered, disabled, minority, rural, poor, young, and older women."[133] As well as the tangible recommendations that, it was hoped, would form the basis of future legislation and government policy, the Houston Conference also served a broader purpose—empowering individuals, fostering a sense of community and common purpose, and encouraging further activism.[134] Ida Castro, an alternate delegate from the Garden State, explained that "It was a total high to get together and discover so many people who agree on so many issues, and finding that I am not alone." Similar sentiments were expressed by Sharon Talbot, a nineteen-year-old student from Smith College, who described how "Before I went, I hadn't really decided where I stood. Now I know that all those other women feel the same way I do, so if they call themselves feminists, or whatever, then that's what I am too."[135]

Patriotism was much in evidence at Houston. The conference's slogan—which appeared on posters, badges, and banners—was "to form a more perfect Union," and these words from the Preamble to the Constitution also formed the title of Maya Angelou's updated "Declaration of Sentiments," written especially for the conference. The "Declaration of American Women," which formed the preamble to the "National Plan of Action" adopted in Houston, ended with the words: "We pledge ourselves with all the strength of our dedication to this struggle 'to form a more perfect Union.'"[136] On Saturday 19 November the conference's first plenary session opened with the Pledge of Allegiance and the singing of the national anthem. Commissioner Gloria Scott, an assistant to President Carter and professor of higher education at Texas Southern University, then delivered a speech in which she explained that they were gathering in the aftermath of the Bicentennial to "focus nationwide attention on a most important resource that has helped to make and keep America great from the time of its founding—our American women." She argued that they had gathered in Houston "in the true spirit of American democracy" in order to help the nation "move closer to the possibility of what America can be."[137] A similar note was struck by Barbara Jordan in her plenary address. Jordan, the first southern black women to be elected to Congress, explained that "None of the goals stated in this conference are incompatible with the goals of America.

The goals of this conference, as a matter of fact, sound like stanzas to 'America the Beautiful.'"[138]

Later that day delegates debated the ERA, one of the more controversial issues under discussion. The draft pro-ERA plank stated that:

> Women have waited more than 200 years for the equality promised by the Declaration of Independence to all men. Two years after the United States of America celebrated its Bicentennial, it is time to extend democracy to all American citizens and to put women into the Constitution at last.[139]

After the resolution in support of the ERA was passed in an "enthusiastic and noisy standing vote that appeared to be almost five to one," women sang "God Bless America" before the conference was adjourned. The spirit of patriotic protest that animated the conference was perhaps summed up best by a banner that was carried by delegates from Wisconsin, which read "Women's Rights: As American as Apple Pie."[140]

In many ways the Houston gathering represented the high point of the women's movement: a moment when radical change and the achievement of genuine equality seemed possible. The confidence of the time was encapsulated by the remarks of Susan B. Anthony II who, at the opening ceremony, repeated the words made famous by her great aunt—"Failure is Impossible."[141] Feminism, of course, did not disappear after Houston; indeed, there would be further victories and key successes. But, in truth, it was the conservative opponents of the National Women's Conference who would seize the initiative in the years ahead as the "pro-family" movement used radical feminism as a boogeyman around which to mobilize public opinion and, perhaps more critically, accumulate political capital. In fact, as the conference got underway conservative groups took out a prominent advertisement in the *Houston Post* which featured a little girl holding a posy and the headline "MOMMY, WHEN I GROW UP CAN I BE A LESBIAN?"[142] 13,000 attended a counter-rally across town, organized by the Eagle Forum, where they heard Phyllis Schlafly claim that supporters of the ERA "want to reconstruct us into a gender-free society, so there's no difference between men and women" and Californian congressman Robert Dornan attack the conference participants as "sick, anti-God, pro-lesbian and unpatriotic."[143] Politically, the major beneficiaries of such tactics were conservative Republicans. As Ruth Rosen has written, "with the election of Ronald Reagan in 1980, memories of Houston would quickly come to seem like a dream from a distant past."[144]

Chapter 4

The Battles over Busing

Our cause is to retain freedom, just like George Washington.
— Irene McCabe, anti-busing activist, Pontiac, Michigan

The Anti-busers did not choose this issue. It came to us with our American heritage of liberty.
— Sal Giarratani, Boston journalist and activist

As the first of the bright yellow school buses rolled up outside South Boston High School on the morning of Thursday 12 September 1974 it was greeted by an angry mob. Chants of "Go home nigger," and "Turn the bus over" erupted from the watching crowd of 500 or so whites. As a rock bounced off the side of the bus "a cheer arose from the youths on the sidewalks." One bystander, described as a "pudgy man in a pork-pie hat," announced that "any white kid that goes to school out of his neighborhood should be shot, and any black kid that comes out of his neighborhood to school here should be shot." As the buses continued to arrive, some of them containing only a handful of "neatly dressed, silent, often wide-eyed black students," the crowd frequently burst into refrains from South Boston High's football chant—"Here we go, Southie, here we go."[1] Meanwhile in the Hyde Park district—a "pleasant middle-class neighborhood of leafy streets lined with modest but attractive homes"— there was little violence.[2] The local population, primarily "third and fourth generation Bostonians, many of Irish and Italian extraction,"[3] preferred to support a boycott that saw local school attendance plummet by 50 percent that opening day.[4] Although the response in Hyde Park may have been more restrained, white resentment was still much in evidence: "Sullen groups of white parents watched from lawns and sidewalks and complained bitterly about losing their 'freedoms'."

In 1968, fourteen years after its historic decision in *Brown v. Board of Education* that segregated schools were "inherently unconstitutional," and aided by a Department of Health, Education and Welfare threatening to withhold funding from segregated school districts, the U.S. Supreme Court had finally moved to bring an end to the tokenism, obfuscation, and delay that had prevented meaningful integration from taking place.[5] In *Green v. County School Board of New Kent County*, the nine justices ruled that school boards had an "affirmative duty" to take steps to ensure that segregation was "eliminated root and branch." Moreover, they declared, school boards had to produce realistic plans for desegregation that promised to "work *now*."[6] In 1971, in *Swann v. Charlotte-Mecklenburg Board of Education*, the Supreme Court upheld large-scale busing as a means to achieve integration and stated that school boards would be judged on whether they had managed to achieve "the greatest possible degree of actual desegregation."[7]

Beginning first in the South before moving north and west, busing— whether initiated by local school boards or mandated by the courts—was used as a means of desegregating the nation's schools. Busing, and especially "two-way" busing (which involved the transfer of white children in addition to assigning black children to previously predominantly white schools), proved extremely controversial. Indeed, almost everywhere it was instigated whites (and some blacks) resisted it by marching, petitioning, withdrawing their children from the public schools, or moving to unaffected suburbs. Sometimes the protests became violent. In Lamar, South Carolina, in March 1970, a mob of 200 whites attacked two school buses that were transporting black students to a newly desegregated school. A *Newsweek* report described how "the whites broke through police lines and swarmed over the buses, smashing windows and ripping out ignition wires," as the terrified black passengers "ducked behind seats and dived to the floor as rocks and clubs crashed through the windows."[8] In September 1975, anti-busing protesters attacked the police and set fire to school buses in Louisville, Kentucky.[9] As J. Harvie Wilkinson, a circuit court judge and historian of school desegregation, has commented, the seemingly innocuous yellow school bus became the "flash point of domestic policy in the early 1970s" as busing "rubbed the raw nerve endings of American life."[10]

Boston, with its tightly demarcated ethnic enclaves and fiercely parochial neighborhoods, generated the nation's most virulent and most violent opposition to the busing of students to bring about school desegregation.[11] The city's public school system was highly segregated—in 1972-73 more than 80 percent of African American pupils attended majority-black schools, and more than half were enrolled at schools that were 90 percent black. This was despite passage of a Racial Imbalance Law in 1965, designed by the commonwealth's lawmakers to eliminate such de facto segregation. Indeed, the Boston School Board's delaying tactics had actually seen segregation in the school system increase during the intervening years.[12] In June 1974, federal judge Arthur W. Garrity, a Harvard graduate renowned for being "meticulous, thorough and exacting," found the board guilty of having "knowingly carried out a systematic program of segregation affecting all of the city's students, teachers and school facilities and hav[ing] intentionally brought about and maintained a dual school system." His 152-page opinion boiled down to one very stark conclusion: "the entire school system of Boston" was "unconstitutionally segregated." Garrity thus ordered the city to desegregate its schools and, since the School Board had steadfastly refused to draw up its own plan, he found himself compelled, just months before the beginning of the new school year, to support the only comprehensive desegregation plan on the table. Drawn up in early 1973 by Charles Glenn, an Episcopal priest, it involved busing some 18,000 students (almost half of them white) in order to achieve desegregation. With the city's middle-class suburbs unaffected by the ruling, the white burden fell disproportionately on working- and lower-middle-class Bostonians. Most controversially, the plan paired South Boston High School, embodiment of the area's working-class Irish heritage, with Roxbury High, in the heart of Boston's black ghetto. This was an incendiary decision that, perhaps unsurprisingly, proved a "social and political disaster."[13] Between 1974 and 1976 Boston saw mass rallies, arrests, brawls, vandalism, and incidents of serious violence. It was, in the words of one historian, a "national tragedy of the first rank."[14]

There were numerous reasons behind the high levels of white hostility toward busing, even among those who professed to favor integration.[15] Real concerns existed about the impact busing might have on educational attainment—in terms of the deleterious impact of longer school journeys, especially on younger children, as well as the consequences of reassigning white students to formerly black schools. While some whites sympathized with the rationale for transferring black students from working-class areas to (largely white) middle-class schools, they found it difficult to identify clear educational benefits when that process was reversed.[16] African Americans had little doubt that racial prejudice played an important part in motivating white opposition—one NAACP report on busing, for instance, was provocatively entitled "It's Not the Distance, It's the Niggers."[17] Some of the slogans used by anti-busing protesters were clearly racist, while white fears about crime and low educational performance derived, at least in part, from racial stereotyping. As one white Bostonian put it, "the question is: Am I going to send my young daughter, who is budding into the flower of womanhood, into Roxbury on a bus?"[18]

There was also genuine support for the notion that schools should have strong connections with, and reflect the values of, the communities in which they were situated.[19] Indeed, assaults on "neighborhood schools," and removing the right of parents to exercise control over where their children were educated, were often portrayed as attacks on the American Dream itself. An editorial in the *Mobile Press-Register* on 30 July 1968, for example, spoke of leftist liberals wreaking "havoc to the American way of life,"[20] while Don Roberson, an anti-busing leader in Charlotte, North Carolina, "couldn't believe such a thing could happen in America." He explained that many parents purchased their homes "primarily on the basis of their location with regard to schools. It seemed like an absurdity that anyone could tell us where to send our children."[21] Meanwhile Bostonian activist Thomas O'Connell characterized opponents of busing as "people who work hard their whole lives. My wife and I denied ourselves a lot of the frills of life for our dream of a beautiful house. We like the schools and wanted to stay."[22] Neighborhood schools such as South Boston High served to inculcate pupils with a sense of community and reinforce shared values, and they were often regarded fondly irrespective of academic standards.[23] It was, then, not hard to see how busing might be seen as a challenge to a community's traditions, history, and customs.

Moreover, many white critics viewed court-ordered busing as an undemocratic violation of their civil rights; indeed it was often condemned as an act of judicial "tyranny" that threatened America's historic promise of liberty.[24] In Charlotte, North Carolina, where comprehensive two-way busing began under court order in 1970, a flyer produced by the Concerned Parents Association (CPA) explained that "The plain and tragic fact is that, in this vital and major area of life, freedom of decision is being taken away from the American people."[25] Peg Smith, a resident of Boston's Charlestown neighborhood, explained, "I want my freedom back. They took my freedom. They tell me where my kids have to go to school. This is like living in Russia."[26] Perhaps fellow Bostonian Clarence McDonough, a "tall, handsome Irishman with curly, reddish hair," encapsulated best the visceral reaction of many whites who were suddenly faced with the prospect of busing:

> They did it to me. They went and did it to me, those goddamn sons of bitches. I told you they would. I told you there'd be no running from 'em. You lead your life perfect as a pane of glass, go to church, work 40 hours a

week at the same job—year in, year out—keep your complaints to yourself, and they still do it to you. . . . Someone's got to explain it to me . . . how this Garrity guy . . . gets all the power to move people around, right the hell out of their neighborhood, while everybody else in the world comes out of it free and equal.[27]

For many whites, the "forced busing" of their children represented a profound loss of control. It was seen, along with such things as growing cultural permissiveness, outlawing of school prayer, and new rights for criminal defendants, as a further sign of a widening gulf, real or imagined, between "the people" and the government. In some ways the anti-busing protesters of the 1970s were championing the principle of participatory democracy that had been advocated by the 1960s New Left—the idea that the individual should "share in those social decisions determining the quality and direction of his life"[28]—to counter a policy they viewed as being imposed unfairly by judicial, bureaucratic, and political elites.[29] Indeed, anti-busing campaigns were motivated, at least in part, by activists' sense of powerlessness *and* a desire to (re)assert their influence: something symbolized neatly in the decision to name Boston's main anti-busing organization ROAR (Restore Our Alienated Rights).[30] As a New York City radio talk show host saw it, "This is a government for the people. We are the people. America is opposed to busing"—and yet busing still happened because of a failure of ordinary Americans, the "hard-working backbone" of the country, to organize and mobilize. As he put it, "The squeaky wheel gets the grease, and you people don't squeak."[31]

A central tactic of the anti-busing movement was to attempt to craft both a language and a style of protest that was unequivocally patriotic. In the words of one activist, busing was a "red, white and blue issue," not a "black and white" one.[32] Anti-busing leaders sought to define the terms of the debate in a way that demonstrated clearly that it was they who were standing up for quintessentially American ideals (liberty, freedom, and justice) while busing itself was "un-American." At a meeting of the Mobile school board on 23 July 1969 to discuss school desegregation, for example, W. B. "Bill" Westbrook declared "We are willing to go to jail by hundreds if necessary to back our wishes and demands for freedom-of-choice." "This," he said, "is what America was founded upon and we . . . will settle for nothing less." Westbrook, one of the city's leading anti-busing activists, concluded, "This is still America, we are still free, and we intend to remain free."[33] In March 1970 some 1,500 parents crammed into Nashville's War Memorial Auditorium for an anti-busing rally. There, they heard council member Casey Jenkins, a leading opponent of busing, denounce it as an "ugly creature" that was "unconstitutional . . . [and] deprives us of our freedom of expression, of our freedom of choice, of our property rights and our civil rights."[34] In Charlotte the CPA declared that, "A Struggle for Freedom is Coming. Where Will You Stand?" The organization argued that if pro-busing judges succeeded, "this Nation will cease to be a 'Land of Liberty'."[35]

Attempts to fashion a patriotic dissent for the anti-busing movement, and activists' efforts to invoke the principles of Americanism in their cause, can be seen clearly in the numerous public protests that were staged. In Charlotte, for example, a major anti-busing rally was held at the county fairgrounds to the north of the city on Tuesday 8 September 1970—the day before the new school year, and the city's comprehensive busing plan, was to start. The rally opened with prayer and the playing of both "Dixie" (unofficial anthem of the Confederacy) and the "Star-Spangled Banner." A *New York Times* reporter noted that the cheering crowd of 10,000 were told that it was their "patriotic as well as their strategic duty to peacefully disrupt the busing plan by keeping their children home." Dressed in red, white, and blue, Jane Scott, wife of CPA vice-chairman Jack Scott, declared that she believed busing violated the Constitution and that she would therefore be keeping her sons at home. She then closed the rally by leading the crowd "in a rousing version of 'God Bless America'."[36]

As busing moved north in the early 1970s, anti-busing protest quickly followed. In Pontiac, Michigan—where most of the nation's school buses were made—the campaign was led by Irene McCabe, a "fiery 36-year-old housewife" and mother of three, who believed that the neighborhood school was a vital component of the "American way of life." Protesting outside Lincoln Junior High on 8 September 1971, many anti-busing activists carried American flags and they recited the Pledge of Allegiance and sang "God Bless America." One woman even attempted to use the flag to protect her from the scourge of busing: standing in front of a school bus she waved Old Glory and taunted a bus driver with the words "you can't run over the American flag," before being removed by the police. A week later, on 14 September, McCabe succeeded in shutting down production at the town's General Motors plant after more than half of the 2,000-strong workforce defied United Auto Workers instructions and refused to cross an anti-busing picket line made up of hundreds of local women and children.[37]

In March 1972 McCabe launched her own march on Washington in an attempt to rally congressional support for a proposed anti-busing amendment to the U.S. Constitution. Declaring that "our cause is to retain freedom, just like George Washington,"[38] McCabe and her five fellow marchers set off from Pontiac on 15 March. Eight days into the march, one of their number fell ill and had to be hospitalized in Norwalk, Ohio, leaving the remaining women to complete the 620-mile journey. McCabe explained to reporters covering the march that the neighborhood school was an extension of the family, and "the one thing that separates our government from totalitarian governments." Her assertion that their anti-busing activism was a form of patriotic protest did not wash with everyone, however. During an altercation at a rally held in Akron, Ohio, on Tuesday 28 March, several blacks carried placards declaring "Bigots in PTA Clothing." Meanwhile Dick Reinhold, a white law student, challenged McCabe to "drop America and the flag and say what you really mean." McCabe responded, "I'll never drop America and the flag."[39] Arriving in the nation's capital on 27 April, McCabe and her fellow activists were joined by more than 100 supporters for the final 30-block walk to the Capitol building. There, joined by a further 100 activists, they were greeted by congressional representatives including House Minority Leader Gerald Ford, who commented "you've got a good deal of support. I think you're going to be successful." Later that afternoon a "tired, tanned," limping McCabe addressed a rally of 2,000 supporters at the Sylvan Theater, where she announced that the anti-busing crusade marked "the rebirth of American grass-roots involvement in politics."[40]

Given its prominent role in the American Revolution it was perhaps inevitable that Boston, the "cradle of liberty," provided the richest evidence of the anti-busing movement's engagement with Americanism. Indeed, from the very start Boston's anti-busing forces sought to identify themselves and their cause with patriotism, a desire that was only reinforced by the impending celebration of the U.S. Bicentennial.[41] U.S. flags, the singing of "God Bless America," and recitations of the Pledge of Allegiance were commonplace at the numerous anti-busing rallies that occurred during 1974-1976.[42] One of the largest demonstrations took place on Monday 9 September 1974, shortly before Judge Garrity's busing plan came into effect. It was organized by John R. Kerrigan, a "stout, nattily dressed man with quick, shrewd eyes and a salty vocabulary" who was chairman of the city's school board, and city councilman Albert L. O'Neil.[43] Between eight and ten thousand assembled on Boston Common before marching to City Hall plaza for a rally. There, Senator Edward M. Kennedy attempted unsuccessfully to address the crowd before beating a hasty retreat to the relative sanctuary of the Federal Building while dodging a volley of eggs and tomatoes.[44] As well as such raucous behavior, the rally illustrates perfectly how the city's anti-busing activists attempted to draw on the heritage of the Boston Tea Party and War of Independence. One reporter described a "forest of American flags" with speakers making "many references to Constitutional rights—

nothing very specific. The Constitution means the government is not supposed to tell you what to do—it's a free country."[45] Another noted that "several women wore small flags or tea bags in their high, sprayed hair-dos as protest symbols." The Pledge of Allegiance was recited several times—with particular emphasis on the final two words of the phrase "with liberty and justice for all."[46]

Early on Friday 4 October 1974, a "bright, crisp, fall day," the crowds began gathering at South Boston's Marine Park for a parade. Louise Day Hicks, whose anti-busing political odyssey had taken her from the Boston School Board to the U.S. House of Representatives and Boston City Council,[47] was the "Mother Superior" of anti-busing. Described as the embodiment of "maternal, lace-curtain propriety" who looked as if she was "perpetually en route to a . . . christening,"[48] Hicks "was cheered as she arrived behind a color guard in Revolutionary tricornered hats." Before the march began, the demonstrators recited a special version of the Pledge of Allegiance—"I will not pledge allegiance to the court order of the United States District Court, or to the dictatorship for which it stands, one law, incontestable, with liberty and justice for none."[49]

Boston's anti-busing activists made frequent references to the city's Revolutionary heritage, even on occasion going so far as to dump copies of the *Globe* (which anti-busers accused of liberal bias) into Boston Harbor.[50] ROAR's anthem (sung to the tune of "Colonel Bogey's March") was "Boston was the first in liberty; Boston, the one that first was free; Boston, again in Boston; The people will lead the whole country"[51] and in March 1976 the *Boston News Digest*, the organization's official publication, ran a cartoon featuring Paul Revere riding on a horse called "Never" past the city's Callahan Tunnel, crying "The Buses Are Coming."[52] At a December 1974 protest on Boston Common, State Representative Raymond L. Flynn reminded the 6,000-strong crowd that "It was here in Boston that the cherished banner of liberty was first unfurled." Flynn, who represented the constituents of South Boston, declared that there should "be no bicentennial celebration at all while the sacred principles on which this nation was founded are threatened by a new tyranny, a tyranny dressed in judicial robes."[53] When Pulitzer Prize-winning journalist J. Anthony Lukas visited the headquarters of the anti-busing South Boston Information Center in spring 1975, he discovered that it was decked out with patriotic regalia—"red, white and blue bunting drape[d] the windows" and the walls were filled with the words of James Madison, Benjamin Franklin, and the Declaration of Independence. Tellingly, Franklin's assertion that "Those who would give up essential liberty to purchase a little temporary safety deserve neither liberty nor safety" had been amended, with the word "safety" crossed out and replaced with "education." The center's Nancy Yott told Lukas that she and her fellow anti-busers were "being denied the very rights we fought for in the revolution." She explained that "We've been denied the right to peaceably assemble. We've been denied the right to free speech and the right to walk the streets. Police come in here escorting the buses and everything else has to give way." Judge Garrity, meanwhile, was viewed as the equivalent of a king—"He's not elected by the people. He rules for life. . . . His word is final." But the women resisted being characterized as "revolutionaries"—that label, they claimed, applied to the leftists; they insisted that they were conservatives who simply "want to go back to the old way."[54] A few months after Lukas's visit, on the first day of the school year, an estimated 500 activists led by Louise Hicks walked along Broadway to protest busing. One mother, pushing a baby carriage, wore a large badge displaying the slogan "South Boston—1775-1975—Resist.'[55] The previous day, Sunday 7 September, more than 1,000 protesters from Charlestown had marched behind American flags turned upside-down (to signal distress) and a "banner like that used during the Revolutionary War at the Battle of Bunker Hill."[56]

Of course, the battles over busing symbolized a clash of *competing* principles, and both sides in the school desegregation struggle appealed to Americanism in support of their cause. Opponents of busing emphasized individual liberty, the right to exert control over their children's schooling, and small-town notions of democracy. As Louise Day Hicks explained, America was the "land of the free" and court-ordered busing was "certainly never intended by the Bill of Rights."[57] Similarly, a leader of the Positive Action Committee, an anti-busing organization in Wilmington, Delaware, argued that "In slightly over 200 years we have regressed to the sort of tyranny and injustice that the British government imposed on the people of that time."[58] But busing was itself designed to roll back decades of racial discrimination, both de jure and de facto: discrimination that had denied African Americans equal educational opportunities. Busing, then, was conceived as a means to help achieve justice and equality for the Republic's black citizens. Roy Wilkins, head of the NAACP, invoked the nation's founding principles as part of his efforts to prevent the passage of legislation designed to curtail busing. In September 1972 he wrote Rhode Island's Democratic senator Claiborne Pell, to "urge your steadfast opposition to those who would flagrantly violate both the Constitution and the Bill of Rights by rolling back the clock to another era."[59] Reporting on two busing rallies held in Boston on 18 May 1975 (one a ROAR convention, the other a pro-busing "March Against Racism") John Kifner of the *New York Times* explained that they were both "made up of people feeling left out of the American dream."[60]

The anti-busing movement's attempts to lay claim to America's founding ideals was, however, done grievous harm by a single photograph.

Monday 5 April 1976 was a mild, clear day and many South Boston students wore light jackets and windbreakers as they attended one of the regular mass anti-busing rallies at City Hall Plaza. That same morning Theodore Landsmark, a Yale-educated lawyer working for the Contractors Association, was heading to City Hall for a meeting to discuss minority hiring in the construction industry. A native of Kansas City and the grandson of a follower of Marcus Garvey, the twenty-nine-year-old Landsmark had marched from Selma to Montgomery in 1965 and, under the mentorship of William Sloane Coffin, protested the war in Vietnam. But Landsmark was attacked that April morning not because of his civil rights activism, support for affirmative action, or stance on busing. He was attacked because he was a black man who simply happened to be in the wrong place at the wrong time. As he approached City Hall Landsmark, who was running a little late, had the grave misfortune to run into the 200-strong anti-busing crowd. Within moments of being spotted, several protesters turned on him. As one tried to trip him up, others shouted "Get the nigger" and the smartly dressed lawyer was jumped, kicked, and punched while Joseph Rakes, a seventeen-year-old student and anti-busing regular, "circled around" and began swinging a large American flag he had taken from his family's third-floor apartment in South Boston earlier that morning. The incident, which lasted no more than twenty seconds, left Landsmark bloodied, dazed, and with a broken nose. Watching from his office window nearby, mayor Kevin White had been afforded a bird's-eye view of events. As he recalled, "This man, as I could see with my own eyes, had been walking calmly, quietly, and alone across City Hall Plaza right under my window when he was attacked. He was taking no part in any demonstration, yet he became a victim because he was a black man who came in contact with a bunch of hooligans." Landsmark himself knew only too well that someone had "tried to kill me with the American flag" not because he "was somebody but because I was anybody. . . . I was just a nigger they were trying to kill."[61]

While Ted Landsmark had been exceptionally unlucky, the gods were smiling on Stanley Forman that warm April morning. If the thirty-year-old photographer for Boston's *Herald American* had not decided to drop in on his girlfriend to deliver an apple and have a quick chat on his way to City Hall Plaza, he would almost certainly have missed his opportunity. As it was, arriving a little late to the anti-busing rally, Forman found himself in prime position to capture the attack on Landsmark. His iconic photograph was printed on newspaper front pages around the nation and the world, and won him the 1977 Pulitzer Prize for spot news photography. As the image's historian, Louis Masur, has explained, Forman's photograph "presents a sickening sight." A "well-dressed black man is being grabbed from behind. He seems to be struggling to free himself.

His satchel lies behind him at his feet. A large crowd, composed mostly of high school students, looks on. The flag bearer's feet are planted, his hands firmly grasping the staff, his eyes focused on his target. His hair flows back as he prepares to lunge forward." Masur explains, "attacker and victim are forever frozen in time" and the viewer is trapped—"we can glance away, but we cannot escape the horror of what we imagine the next instance will bring."[62]

That Landsmark was attacked with an American flag in Boston, the "cradle of liberty," literally in the shadows of the site of the Boston Massacre, during the year the nation was celebrating its Bicentennial, served only to magnify the power of Forman's remarkable photograph. Numerous commentators observed that the incident reflected very badly indeed on the city of Boston. An editorial in the *Boston Globe* on 7 April, for example, deplored the damage that was being done to "the spirit of the city, the psyche of its citizens and its reputation across the nation and throughout the world." And it was not surprising that many drew unfavorable parallels between Boston's historic role in the American Revolution and its more recent racial troubles, with one journalist describing Forman's photograph as "the shot heard around the world for its indelible portrait of American racism."[63] One letter-writer to the *Globe* declared that "the black people of Boston have very little reason to celebrate the Bicentennial, for they still are not free to safely walk the streets of this city," while another viewed the attack on Landsmark as an "assault . . . on the foundations of American democracy" itself.[64] As well as casting a pall over the city's plans to celebrate the 200th anniversary of the nation's birth, the photograph also proved to be a key turning point for Boston's anti-busing movement. As Masur has argued, "in one click of a photographer's shutter, the anti-busing claim that the movement was not driven by racism, and that protesters were patriotic defenders against tyranny, came undone."[65] While they might argue forcefully that they were motivated by issues of class and neighborhood rather than race, and that in fighting for their liberty they were laying claim to the nation's heritage of resistance against tyranny, Boston's opponents of busing were unable to overcome the powerful resonance of Stanley Forman's photograph, which he entitled "The Soiling of Old Glory."[66]

Opponents of busing lived in a world the 1960s had made. While viewing themselves as fighting against many of the social, cultural, and political changes commonly associated with that decade,[67] they simultaneously deployed 1960s modes and styles of activism. In the words of historian Ronald P. Formisano, anti-busing activists were "children of the 1960s."[68] Indeed, they drew quite self-consciously on the civil rights, New Left, and antiwar movements for both legitimacy and tactics. In

Charlotte during the 1969-1970 school crisis, for example, Don Roberson, a local physician who was vice-chairman of the CPA, explained that
the "silent majority" was "about ready to take to the streets with tactics
that have seemed to work so effectively for the vocal minority groups."[69]
In 1978, Boston activist and journalist Sal Giarratani referred explicitly to the struggle against the war in Vietnam in seeking to justify the
actions of the anti-busing movement—"The Anti-War Movement took
a stand against the Vietnam War because they felt obliged to do so.
So to[o] with the Anti-Busers is forced busing opposed."[70] Moreover,
Boston's anti-busing leaders invoked the African American civil rights
movement repeatedly when promoting civil disobedience, urging, for
instance, that it was time to "take a leaf out of Martin Luther King's
book." In March 1975 they even sought (albeit unsuccessfully) to repli-
cate the August 1963 March on Washington.[71] The language of "rights"
developed by the black movement was also co-opted by anti-busers—in
Richmond, Virginia, Citizens Against Busing, which organized rallies,
drive-ins, and boycotts to oppose busing, claimed that white southerners were being treated as "second-class citizens."[72] Anti-busing activists
in Canarsie, New York, spoke of the need to win "rights" for white ethnics and to follow the example of other groups, particularly black civil
rights organizations, by organizing and mobilizing.[73] In one of history's
ironies, "We Shall Overcome," the iconic anthem of the black freedom
struggle, was sung at anti-busing protests in several American cities,
including Boston and Charlotte.[74]

Many of the tactics—petition drives, marches, sit-ins, and rallies—
deployed by anti-busing forces across America in places like Boston,
Charlotte, Canarsie, Corpus Christi (Texas), and Wilmington (Delaware), had been pioneered by the civil rights and student protest movements.[75] In July 1975, thirty-four demonstrators led by Louise Day Hicks
held a sleep-in at the Boston Sheraton, which was hosting the national
Conference of Mayors. That September, in a protest that echoed the
Berkeley antiwar activists who had lain in front of troop trains, a group
of anti-busing protesters lay down in front of trucks that were distribut-
ing the *Boston Globe*. In December, fifty ROAR activists staged a sit-in at
the offices of the state's congressmen at the Federal Building.[76] Boston-
based journalist Alan Lupo later recalled that "it was an ironic thing to
watch and listen to the people actively opposing busing. A number of
them said, essentially, "If Martin Luther King was a hero for sitting on
the street, or blocking traffic, or picketing or demonstrating, how come
we're not heroes? How come the media are treating us differently than it
did the white college students who opposed Vietnam, or the blacks who
had sit-ins?" Lupo felt that, while many may have been sincere in expressing such sentiment, genuinely believing that their "civil rights" were at

stake, others were perhaps simply "being cute" and seeking to "run that guilt trip on the media," "playing it for all it was worth."[77]

Often the style of the anti-busing movement reflected the 1960s fashion for (counter)cultural activism—especially the use of street theater as political protest. An October 1970 "Fathers' March" in Mobile, for example, saw protesters carrying caskets labeled "Freedom of Choice" and "Neighborhood Schools." A boy, aged fourteen, "played *Taps* as the caskets were placed on the steps of the Federal Building."[78] A popular tactic in Boston was to hold large, loud convoys as an expression of community solidarity. In South Boston, on the afternoon of Sunday 15 September 1974, for example, "hundreds of people gathered on street corners as a horn-honking procession of cars from other sections, led by a hearse, drove through in an expression of solidarity."[79] The funereal theme was reprised on 5 March 1975, when 400 anti-busing protesters marched behind a coffin that represented the death of liberty. Waving placards that read "Boston Mourns Its Lost Freedom," they chanted "Garrity's killed liberty." The protesters then attended a reenactment of the Boston Massacre sponsored by the Charlestown Militia Company; as the fateful shots were fired, all 400 fell to the ground.[80] Boston also saw anti-busing forces co-opt the antiwar slogan "Hell, no! We won't go," and t-shirts bearing the slogan "Hell, No, Southie Won't Go" became fixtures at local anti-busing rallies.[81] In a further reflection of 1960s influence, police in Boston and Louisville were subjected to the "pig" epithet by protesters.[82] Lupo explained how, in Boston, clashes between police and protesters—who often charged police brutality—were "sort of a replay of the white college kids fighting with cops earlier."[83] All this was not lost on perceptive contemporary observers. Indianapolis resident Charles A. Modernne explained in a letter to *Time*, "during the antiwar years, protesters were called subversives and Commies for speaking out against the Viet Nam War and turning the American flag upside down." Now "those people who supported that . . . war (silent majority, etc.) are out protesting busing, burning buses, turning cars and the American flag over."[84]

The anti-busing movement of the 1970s is illustrative of the unraveling of the electoral coalition Franklin Roosevelt had first assembled during the Great Depression; indeed, opposition to busing formed an important part of a wider populist revolt against the liberal politics of the postwar era. At one level, anti-busing demonstrates the growing antagonism between ordinary white working-class Democrats and the party's leadership— encapsulated in the hostility directed toward Bay State senior senator, Ted Kennedy in September 1974. One South Boston father explained, "These people are always fine to tell you that it's all right for you. But it's the double standards. 'Your kids'll go to Roxbury and mine'll go to

Milton Academy' [an elite private school]."[85] During the late 1960s and 1970s many white working-class Democrats reacted against their party's identification with African Americans, minorities, and interventionist liberal welfare and social policies and began a historic move away from the party of Franklin Roosevelt toward the party of Ronald Reagan.[86]

The GOP both benefited from this political shift and sought actively to exploit it. Richard Nixon's 1968 and 1972 election victories, for example, were based on appeals to the "forgotten," "ordinary," "hard-working" Americans—those he would term "the Silent Majority." In fact Nixon and his party planned to forge a new Republican electoral majority that would include white voters in the Sunbelt suburbs of the South and West as well as disaffected northern ethnics. Nixon tapped into the growing opposition to federal government interventionism over race by championing an America that was a "land of opportunity" rather than a "land of quotas and restrictions."[87] When it came to school desegregation, Nixon sought to chart a middle course. He repeatedly emphasized his endorsement of the *Brown* decision and backed efforts to eliminate de jure segregation in the South. But he opposed the use of busing to counter de facto segregation in the North, instead supporting the idea that children should attend neighborhood schools on a nonsegregated basis.[88] In a statement issued 24 March 1970, Nixon argued that resources would be better spent on improving educational facilities than on "buying buses, tires and gasoline to transport young children miles away from their neighborhood schools." He also explained that "in a free society there are limits to the amount of government coercion that can reasonably be used."[89] Two years later, in a nationally televised address on 17 March, Nixon called on Congress to implement a moratorium on busing.[90] In political terms Nixon viewed busing as a "wedge issue" that could be used to divide the Democrats and reap electoral rewards by recruiting elements of the old New Deal coalition—especially traditional blue-collar workers and those suburbanites who had only recently managed to escape the inner cities—to the ranks of the Grand Old Party.[91] He believed, crudely, that opposing busing in public would "make those bastards [in the Democratic Party] take a stand and it's a political plus for us."[92]

From the late 1960s onward conservatives based their appeal, in part, in attacks on what they viewed as the misguided efforts of liberals to effect social change—efforts they believed undermined traditional American values.[93] Busing was a favorite liberal boogeyman, and conservatives assailed it with great relish. During the 1976 campaign for the GOP presidential nomination, for example, Ronald Reagan declared that "for too many years a philosophy of government has dominated Washington . . . that works against the values of the family and the values that were so basic to the building of this country."[94] It was a theme he repeated during his 1984 campaign for reelection: the Gipper attacked the Democrats for supporting "busing that takes innocent children out of the neighborhood school and makes them pawns in a social experiment that nobody wants. We found out it failed."[95] Indeed, busing did much to undermine popular faith in "experts" and conservatives were able to reap electoral success by tapping into this burgeoning anti-intellectual sentiment, helping set the stage for Reagan's famous pledge to lead a "crusade" to "take Government off the backs of the great people of this country."[96]

In March 1972 Irene McCabe had declared that the movement against busing represented "the rebirth of American grass-roots involvement in politics."[97] While this may have been an exaggeration, McCabe's bold statement contained a kernel of truth. As historian Matthew Lassiter has argued, in explaining the rise of the new conservatism scholars have tended to focus heavily on national leaders, such as Barry Goldwater, George Wallace and Richard Nixon. In so doing they have obscured the critical role played by the "suburban warriors" and grassroots activists who, based around local churches, PTAs, and neighborhood associations, helped to both remake the national political landscape and effect a profound electoral realignment that shattered the liberal consensus and fueled the rise of the New Right.[98]

The grassroots activism of the anti-busing movement generated a new political language that downplayed race in favor of an emphasis on rights based on citizens' status as homeowners, taxpayers, and parents. In this emerging discourse, "freedom of choice" and "neighborhood schools" were cast as fundamental rights to be defended from unelected bureaucrats and judges as the legitimate fruit of the American Dream. For Matthew Lassiter, the activism that materialized in the Sunbelt suburbs of cities like Charlotte during the early 1970s, and the "color-blind" political language that it pioneered, played a decisive role in the rise of the new conservatism. It produced, he has written, a "suburban blueprint that ultimately resonated from the 'conservative' subdivisions of Orange County to the 'liberal' townships of New England: a bipartisan political language of private property values, taxpayer and consumer rights, children's educational privileges, family residential security, and middle-class historical innocence."[99]

Moreover, the anti-busing cause mobilized new constituencies of political activists and provided a route to other forms of conservative action that spilled over into the "culture wars" of the 1980s. In both Richmond, California, and Erie, Pennsylvania, anti-busing activists also challenged sex education in schools, fought against literature deemed to be "indecent," and urged "back-to-basics" curricula.[100] The *Boston News Digest*, official publication of ROAR, ran articles on a myriad causes besides busing, including opposition to gun control and the Equal Rights Amendment and more general attacks on liberalism and big government. It also offered support to conservative candidates for political office.[101] Meanwhile STOP, an anti-busing organization based in South Boston, recognized the "importance and necessity of addressing other inter-related problems (e.g. ERA, Textbooks, Gun Control, Pornography, Abortion, Communism, Prayer in Schools et al.)." It went on to urge opponents of busing "to "make the good fight" with us by participation with those organizations existing in your own area . . . and nationally."[102]

Increasingly, New Right strategists themselves placed opposition to busing within a broader constellation of concerns—social, economic, political, and cultural—that they believed would appeal to a critical mass of ordinary Americans. The Conservative Caucus, created in November 1974 by Howard Phillips, a founder of Young Americans for Freedom and director of the Office of Economic Opportunity during the Nixon administration, provides a good illustration of this trend.[103] The Caucus, which recruited some 73,000 members in its first year of operation, aimed to roll back the liberal tide by organizing conservative strength "in the places where conservative influence is greatest—at the grass roots level, in the communities where we live and work, all over America."[104] To help achieve this, it intended to build organizations in each of the nation's 435 congressional districts to mobilize local conservatives and wield decisive influence over members of Congress.[105] The Caucus's ambition was matched by its rhetoric: the organization saw itself as part of a "great crusade to gain control of our government from radical politicians and bureaucrats, and restore it to its rightful owners, the citizens of the United States."[106] In a fundraising and recruitment letter written by the Caucus's first national chairman, New Hampshire governor Meldrim Thomson, Jr., opposition to busing was linked to a broader disillusionment with liberalism:

> Are you opposed to forced busing?
>
> Are you tired of liberals telling you how to run your life?
>
> Are you opposed to liberal politicians' wild spending which cause higher taxes, inflation and depression?
>
> Are you tired of liberals forcing your children to study from school books that are anti-God, anti-American and filled with the most vulgar curse words?
>
> Are you tired of feeling no power to change things?
>
> If so, why don't you join the Conservative Caucus?[107]

It was a heady conservative brew that would ultimately yield considerable political reward for the New Right.

In addition to introducing activists to, and generating increased support for, new political issues, anti-busing campaigns also enabled conservatives to challenge liberal control at the community level. In Richmond, California, conservative candidates opposed to busing buried the school board's liberal incumbents in a landslide during the April 1969 election.[108] In Canarsie, meanwhile, the power of the Jefferson Democratic Club was tested by anti-busing insurgents when, in 1976, Alan Erlichman took on state assemblyman Stanley Fink. Fink, a graduate of NYU Law School and a liberal who was also schooled in the practical arts of pork barrel, was a rising star in the Jefferson machine. Erlichman, a "large, brawny man" who sported a "bushy Fu Manchu mustache," had led Canarsie's anti-busing forces during 1972-73. Presenting African Americans as direct competitors with white ethnics, Erlichman's campaign played heavily on racial fears—as he explained, "when my nine-year-old can walk through Harlem safely, then I'll consider integration." Although Fink won the election, Erlichman performed well in the forty or so Canarsie election districts—beating Fink in four and holding him to majorities of 60 percent or less in a further fifteen.[109] In Boston, anti-busing appeared to have run out of electoral steam by 1977, when Louise Day Hicks failed in her bid for reelection to the city council. Nevertheless, some who had achieved prominence during the battles against busing were able to enjoy further electoral success. In 1977 former state assemblyman Ray Flynn was elected to the city council (as the second most popular candidate), in part by broadening out his political appeal by opposing abortion.[110] In 1983 he became the first Southie to be elected mayor.[111] That same year, former ROAR leader James Kelly was elected to the city council as a self-styled "union-oriented Reagan Democrat" (who supported gay rights but opposed rent controls).[112]

Democratic politicians at the local level were generally able to survive the conservative revival by utilizing the advantages of incumbency and developing policies that were more attuned to the feelings of their constituents. It was at the national level, and especially in presidential elections, that the Democratic Party suffered at the hands of a conservative politics that emphasized race and lifestyle issues. Conservative national candidates, whether Republicans like Richard Nixon and Ronald Reagan, or Democrats like George Wallace and Henry "Scoop" Jackson, polled increasingly well in working-class and lower-middle-class districts. In the 1976 Massachusetts Democratic primary, for instance, Jackson won with 23 percent—while Wallace scored over 60 percent of the vote in both of Boston's Southside wards.[113] Canarsie, meanwhile, saw growing levels of electoral support for first Nixon and then Reagan among the traditionally Democratic electorate (the former winning 60 percent of the vote in Italian areas of the city in 1968).[114] In Boston, between 1964 and 1980, the Democrats hemorrhaged votes in presidential elections at an alarming rate—their share slumping from 86 percent to 53 percent. The decline was even more dramatic in the Southside wards where opposition to busing had been so fierce—in Ward 6 it declined from 90 percent to 38 percent, and in Ward 7 from 89 percent to 44 percent. While the city remained Democratic, the party's increasing inability to win the support of working and lower-middle class voters proved catastrophic nationally, helping explain why the party won the White House just once between 1968 and 1992.[115]

Chapter 5

The Tax Revolt

Save the American Dream: Yes on 13
—Proposition 13 Bumper Sticker, 1978

We knew we had to prove again that the American system of freedom
and liberty is the greatest in the world.
—Howard Jarvis, Proposition 13 leader

Liberty and Economic Justice for All!
—Citizens Action League slogan

On the morning of Wednesday 20 April 1977 about fifteen senior citizens, led by Roger Sutton of California's Citizens Action League (CAL), assembled on the steps of the old courthouse building in Redwood City to demand property tax relief for the state's low-income citizens. In a dramatic show of protest that was reminiscent of the draft card burnings of the 1960s, the group of San Mateo County activists set fire to their tax assessment notices in an upturned hubcap, before carrying the ashes to the office of the county assessor, Jack Estes. Marvin Rexford, a retired switchman on the Southern Pacific Railroad, spoke for many who were faced with rising property tax bills as a result of increasing real estate values: Rexford explained that his retirement pay "should be enough to take care of my wife and I—but when we have to pay $200 to $250 per month to live in our home . . . I'd like to enjoy a little of my railroad pension rather than pay it all out in taxes."[1] Little more than a year later, Californians' mounting frustration with rising property tax bills was vented in spectacular fashion. By a margin of almost 2-1, voters passed Proposition 13—a ballot initiative which established a 1 percent limit on the property tax rate, rolled back the assessed value of property to 1975 levels and mandated yearly increases in a property's assessed value of no more than 2 percent irrespective of rises in the price of real estate. It also amended the state constitution so that a vote of two-thirds in the legislature was required to approve any increases in state taxation. Proposition 13 delivered an immediate reduction in property taxes of some 57 percent, returning $7 billion in tax revenues to the people. It was, wrote the editors of *Time* magazine, the political equivalent of a "Pacific tidal wave threatening to sweep across the nation." While John Peterson, an official of the Municipal Finance Officers Association denounced Proposition 13 as "a Frankenstein, a green hulk emerging from the swamps of the West"[2] Howard Jarvis, the high-profile leader of the Proposition 13 campaign, was understandably more upbeat. Sipping scotch in downtown Los Angeles' Biltmore Hotel, he claimed "victory against money, the politicians, the government." For Jarvis, the passage of Proposition 13 was a "second American Revolution" in which ordinary taxpayers in California had, through their organizing efforts, "re-established the definition of what freedom is, what it is worth and what it takes to keep it."[3]

The tax revolt was no one-off protest; it was a social movement that was sustained by tens of thousands of ordinary people who picketed, demonstrated, petitioned, supported tax strikes, and cast ballots against high property tax bills, and it was active—and sometimes successful— right across the nation during the second half of the 1970s. In 1978 and 1979, for instance, 37 states passed laws reducing property taxes while 28 reduced income tax. Wisconsin residents enjoyed a $942 million tax cut, those of Minnesota and Oregon cuts in excess of $700 million. In 1980, voters in Massachusetts endorsed Proposition 2½, which reduced property taxes by $1.3 billion.[4] The tax rebels helped to transform the American political landscape, encouraging the political class, and Republicans in particular, to adopt populist tax-cutting policies and endorse the fashionable new theories of "supply-side" economics and monetarism.[5] According to Californian journalist Peter Schrag, Proposition 13 "set the stage for the Reagan era" and symbolized a radical shift comparable with the New Deal.[6] And while it is usually viewed as a grassroots conservative groundswell, the tax revolt actually had rich and complex connections with the social protest movements of the 1960s. Indeed, tax rebels drew extensively on direct action tactics and political ideologies that had been popular among 1960s radicals—even as many of them railed against Sixties notions of "big government' and "welfare." Given the nation's origins in bitter protests against colonial taxation it is perhaps not surprising that tax protesters employed patriotic dissent extensively and sought to portray their efforts as a defense of traditional American freedoms. Ultimately, the tax revolt played a decisive role in the conservative realignment that transformed American politics during the 1980s.

The tax revolt flared first and most intensely in California—where dramatic increases in real estate values after World War II resulted in soaring property tax bills for many homeowners even though the actual rate of taxation changed little.[7] During fiscal years 1949-1958 more than 20,000 people participated in tax protests.[8] In 1957, homeowners in the San Gabriel Valley rebelled against increases in their property tax assessments of between 30 percent and 50 percent—the protests culminated in a rally of 6,000 at the L.A. Coliseum.[9] The property tax, the oldest tax in the United States with links to the colonial era, was problematic in a number of ways. It was, for example, not based on a person's ability to pay—so those on low incomes whose home had increased in value dramatically in the years after purchase could quite easily find themselves struggling to pay their bills. There was also a lack of uniformity and fairness in the way that the tax was applied—with plenty of room for corruption. Indeed, in 1965 the *San Francisco Chronicle* published an expose of Russell Wolden—a socialite, dandy, and tax assessor for the City and County of San Francisco. Wolden, a "dapper dresser" whose office apparently "had the prettiest secretaries and the best-stocked liquor cabinet," had basically been operating a protection racket, setting high valuations for commercial property and then offering reductions to some in return for campaign contributions, bribes and kickbacks. Despite California's constitution requiring that property be assessed at "full cash value," Wolden had tended to value residential property at about 10 percent of its market price. The story led to a series of investigations and criminal trials that exposed further abuses and helped to discredit the state's tax assessment system.[10] The level of abuse was in many ways not entirely unexpected: tax assessors were elected by the same constituents whose property they assessed, so there was a strong incentive to under-assess residential property values. Indeed the practice of fractional assessment, in which people were taxed on a fraction of the real value of their property, was widespread—and constituted a valuable and valued "informal tax privilege." While fractional assessment was legal in only 22 states, it was "nearly universal in practice"; in 1971 it is estimated that it was worth some $39 billion to American homeowners.[11]

During the 1960s, under pressure from investigative journalists, criminal investigations, and the courts, states began to modernize the property tax by imposing centralization, professionalization and standardization. Designed as a progressive measure to insure fairness and uniformity, these reforms had unintended consequences and played a critical role in spurring nationwide tax protests.[12] As historian Isaac Martin has shown, the "movement against property taxes was . . . concentrated in states that did the most to modernize property tax administration"—such as California, Idaho, and Oregon. The one exception was Massachusetts, though here it was the threat of impending modernization that seems to have been significant.[13] In California, modernization came in the form of the Petris-Knox Act, passed by the state legislature in 1966, which required uniform assessment of all property at 25 percent of actual value. The bill also stipulated that reassessment had to take place every three years, and it reduced the discretionary powers of local tax assessors significantly. The reforms actually resulted in large tax cuts for many businesses—which had been over-assessed as a way to keep homeowners' tax bills low (and their votes secure).[14] It did not take long for taxpayers to begin organizing—in 1966 the United Organization of Taxpayers (UOT), a coalition of neighborhood organizations based in L.A., called for a property tax strike. The following year they attempted to abolish the property tax altogether, but could gather only 100,000 signatures in support of placing the measure on the state ballot. In 1968, a proposal from L.A. tax assessor Philip Watson did make it onto the November ballot. Proposition 9 called for a cap of 1 percent of full market value and limiting the property tax to fund only local, "property-related" services (such as sewers, roads, and fire protection). Both Proposition 9 and a similar measure in 1972 were defeated.[15]

All the while property tax bills in the Golden State continued to rise—fueled by both modernization (including the use of computerized regression analysis that made possible for the first time widespread reassessment of property values) and inflation. Between 1972 and 1978 prices for single-family homes in California increased at an annual rate of 18 percent, with much of the growth centered in the Los Angeles area. Indeed, a 1977 survey revealed that between 1971 and 1976 the appraised value of residential property in L.A. County had risen by more than 40 percent. For the 1977 fiscal year, valuations in Northridge increased by 111 percent, Studio City by 88 percent, and Venice by 88 percent. Throughout the state assessed values for owner-occupied homes increased by 111 percent between fiscal years 1975 and 1978. Given that rising property values meant ever-higher property tax bills, it was hardly surprising that many California taxpayers were, in the words of Howard Jarvis, "mad as hell."[16]

Howard Jarvis was widely viewed as the driving force behind Proposition 13, and he was certainly the tax revolt's most high-profile leader—he made the cover of *Time* magazine in June 1978 and was a runner up for the magazine's "man of the year" award that same year (losing out to Chinese Premier Deng Xiaoping). Aged seventy-five in June 1978, Jarvis had been active in the tax protest movement since the early 1960s—becoming head of the UOT in 1965. Often viewed as a crank and a curmudgeon, Jarvis was a colorful character whose life seemed to have been lifted from some extraordinary work of fiction. He hailed from the little mining community of Mercur, Utah, some 50 miles west of Salt Lake City. In September 1903, just a week or so after his birth, the town burned to the ground—precipitating a move to Magna, population 250. The Jarvises owned a small farm and his father, a "stern, righteous, but fair" man, also worked as a carpenter, taught himself law and eventually became a judge. Jarvis studied law at the University of Utah, and took a series of summer mining jobs to help pay his way. Jarvis came close to losing his life on no less than two occasions: first when a mine shaft in Eureka, Utah, collapsed, trapping Jarvis and two others for almost three days; second, when a plane in which Jarvis was traveling crashed in heavy snow into a mountain near St. George, Utah, and the passengers had to wait almost 48 hours before a rescue team arrived.

A keen sportsman—in addition to playing semi-professional baseball he also managed to box with Jack Dempsey, play golf with Ben Hogan, and watch the Notre Dame-USC football game with Will Rogers—Jarvis was a self-made man. After making his first fortune as a newspaperman in Utah, he was persuaded by no less than Earl Warren to move to California in 1935. Once in the Golden State, Jarvis helped J. Paul Getty, III, to write his family history and developed a wide range of successful business interests—including manufacturing car coolers, gas heaters, flatirons, garbage disposals, and aircraft parts and assemblies. Alongside his business interests, Jarvis had a long-standing commitment to the Republican Party—in 1932 he had served as Herbert Hoover's press man on his campaign train from Des Monies, Iowa, to Elko, Nevada, where his major responsibility appears to have been to use a cushion to protect the president from the rotten eggs and tomatoes that the Depression-era crowds loved to hurl at him. In California, Jarvis immersed himself in GOP politics, assisting in the recruitment of Richard Nixon as a congressional candidate in 1946 and helping to run a series of election campaigns (including those of Earl Warren, Dwight Eisenhower, and Bill Knowland). Jarvis himself ran for office several times, including the U.S. Senate in 1962 and mayor of Los Angeles in 1977, always without success.[17]

Much of Jarvis's appeal came from his cranky populism—he described himself as a "rugged bastard who's had his head kicked in a thousand times by the government" and explained that one of Proposition 13's aims was to "forge a chain around the necks of all elected officials and their coteries of bureaucrats so that they could be dragged away from the feedbag." He dismissed a report from the UCLA Graduate School of Management that claimed passage of Proposition 13 would double unemployment and cost more than 400,000 jobs, as the work of a "bunch of punk students that knew as much about economics as a mud turtle." With his bulldoggish face and gruff voice Jarvis seemed to be a "rumpled throwback to [H. L.] Mencken's soap box demagogues."[18]

After property tax reduction measures had failed to qualify for the ballot in 1976 and 1977 by narrow margins (respectively 10,000 and 1,400 signatures short)—in part because of tactical divisions and personality clashes among California's anti-tax forces—a renewed attempt at cooperation by Jarvis and Sacramento activist Paul Gann, a soft-spoken former auto dealer and realtor, succeeded. With Jarvis heading the drive in southern California and Gann taking the north, the largest petition drive in California's history was launched in July 1977. On 2 December Proposition 13 (known popularly as the Jarvis-Gann amendment) qualified for the June ballot with more than a million signatures (there were, apparently, some 300,000 more that they had not been able to process in time). The cost of this impressive organizing feat: just $28,500.[19] After years of failing to do very much in response to the tax protests California's political class responded to Proposition 13 with a proposal of their own. The Behr bill promised to reduce taxes by 30 percent and expand tax relief for seniors, while an amendment to the state constitution would allow "classification," thereby enabling business and tax property to be taxed at different rates.[20] But many Californians were suspicious of this measure—full of legal jargon, it was extraordinarily hard to understand, and the tax cut that it promised was in any case a temporary one.[21]

Having spent the best part of two decades fighting against high property taxes, Howard Jarvis threw himself into the campaign to pass Proposition 13. He was "on the road constantly.... On a typical day ... I would do a couple of interviews with the press, give a speech at a lunch, cut a radio or TV spot, have dinner with the local tax leaders in whatever area I was in, and appear at an evening rally." Much of the state's political establishment, Democrat and Republican, were against Proposition 13. Governor Jerry Brown, for instance, claimed that it would replace "one monster with another," while the AFL-CIO, California Teachers Association, California Fire Services Coalition, almost every major state newspaper, Bank of America, the Southern Pacific Railroad, and Standard Oil of California were among whose who lined up against the measure.[22]

Opponents of Jarvis-Gann claimed that, if it passed, schools might have to close, thousands of public employees would lose their jobs, and police and fire services would be slashed.[23] Jarvis responded that his critics were "horses' asses," "marinated bureaucrats and over-animated popcorn balls." He counter-claimed that, if Proposition 13 did not pass, property tax bills would increase massively.[24] Jarvis's arguments appeared to be supported by the actions of politicians: San Diego city council voted to raise their salaries by 53 percent, which seemed to validate Jarvis's call for a fence "between the hogs and the swill bucket."[25] Then, on 16 May 1978, L.A. County tax assessor Alexander Pope announced that residents could check their reassessments by visiting or calling his office (rather than having to wait until July). The average increase in assessed value was more than 100 percent, which, in addition to authenticating Jarvis's warnings, caused panic and chaos among ordinary taxpayers and state politicians.[26] Pope was ordered to cancel the 1978 reassessments while Governor Brown attempted to freeze the entire reassessment process.[27] Public opinion seemed to shift decisively behind Proposition 13 and, on 6 June, more than 4 million Californians voted for it. At his victory celebration at the L.A. Biltmore, Jarvis blew kisses to his cheering supporters and exclaimed "Now we know how it felt when they dumped English tea in Boston harbor!"[28]

The tax revolt was not restricted to California. Voters in Nevada and Idaho approved measures similar to Proposition 13 in November 1978, while limits to restrict state and local spending were enacted in Colorado, New Jersey, and Tennessee.[29] During the 1970s tax protest organizations and campaigns could be found around the country in cities like Boston, Chicago, Detroit, and Pittsburgh; rural areas of Ohio and Wisconsin; and southern states like Arkansas, Texas, and Virginia. In 1972, for example, both the Taxpayers Committee of Cook County and the Citizens' Action Program protested against the property tax in the Chicago area. In June, 200 demonstrated in the office of Mayor Richard Daley to demand a two-year freeze on property tax increases. In February 1973, 700 rallied in Springfield for the same cause. Later in the decade the Taxpayers Protest Committee mobilized more than 1,500 to take part in demonstrations and offer support for a tax strike. In Massachusetts, known as "Taxachusetts" by disgruntled taxpayers, a variety of organizations, including Massachusetts Fair Share and Citizens for Limited Taxation, were active in tax protest.[30]

Although the tax revolt certainly had important roots in the conservative political organizing of the 1950s and 1960s, and has traditionally been viewed by scholars as a manifestation of the new right, it also makes a good deal of sense to view it as a product of the radical 1960s—not least because a number of its activists and organizations grew directly out of that decade's civil rights and New Left movements.[31] Moreover, in their use of protest tactics, in their challenge to established authority and skepticism of political elites, and in their commitment to grassroots organizing and participatory democracy, tax activists drew constructively on the 1960s.

Many of the tactics used by property tax protesters would not have been out of place in the civil rights, New Left, or anti-Vietnam War movements: some protesters burned their tax assessment notices; on one occasion a "mob of homeowners took to the streets" and smashed a mayor's car; activists held rallies and marches, staged guerrilla theater, held candlelit marches, interrupted political meetings, and shouted down elected officials; they staged tax strikes; and they called for revolution.[32] In Georgia, for example, radical folk singer Si Kanh performed a benefit concert for the Fanin County Taxpayers Association. Kanh, a veteran of the Student Nonviolent Coordinating Committee (SNCC), attacked tax breaks that favored wealthy city homeowners at the expense of the rural poor.[33] In Oregon Perry Chesnut, a college drop-out who had opposed the war in Vietnam, was one of the leaders in the campaign for a Proposition 13-style property tax limitation measure that was defeated at the ballot box in 1978.[34]

The "Sixties connection" can be viewed particularly clearly in California. In his 1973 mayoral campaign in Oakland, for instance, Black Panther Bobby Seale condemned rising property taxes and called for the tax burden to be shifted onto big business through the creation of a new tax system.[35] A year later CAL was established by veterans of the civil rights and welfare rights movement, initially to protest against hikes in utility bills before turning its attention to the property tax. One of its founders was Mike Miller, a former member of both SDS and SNCC, who had worked with the legendary community organizer Saul Alinsky.[36] CAL described itself as a "mass-based, multi-issue citizen organization made up of low to middle income families and individuals throughout the State of California" whose purpose was to "build an organization capable of demanding and obtaining accountability from the people in power— the men and women who run the giant corporations, the banks, the bureaucracies and the political organizations that control our lives and the fate of our communities so that greater economic and social justice can be secured for all people."[37] CAL betrayed a clear debt to 1960s-era styles of protest—especially the anti-Vietnam War demonstrations. In the same year that tax assessment notices were burned by some of its members, the group also staged a 21-day vigil outside Governor Jerry Brown's Los Angeles office. In a protest that appears to have been inspired by the November 1969 "March Against Death" (in which the names of American soldiers killed in Vietnam were read out in front of the White House) activists read out the names of the 150,000 LA-area residents who had signed petitions supporting property tax relief.[38] The group's New Leftist origins might also explain its commitment to participatory democracy. A central goal of CAL's organizing strategy was to "give people a sense of their own power"—to show that ordinary people could "win, and see that they have won the reforms through their own power" in order that democracy could become a "reality instead of a myth."[39]

Similar connections can be seen in Chicago, where the Citizens' Action Program (CAP) moved into tax protest after initially campaigning against industrial pollution: it turned out that U.S. Steel's South Works plant contributed far more to the Windy City's toxic air than to its coffers, thanks to a generous underassessment from the notoriously corrupt Cook County assessor and Daley machine operative, P. J. "Parky" Cullerton. Between 1970 and 1973 CAP's co-chairs were Rev. Leonard Dubi and Paul Booth. Dubi, a Catholic priest and native of the city's Southeast, who apparently resembled "a somewhat thinner version of Robert Redford," had moved into political activism after being "excited by the civil rights movement, the peace movement and the war on poverty." His involvement with the CAP grew out of the concerns of his parishioners over "bad schools, filthy air," and "heavy tax burdens." Booth was a New Left veteran, a signatory to the Port Huron Statement who had served as SDS national secretary before working with organized labor and taking up a research fellowship at the University of Chicago.[40] A "militant, democratic citizens' organization," CAP engaged in direct action protests—staging boycotts, demonstrations, pickets, and voter-registration drives, for instance. Influenced by 1960s notions of participatory democracy, the group emphasized organizing at the neighborhood level and it sought to nurture the leadership potential that it believed was present in the local people among whom it worked. As well as highlighting "Parky" Cullerton's underassessments of U.S. Steel and Cook County's five racetracks—exposés that made front-page news in Chicago—CAP also launched an early campaign for tax rebates for homeowners in Beverly and the South Shore, areas that had been "drastically overassessed."[41]

In the Bay State, former SDS activists Mark Splain and Michael Ansara helped to form Massachusetts Fair Share (MFS) in 1973. Expanding from the working-class suburb of Chelsea, it boasted 12,000 members in more than 20 chapters by 1978 and engaged in sustained grassroots community organizing as well as organizing pickets and demonstrations. On one occasion they held "brown-bag lunches outside Jimmy's Harborside Restaurant," an eatery that was popular with politicians, in order to force "prompt payment of the restaurant's taxes."[42] The organization sought to shift the burden of taxation away from low-income homeowners and onto business. It campaigned against so-called "sweetheart deals" for downtown developers and for collection of unpaid taxes from big businesses. It also worked to make taxation more progressive: it proposed cutting property taxes by up to 20 percent and bridging the funding gap through taxes on legal fees, stock transfers, and other services used mostly by the rich.[43]

In 1978, MFS worked tirelessly for a so-called "circuit-breaker" tax relief law that would have provided up to $500 for homeowners and renters whose property taxes exceeded 8 percent of their annual income. MFS bused in hundreds of supporters to the state capital as the legislative session drew to a close to testify and to pressurize legislators into supporting the proposed law. When the televised testimony of MFS's Mike Regan was cut short, the candy factory worker warned the state's lawmakers that "we are just about ready to blow . . . our tops. . . . We are going to blow a fuse"; in a piece of choreographed political theater he approached the committee chair, reached into his pocket, and placed two blown fuses on the table, and 150 fellow activists immediately followed suit. After the law passed the statehouse, governor Michael Dukakis pocket-vetoed the bill; his failure to support property tax reform contributed to his defeat in the gubernatorial primary later that year. MFS, meanwhile, switched tactics to try to secure an amendment to the state constitution that would allow for fractional assessment—something that had been overturned in 1974 by the state Supreme Court in *Town of Sudbury v. the Commissioner of Corporations and Taxation.*[44]

MFS had actually begun as a "pilot organizing project" of the Movement for Economic Justice (MEJ), founded by former civil rights and welfare rights organizer George Wiley in December 1972.[45] MEJ was an "attempt to develop a nationwide, grass-roots movement among the many diverse groups of people who have a direct economic stake in more adequate income, better jobs with decent pay, adequate health care and a fairer system of taxation." Wiley sought to unite the tens of millions of Americans who earned less than $15,000 a year with "millions of middle class citizens who are sincerely concerned about ending poverty, war and social and economic injustice in America." Initially organizing around specific issues—such as "property tax assessments"—it hoped over the longer term to unite these groups "around a common economic agenda."[46]

With his trademark Afro, dashiki, jeans, and scuffed shoes, George A. Wiley does not fit most people's stereotype of the typical property tax protester of the 1970s. But as historian Isaac Martin has pointed out, "from the vantage point of 1973" it "would have been . . . natural" to view Wiley as a preeminent leader of the tax revolt.[47] Born in Bayonne, New Jersey, in February 1931, Wiley was a former chemistry professor who had taught at Berkeley and Syracuse. He became active in the civil rights movement, founding the Syracuse chapter of the Congress of Racial Equality, and in 1964-1966 served as CORE associate national director. After losing out to Floyd McKissick in an internal power struggle to succeed James Farmer as national director, Wiley founded the National Welfare Rights Organization (NWRO) and helped lead efforts to secure economic justice and self-respect for many of America's poorest citizens. At its height, the NWRO had 125,000 members in some 800 chapters, and Wiley gained national prominence by organizing sit-ins of welfare mothers at the offices of mayors and legislators to demand reforms. In 1970 he led the fight against President Nixon's Family Assistance Plan on the grounds that the proposed annual income of $1,600 for a family of four was far below the $5,500 that was required. At the end of January 1972, Wiley stepped down from NWRO to form the Movement for Economic Justice.[48]

Wiley believed that opposition to the property tax could be channeled into a broader movement that would promote progressive taxation and policies of redistribution that would benefit the majority of American citizens, bringing together those on welfare with the working poor, seniors, and middle classes who were increasingly struggling with high property tax bills. Indeed, Wiley was "convinced that the working man and the poor had far more in common in terms of needs and self-interest than they had differences." At a March 1973 conference sponsored by the liberal National Council of Churches, Wiley called for a "taxpayers' revolt" that would be directed "not against welfare mothers" but against the "welfare program that takes care of the welfare of corporations . . . corporate farmers . . . the oil industry" and those living "at the public trough." Wiley's MEJ provided seed money, staffers, and advice on organizing to local taxpayers' groups throughout the country, including MFS and CAL; and it set up tax clinics across the nation to help poor Americans fill out their tax forms (and secure any tax breaks to which they were entitled) and serve as an organizing tool to encourage tax activism. In April 1973 the MEJ sponsored a national conference of taxpayer organizations in an effort to foster a greater sense of coherence and common purpose among disparate local movements. Wiley's tragic death, at just forty-two, in a boating accident in August 1973 robbed the tax protest movement of one its most high-profile, articulate, and talented leaders.[49]

The tax revolt was a movement made up primarily of community-based organizations that mobilized ordinary people in the fight against property taxes.[50] Sometimes tax protest organizations evolved out of existing local groups, such as a neighborhood crime watch organization, a local union branch, or the struggles against school busing or property developers.[51] Alongside this focus on community organizing, many tax rebels of the 1970s shared with the New Left of the 1960s a commitment to participatory democracy—the notion, in the words of the Port Huron Statement, "that the individual share in those social decisions determining the quality and direction of his life" and that "politics be seen positively, as the art of collectively creating an acceptable pattern of social relations." As a number of historians have shown, a common theme among the tax rebels of the 1970s was their firm belief that politicians and government—at the local and state levels—were unresponsive to, indeed often contemptuous of, their grievances. Statistical analysis by political scientists offers support to the idea that the "best predictor of support for tax limitation . . . is the feeling that one is cut off from the political decision-making process."[52] The qualitative evidence also seems persuasive. When David Morgan, a tax activist from Hollywood, attempted to appeal his tax assessment he found the head of the Assessment Appeals Board to be arrogant—"I started to testify and he interrupted me and overruled me and said I couldn't quote the *Wall Street Journal* because it wasn't proper legal authority." San Gabriel Valley activist Richard Carman had a similar experience—he explained that local government "did everything in the world to discourage us . . . everything possible to belittle you."[53] Doubtless many tax protesters came to share the view of one activist that elected officials "were against any controlling of the taxes by the people . . . They felt that has long as they were elected . . . they had the right to do just as they saw it."[54] For Barbara Anderson, a swimming pool instructor and volunteer secretary for the Massachusetts group Citizens for Limited Taxation, the tax revolt was a "populist revolt. It was people who were just tired of being pushed around . . . people who [were] tired of not having their voices heard at high levels."[55] As well as seeking to reduce property tax bills, these 1970s protesters were also demanding that a measure of political power be returned to "the people." The demands of one taxpayers' organization in southern California were typical—it encouraged citizens to participate in politics and declared that "We the people insist on remaining informed so that we may retain control over the instruments that we have created."[56] This demand for control even manifested itself in secession movements in southern California during the mid- to late 1970s: attempts (unsuccessful) to secede from Los Angeles County occurred in the San Fernando Valley, the Santa Clara Valley and the South Bay area of L.A.[57]

Although the tax revolt had important and productive links with the civil rights and New Left movements, a significant number of tax rebels drew strength from engaging in "backlash" politics that attacked both "big government" and the perceived liberal excesses of the 1960s. An interesting early example of this phenomenon comes from the New Right Coalition—an Ayn Rand-inspired offshoot of the Young Americans for Freedom that was founded in the spring of 1971 by college students and young businessmen. The group's "statement of principles" endorsed individual freedom, laissez-faire capitalism, and small government restricted to maintaining law and order and the national defense. Communism and the welfare state were denounced as undermining personal freedom and economic productivity. The NRC argued that "life without freedom is a shallow existence, and we pledge ourselves to the defense of our freedom and the eradication of tyranny."

In the spring of 1972 the organization, based in Brighton, Massachusetts, claimed more than 600 members with chapters at Harvard, MIT, NYU, Boston University, University of Florida, and University of Wisconsin. One of its most innovative tactics was to use "street posters to reach the public with our Capitalist ideology." Indeed, the group claimed to be the "first right-wing organization" to have done this. By February 1972 some 30,000 posters had been "pasted up in Boston, New York City, Chicago, Tallahassee, Washington D.C., Los Angeles, Milwaukee, Manchester (N.H.), and a dozen other cities." The aesthetic of the posters was inspired by the very movements—the New Left, the antiwar movement—that they sought to attack; which they did uncompromisingly. The New Left, for example, was accused of being full of "parasites," "fascists," and "moral barbarians"; the antiwar movement was caricatured as a "Trojan Dove" that supported the Communists. NRC engaged in "pickets, debates, rallies," held lectures, and staged counter-demonstrations against the peace movement, the New Left and welfare mothers. But protesting against high taxation was an early focus. On the morning of Saturday 26 June 1971, for example, a group of about 30 NRC activists staged a picket outside the Massachusetts State House to protest what they termed the "slavery" of taxation. One sign declared "Right On With Taxpayers Liberation" while another denounced Governor Francis W. Sargent as "Massachusetts answer to George III." A series of tax demonstrations were also planned for 15 April 1972.[58] NRC national chairman Don Feder was a veteran of the 1964 Goldwater campaign who went on to become a prominent conservative commentator and activist. His commitment to reducing taxation endured, and he was involved heavily with Citizens for Limited Taxation in the late 1970s.[59]

As historian Clarence Lo has observed, many affluent activists objected to the fact that their high property taxes did not benefit them directly, but instead funded welfare and other social programs. The editor of *Taxpayer's Watchdog*, a southern California newsletter, explained, "[what got people the maddest was] the greed of government and the careless way they spent the fruits of our labors."[60] In California in particular, attacks on "big government" and "welfare" seemed to go down well: by 1978 there were 1.5 million government employees (or 1 for every 15 residents), and food stamps cost the state $5.5 billion.[61] During the 1960s, Ronald Reagan's attacks on welfare mothers (and campus radicals) contributed significantly to his electoral appeal. In a 1964 speech, for example, the Gipper explained that "Today there is an increasing number who can't see a fat man standing beside a thin one without automatically coming to the conclusion the fat man got that way by taking advantage of the thin one." He warned that, having "laid its hand on health, housing . . . commerce [and] education," the government was threatening the very principles of freedom on which the nation was founded. By tapping into this emergent backlash, Reagan was able to with the governor's mansion in 1966 by more than a million votes, defeating liberal incumbent Pat Brown.[62]

The growing power of public unions in the Golden State also provoked resentment at the perceived abuses—such as "phony sick leaves" and generous benefits.[63] Howard Jarvis epitomized the populist, "backlash" strain of the tax revolt—he denounced the "Powerful public employee unions, influential politicians, and ultra-liberal social activists" who had "launched a multi-million propaganda campaign against Proposition 13,"[64] and he attacked the "bums" of Santa Cruz who "surf eighteen hours a day, thirty-seven days a month" while drawing "welfare and food stamps." Jarvis promised that "after [Proposition] 13 passed, the sun was going to come up and all the surfers were going to evaporate."[65]

Like many other social movement activists, those involved in the tax revolt sought to ground their demands firmly within America's ideals of freedom and equality and attempted to present their protests as patriotic. Naturally, tax revolt activists were attracted to the legacy of the Founding Fathers—who had emphasized the importance of property rights and defined a government's legitimacy, in part, by its ability to protect them.[66] And they were also able to invoke the American Revolution itself, particularly its origins in colonists' opposition to what were viewed as unfair and excessive imposts. The tax protesters of the 1970s made numerous references to the Boston Tea Party—some went as far as to dress up in colonial garb and reenact some of the famous scenes from the nation's birth—while opposition to the property tax was portrayed as a legitimate defense of the American dream itself.[67]

One does not have to look particularly hard to find evidence of the tax revolt's use of patriotic protest. While Jarvis had little time for the use of "gimmicks," such as using tea bags as symbols of the tax revolt, he placed patriotism and love of country at the heart of his own anti-tax rhetoric.[68] He claimed repeatedly that the tax rebels were following in the "hallowed tradition" of the American Revolution and that Proposition 13 was, like the famous first shot at Lexington and Concord, "heard around the world."[69] In his autobiography Jarvis explained that "The last lines in our national anthem . . . are: 'The land of the free and the home of the brave.' These words mean that the people cannot be free if they are not brave. Our small group of taxpayers in California consisted of brave souls who eventually slew the giant. They had the will, the persistence, and the guts to fight and win against great political odds. They reestablished the definition of what freedom is, what it is worth and what it takes to keep it."[70]

The American Tax Reduction Movement celebrated the November 1978 election of Democrat Edward J. King to the governor's mansion in Massachusetts on an anti-property tax platform.[71] An article in the group's newsletter described King's victory as "another Boston Tea Party" and argued that a "new breed of Democrats" were "bringing their party home to Tom Jefferson's ideal of limited government."[72] On the other end of the political spectrum, the MEJ organized for fairer taxes under the slogan "Fair Taxation or New Representation" and, "Remember the Boston Tea Party." In its 1973 campaign to make the critically important executive session of the House Ways and Means Committee open to the press and public, the group suggested that local activists concentrate on property tax assessments as an "organizing focus" and urged them to stage a "major publicity event around the 200th Anniversary of the Boston Tea Party."[73] On 18 March 1974—the 198th anniversary of the evacuation of British troops from Boston, activists with the Massachusetts People's Bicentennial Coalition held a "Taxpayers' Town Meeting" in Boston's historic Faneuil Hall and a march to the Federal Building to demand a fairer and more equitable tax system. Angered by recent revelations that President Nixon had used the donation of his vice-presidential papers to secure a generous tax break, they demanded the "impeachment of King Richard" and pledged to "expose the loophole-filled tax system which allows the wealthy and oil corporations to amass fortunes at our expense."[74]

Back in 1964 ordinary citizens had engaged in property tax protests in Alhambra, California, under the leadership of Mike Rubino, a beer delivery truck driver who was one of the tax revolt's first leaders. An article in the *Alhambra Post Advocate* in March 1965 explained that "Our tax protest movement has been characterized as a grass roots revolution set in motion by a beer truck driver in Alhambra. It's true and thank God for people like Mike. We hope that it is never forgotten that the American Revolution was started by farmers in work clothes."[75] A year later, in Culver City, California, the county tax assessor was booed by a crowd of 700 who cried "Taxation without representation" and "Remember the Boston Tea Party!" In the spring of 1978, disgruntled taxpayers in Glendale, California, shouted, "Taxation without representation is tyranny" and dumped tea bags at the office of the county assessor.[76] In Maricopa County, Arizona, tax protester L. Marvin Cooley had written a handbook for tax resisters that was entitled "Tea Party 1976."[77] In the Garden State during the summer of 1976, the New Jersey Tax Revolt Association, led by Thomas Caslander, and Ralph Fucetola's New Jersey Tax Federation, were leading the campaign to repeal the state's recently enacted income tax law. On 18 September more than 350 demonstrators carried a crate of tea through the streets of Princeton and placed it at the doorstep of the governor's mansion. At a rally earlier that day outside the State House in Trenton, which attracted a crowd of some 5,000, comparisons with the Boston Tea Party were made. Later that afternoon one particularly enthusiastic tax rebel dressed up as a colonial-era town crier and, after ringing his hand bell, called for an end to the "oppressions visited upon us by runaway officialdom."[78] At a national tax limitation conference held in St. Louis on 29 July 1978, the meeting's convener, conservative Republican Representative Philip M. Crane (Illinois) drew comparisons with the American colonists' anger over taxation without representation and warned that the anger driving the tax revolt would lead to a "second American revolution."[79] Dallas's tax revolt organization, the Dallas Tax Equality Association, was known as the TEA Party.[80]

During the second half of the twentieth century home ownership, and the ability to enjoy the "advantages of the good life that had motivated years of hard work"—such as family vacations, consumer goods, and quality education for one's children—lay at the very heart of the American Dream; rising property tax bills were seen by many as a direct assault on this ideal.[81] Jarvis explained that "I have always believed that private ownership of property and the idea that a man's home was his castle made the United States the greatest and freest country the world has ever known. If you destroy the residential property base, you destroy the country." For Jarvis, "the American dream of home ownership for everyone was being sabotaged by exploding property taxes."[82] Similarly, the editor of *Taxpayers' Watchdog* argued that "Everything that we have in this country flows from our right to own private property. When . . . [that] right . . . is taken, everything else, every other freedom falls behind it."[83] As a pro-Proposition 13 bumper sticker put it, "Save the American Dream: Yes on 13."[84]

According to *Newsweek* the passage of Proposition 13 signified a "reaffirmation of free-enterprise priorities. . . . Just as the New Deal of the 1930s launched Big Government, the Great Tax Revolt of 1978 may herald a conservative reaction."[85] Many commentators have agreed, viewing the tax protests of the 1970s as a critical component of the New Right's rise to power and a contributor to the conservative political realignment that swept away the old New Deal order. According to Thomas and Mary Edsall, for example, the tax revolt helped to "catalyze . . . the mobilization of a conservative presidential majority," providing the emerging conservative coalition with "new muscle and a new logic" and enabling it to make significant political capital by portraying the (liberal) government as the enemy.[86]

The year 1978, dubbed the "Year of the Taxpayer," certainly provided plenty of evidence that cutting taxes was popular among the electorate. In Michigan, for instance, voters endorsed the Headlee Amendment which limited state taxes to 9.5 percent of personal income, linked property tax increases to the rate of inflation, and required voter approval for other tax increases. In Ohio, voters defeated proposals for school tax hikes, while Edward King, running as a tax cutter, usurped Michael Dukakis as Massachusetts governor. In a stunning upset in New Jersey, Jeffrey K. Bell defeated four-term incumbent senator Clifford P. Case in the GOP primary election on a platform that called for a 30 percent cut in federal income taxes.[87] Proposition 13-style measures were enacted in Idaho and Nevada, and, over the next few years, at least eighteen states voted to cut or limit taxation. In 1980, the citizens of Massachusetts voted for Proposition 2½, which reduced property taxes to 2.5 percent of market value and delivered a $1.5 billion tax cut.[88] That same year, conservatives won national power with the election of Ronald Reagan to the presidency and the GOP capture of the Senate. A year later, Congress passed the Economic Recovery Tax Act—which delivered the largest income tax cut in U.S. history, 25 percent over three years.[89]

Opposition to high taxation—which was seen as harming economic growth and impinging on individual freedom—and excessive government spending on social programs had long been a staple in conservative circles. Indeed, conservatives had denounced both the "dime store" New Dealism of the Eisenhower administration and the Great Society reforms of LBJ. When Republican president Richard Nixon announced, in 1971, that he was "now a Keynesian" and introduced wage and price controls, many conservatives fumed.[90] In the March 1974 edition of her *Report*, Phyllis Schlafly had called for an end to deficit spending and for "restraints on an unbalanced budge by making it illegal unless we are in a war declared by Congress." She had also called for conservatives to vote "against any politician who votes for any tax increase."[91]

Politicians' preoccupation with tax cuts was, however, a relatively new phenomenon.[92] As governor of California, Ronald Reagan had actually opposed the property tax limitation initiatives of 1968 and 1972. Though committed to reducing the size of government, he feared that limiting property taxes would simply result in the burden being shifted onto other forms of taxation. Reagan instead emphasized limiting spending and balancing the budget, and in 1973 he introduced Proposition 1, a measure that would have limited state spending to 8.3 percent of personal income and required annual reductions in spending by 0.1 percent until it reached 7 percent (it was defeated by 54 percent to 46 percent in the November election). By 1978, though, Reagan had converted—he signed a petition to place Proposition 13 on the ballot and justified his switch by invoking supply-side economic theory. Popularized by the likes of Arthur Laffer, and Jude Wanniski, the advocates of what George H. W. Bush famously referred to as "voodoo economics" argued that tax cuts would stimulate economic growth and ultimately perhaps even deliver more tax revenues to the government.[93] Reagan's shift was symptomatic: politicians were eager to harness the proven electoral popularity of tax cutting and they took to heart Milton Friedman's prophecy that the "wave of taxpayer protest can carry politicians who learn to ride it to the highest offices in the land."[94] There was much talk in the media about the "Proposition 13 babies," Republican freshmen who "rode into office on the same antigovernment, pro-austerity sentiment" that fueled the tax revolt. Many of these young legislators, including future House speaker Newt Gingrich, were committed firmly to reduced government spending and achieving a balanced budget and they believed that these policies could lay the basis for a new Republican majority.[95]

Tax cuts were often used as a conduit to a broader array of conservative issues—such as opposition to busing, affirmative action and welfare, and concerns about moral decline. The Conservative Caucus (CC), a New Right organization founded in 1974, worked hard to promote conservative causes and to organize at the local level to elect conservative candidates to office. A year after its founding it boasted 47 state coordinators, 125 congressional district directors and more than 70,000 dues-paying members.[96] Its national director, Howard Phillips, was a Harvard graduate and founding member of YAF who had been elected chair of Boston's GOP in 1964, at the age of just 23. A leading figure in the New Right, Phillips had briefly headed the Office of Economic Opportunity under Nixon.[97] CC's national chairman was New Hampshire governor Meldrim Thomson, a "successful businessman, publisher, and attorney" who had emphasized "no new taxes" in his 1972 election campaign.[98] The CC was keen to place the question of tax cuts within a broader array of conservative causes, and one of the organization's recruiting letters from 1975, for instance, linked the issues of "forced busing," and progressive education (particularly school textbooks that were "anti-God" and "anti-American") to tax-and-spend liberalism. The CC sought to take power away from the "'we know what's best for you' liberal bureaucrats and social planners" and return it to "average, law-abiding, taxpaying Americans." CC leaders argued that since the "voice of the people" was too often "drowned out by special interest groups in Washington" it was necessary to focus organizing efforts at the local level where, they claimed, conservative influence was at its greatest.[99]

In the mid-1970s it was far from clear that the major beneficiaries of the tax revolt would be conservatives. A number of high-profile Democrats, recognizing that the United States had entered an era of limits, endorsed fiscal conservatism. In 1974, for example, New York's Democratic governor Hugh Carey announced an end to "the days of wine and roses." Carey sought to revive the Empire State's ailing economy, and stave off bankruptcy in the Big Apple itself, by cutting taxes, balancing the budget and encouraging business investment. After more than a dozen years of tax rises, Carey cut corporate taxes from "14 percent to 10 percent, personal income taxes were capped at 9 percent, capital gains taxes were reduced, and generous tax credits were offered to encourage new investment."[100] In California, Jerry Brown won plaudits for his adroit handling of Proposition 13's aftermath. Although he had opposed the measure, Brown acknowledged that "We have our marching orders from the people. This is the strongest expression of the democratic process in a decade." Brown, conscious that his ambitions for national office were on the line, declared that although Proposition 13 created "problems" it also provided "an opportunity to make government in California a model for people all over the country."[101] Helped by its considerable accumulated budget surplus, the state government was able to make up for the shortfall in property tax revenues and thus minimize cuts in services—at least in the short term.[102] Howard Jarvis was so impressed that he voted for Brown in the November 1978 election, in which the governor won a second term by more than a million votes.[103] The president himself also symbolized this development; Jimmy Carter had emphasized the need for a balanced budget during the 1976 campaign, and he had sought to reduce government spending which was seen as a significant contributor to the high inflation that, according to the president, bred a "politics of fear."[104] A week after Proposition 13's victory, Carter reiterated an earlier call for Congress to cut income taxes by more than $20 billion.[105]

It was Proposition 13 itself that helped to turn the tide in favor of conservatives. Before June 1978, state governments had tended to deal with rising discontent about high property tax bills by enacting progressive measures, typically so-called "circuit breakers," which granted tax relief to those on low incomes. After June 1978, attention became focused on the electoral popularity of tax cuts and tax limitation measures, not circuit breakers or alternative redistributive policies, became the remedy of choice.[106] The fact that Proposition 13 had occurred in California—an influential state that was important electorally and was renowned for its innovation and its liberalism—and that it had been enacted by a popular vote led many to conclude that a conservative resurgence was underway.[107] For many property tax payers, frustrated with years of government inaction, the message of Proposition 13 was clear enough: tax limitation measures worked. Pro-business conservatives and ambitious Republicans, meanwhile, noted that tax cutting was a clear electoral winner and embraced it with relish.[108] Indeed, in the aftermath of Proposition 13,

GOP leaders "took to flying around the country in a Boeing 727 nick-named "The Republican Tax Clipper.""[109]

It also suited conservatives' broader interests to portray Proposition 13, and the wider tax revolt, as part of a "backlash' against big government liberalism. Howard Jarvis claimed that voters had opted for "Life, Liberty, and the Pursuit of Happiness," rather than "Life, Liberty, and Welfare or Food Stamps," while Ronald Reagan interpreted Proposition 13 as a rebellion against "costly, overpowering government."[110] But according to revisionist historian Isaac Martin, "the welfare backlash was not the tax revolt, and it did not cause the tax revolt." He has pointed out that the target of tax protesters in 1978 was the local property tax, not federal welfare programs and that an important segment of the tax revolt (which might be described as the George Wiley wing), sought redistributive remedies to the inequities of the property tax—though the possibility must remain that, for many, opposing the property tax also served as a protest against liberalism.[111] As has already been noted, the tax revolt—both nationally and in California—was in part forged in the crucible of 1960s radical activism and progressive politics. After Proposition 13 had passed, Tom Hayden, the former SDS firebrand and Californian political activist, "said that he regretted that the measure had been sponsored by wealthy conservatives . . . rather than by his own constituents who had been fighting corporate power."[112] More important than this—after all, most of those who voted for Proposition 13 were not former New Left organizers—opinion polls found little appetite for hacking back the state and reducing government to a rump. While large majorities of California's electorate desired cutbacks in government spending, lower taxes and a less powerful bureaucracy, they did not want cuts in fire, police, public transportation, education, mental health and recreational facilities. Indeed, in "most areas of government responsibility" they appeared to want at least the same level of service. Californians—and voters in many other places—believed that efficiency savings and the elimination of waste would allow them to have their cake and eat it too.[113]

The two areas where the public did appear to favor cuts, though, were in welfare and public housing.[114] By 1978 California was spending more than $5 billion on Food Stamps and $21 billion on Medicare and polls conducted between July 1977 and November 1979 showed that the state's voters favored cuts in welfare by a margin of 73-27 and in public housing by 54-46 (in contrast, 71 percent favored increases in police spending, and 58 percent supported increases in expenditures on public schools).[115] This suggests the importance of "symbolic racism" to the tax revolt, since minorities (African Americans and Hispanic immigrants) benefited disproportionately from welfare programs—a fact that was emphasized in much conservative rhetoric. As David Sears and Jack Citrin have pointed out, "large numbers of whites remain fundamentally opposed to special government efforts to aid blacks, and that opposition was a central determinant of white support for the tax revolt."[116] Concerned about both the potential impact of the measure and some of the motivations behind it, African Americans were one of the few groups in California where majority opinion did not favor Proposition 13 (the others were public employees and renters).[117] According to Thomas and Mary Edsall, the tax revolt divided the electorate along the lines of taxpayer versus tax recipient with the result that "race melded into a conservative-driven agenda that sought to polarize the public against the private sector."[118]

Despite this, Proposition 13 seems to have captured not a growing revolt against liberalism or a full-fledged embrace of conservatism, but a profound discontent with government itself. The debacle in Southeast Asia and the Watergate scandals had helped to shake the public's confidence in its elected officials, and public opinion in the 1970s seemed decidedly hostile toward the government. Interviewed in October 1975, CAL's Mike Miller claimed that "among a great majority of Americans" there had developed "an alienation from all the major institutions." "They know politicians lie to them, so they don't trust government."[119] In one 1978 poll, for example, only 30 percent said that they trusted the government to do "what is right" most or all of the time, compared with 76 percent in 1964. Confidence in government officials also declined, perhaps in part a consequence of the disputes over busing.[120] Either way, attacks on incompetent "elites" and bureaucrats seemed to go down well with voters in the 1970s. Given that many tax rebels became frustrated and disillusioned with what they viewed as officialdom's lack of empathy and responsiveness, the thesis that the tax revolt should be viewed as a manifestation of growing discontent with government seems persuasive. At his press conference on 28 July 1978 President Carter seemed to recognize this, stating that "I do believe that Proposition 13 is an accurate expression of, first of all, the distrust of the government."[121]

Ultimately, although the tax revolt did have a liberal, even radical, dimension, it helped to fuse together a broad range of conservative causes. As the historian Bruce Schulman has pointed out, it "highlighted the use of tax money for supposedly immoral purposes, like sex education, abortion, and permissive curricula in schools. It dramatized an overweening big government, with briefcase-toting bureaucrats imposing crippling regulations on business and telling ordinary working Americans how to live." In short, high taxes "confirmed the New Right portrait of a government out of touch." It also enabled conservatives to appeal to key segments of the (white) electorate by stressing equal opportunity and economic individualism while simultaneously exploiting latent resentment that the welfare state benefited blacks and racial minorities at the expense of decent, average, hard-working Americans.[122] A formative moment for many young conservatives, the tax revolt of the late 1970s placed tax cuts at the heart of Republican Party policy for a generation and came to symbolize the broader rejection of New Deal liberalism.

Chapter 6

The Anti-Abortion Movement

It is horrifying to realize that a nation committed to life, liberty and justice allows the legal wholesale slaughter of its most precious resource—children.
—Senator Gordon J. Humphrey, March 1987

Oh boy, this is like the '60s revisited
—March for Life participant, January 1993

On Wednesday 22 January 1975, two years to the day after *Roe v. Wade*, a crowd of 25,000 gathered on the steps of the U.S. Congress in Washington, D.C. for the second annual March for Life. The protesters carried "roses and placards—with slogans such as 'Kill Inflation, Not Babies' and 'It's Not Nice to Fool with Mother Nature.'" The day's biggest cheer was reserved for New York senator James L. Buckley, elder brother of *National Review* founder and conservative commentator William F., who told the crowd "that he would introduce tomorrow in the Senate a constitutional amendment banning abortion."[1]

The anti-abortion movement was one of the most prominent social movements to emerge during the 1970s. It is commonly portrayed as part of the conservative realignment in American politics that began at the end of the 1960s and as owing much to the backlash against that tumultuous decade. But in important ways anti-abortion activists were themselves children of the Sixties—a number had been active in the civil rights and peace movements, for example, and they made extensive use of tactics that had been popularized by Sixties protesters. Like other social protest movements, they sought to occupy patriotic terrain by grounding their demands in the language of Americanism. Indeed, anti-abortion activists tended to view their struggle as part of a broader attempt to save the Republic by reclaiming and renewing America's founding ideals. While helping bring about a wider conservative re-alignment in American politics, the anti-abortion movement was not able to secure an end to legal abortion. This failure generated a measure of disillusionment with national politicians among movement activists—a small number of whom turned to extreme violence.

At 10 a.m. on 22 January 1973 the Supreme Court rendered its judgment in *Roe* v. *Wade*. The case involved a twenty-one-year-old Texas woman, later identified as Norma McCorvey, a carnival worker and high school dropout who had agreed to be a plaintiff in a class action suit challenging the state's restrictive abortion laws after becoming pregnant, as the result of a casual affair, for the third time. By a margin of 7-2 the Court affirmed an earlier federal court decision that the Texas statutes were unconstitutional. The majority opinion, written by Nixon appointee and lifelong Republican Harry Blackmun, declared that the "right of privacy, whether it be founded in the Fourteenth Amendment's concept of personal liberty and restrictions upon state action, as we feel it is, or, as the District Court determined, in the Ninth Amendment's reservation of rights to the people, is broad enough to encompass a woman's decision whether or not to terminate her pregnancy." The Court further recognized that a women's right to an abortion was not "absolute" and had to be balanced against "important state interests in regulation."[2] It thus ruled that during the first trimester the right to an abortion should not be regulated in any way; regulation was permitted during the second trimester—but only to protect the life of the mother; in the third trimester, when the fetus was near viability or viable, abortion could be regulated to protect the life of the unborn baby.[3]

Roe v. Wade marked the culmination of a long struggle to reform America's abortion laws—one in which women's rights groups, advocates of population control (most notably Planned Parenthood), and medical professionals all made a significant contribution. The wider context was also important in shaping the debate over abortion reform. The 1960s ushered in more liberal attitudes toward sex among many Americans—symbolized both by the commercial availability of the contraceptive pill beginning in 1960 and the growing counterculture later in the decade that celebrated "free love" and attacked monogamy. The emergence of second-wave feminism, with its (re)assertion of women's rights and emphasis on female empowerment, also played a role. There were more specific developments that informed the debate too. In the summer of 1962 Sherri Chessen Finkbine, a Phoenix mother of four and local children's TV personality, sought an abortion when, after taking Thalidomide, she was informed by her doctor that she had a high chance of giving birth to a deformed baby. Arizona law only allowed abortion to protect the life of the mother, although the rules were known to be applied more loosely in certain circumstances. But after Finkbine agreed to speak to the *Arizona Republic* about the dangers of Thalidomide (leading to the headline, "Baby-Deforming Drug May Cost Woman Her Child Here") a publicity storm ensued and the hospital, fearing prosecution, canceled Finkbine's scheduled abortion. Facing a legal dead end, she eventually traveled to Sweden for the procedure. According to historians James Risen and Judy L. Thomas, the Finkbine case "sensitized the public to the issue of abortion and set the stage for reform." Then, following a rubella epidemic, thousands of women gave birth to babies with birth defects between 1964 and 1966.[4]

Reformers began to push for states to adopt more flexible laws, modeled on plans drawn up by the American Law Institute (ALI), which would allow for an abortion if two physicians agreed that it was necessary to preserve the life or health of the mother, and in cases of rape, incest, or severe fetal abnormalities. On 25 April 1967 Colorado became the first state to pass a reform law, followed by North Carolina on 8 May. That same month, the American Baptist Convention announced its support for the ALI proposals and the American Medical Association promptly followed suit. On 14 June, in a major victory for the abortion reform movement, Governor Ronald Reagan signed into law California's Therapeutic Abortion Act. In November, NOW endorsed abortion reform for the first time and in February 1969 it entered a coalition with public health and population control experts, founding the National Association for Repeal of Abortion Laws (NARAL). New York repealed its restrictions in July 1970. By the early 1970s, then, legal abortions were already available to a large number of middle-class, educated women. Indeed it is estimated that, in 1972, more than 500,000 legal abortions took place nationwide.[5]

While reforms at the state level had met with sporadic and scattered opposition, the aftermath of *Roe* saw the emergence of a forceful anti-abortion movement in which the Catholic Church provided early leadership, valuable resources, and an institutional base for activism. Catholic opposition to abortion was longstanding, based on the belief that the granting by God of a soul began at conception. In 1679 Pope Innocent XI had ruled that abortion to save the life of the mother was prohibited, and in 1869, a reversion to medieval practice, Pius IX imposed excommunication for abortion. Given the reforms of Vatican II, which urged the church to engage more fully with politics, the church was thus primed to enter the abortion debate.[6] Along with financial resources, the church supplied the movement an organizational structure, communications networks, and personnel. The church founded the National Right to Life Committee (NRLC), an independent ecumenical organization to mobilize support through educational outreach, lobbying politicians, and publicity campaigns. It quickly became a highly effective organization—by 1980 it had an annual budget of $1.3 million, a professional staff, and a membership of several million.[7]

For mainstream anti-abortion organizations the Supreme Court's comprehensive ruling meant that there were only two possible avenues to national success: secure ratification of a constitutional amendment that banned abortion, or elect conservatives to national office who could change the political makeup of the Supreme Court, opening the possibility that the *Roe* decision might be overturned. Both had only a very limited chance of success. Ultimately, groups like the NRLC had to settle for "waging small battles on the margins"—such as imposing parental notification on abortions for minors, cutting federal funding for abortions, and placing restrictions on late term abortions.[8] Frustrated by their failure to overturn *Roe*, and with public opinion polls showing strong public support for abortion rights, radical, activist-oriented organizations emerged during the second half of the 1970s. Both John O'Keefe's Pro-Life Nonviolent Action Project, active in Maryland during the late 1970s and early 1980s, and the Pro-Life Action League, founded in 1980 by Joseph Scheidler and based in Chicago, sought more dramatic and confrontational tactics, in particular civil disobedience, in the struggle against abortion.[9] Randall Terry's Operation Rescue, an organization that emerged to coincide with the 1988 presidential election, was the most prominent advocate of militant civil disobedience within the anti-abortion fold.

In an echo of the New Left Weathermen terrorist organization, a small number of extremists engaged in serious violence: locks at abortion clinics were filled with cement; threatening letters were sent to clinic employees; bomb threats were made. In 1977 there were 5 arsons and bombings at abortion clinics, rising to 30 in 1984. The years 1981-1984 saw 273 "acts of violence" (threats, vandalism, arson, and attempted arson/bombing) against abortion facilities, compared with 61 in 1977-1980.[10] On 10 March 1993 David Gunn, a forty-seven-year-old abortion doctor, was shot to death outside a clinic in Pensacola, Florida. Thirty-one-year-old Michael Griffin, a "zealous follower of local anti-abortion leader John Burt," "stepped forward from a group of antiabortion protesters" and fired three shots into Gunn's back at point-blank range. According to a *Washington Post* report the killing was "believed to be the first in the nation's ongoing struggle over abortion." It was not hard to link such appalling violence to the movement at large. While John Burt, who had organized the protest outside the clinic that day, emphasized that his demonstrators had had no intention of harming Gunn, he also stated that "If you start talking about [making it illegal to protest outside abortion clinics], people are just going to find other ways of dealing with it." The *Washington Post* also reported that, at an Operation Rescue rally in Montgomery, Alabama, the previous summer, an "old-fashioned 'wanted' poster . . . was distributed . . . [that] included a picture of Gunn, his home phone number and other identifying information." The posters were apparently designed "to encourage abortion opponents to harass doctors working at clinics operated by Gunn in Alabama." Meanwhile Andrew Burnett, an Operation Rescue stalwart, explained that "the death of an abortionist has caused me to re-examine my own convictions. Was his life really more valuable than the lives of his thousands of victims?"[11]

While *Roe* has remained the law of the land the anti-abortion movement has enjoyed some significant successes. In 1976 Henry Hyde, a freshman Republican representative from Illinois who later, as chairman of the powerful House Judiciary Committee, assumed a leading role in the 1998 impeachment of President Clinton, introduced an amendment to the Social Security Act that prohibited use of public money for abortions. Passed by the Congress, which made exceptions for cases of rape, incest, and when a mother's life is in jeopardy, the amendment was upheld by the Supreme Court in a controversial 5-4 decision in 1980.[12] The Hyde Amendment has served to eliminate Medicaid-funded abortions in most states, significantly reducing poor women's access to abortion. In 1983 the Supreme Court upheld a Kansas law that required minors seeking an abortion to secure parental consent, but only because they were able to seek the approval of a judge as an alternative.[13] In April 2007, in a 5-4 decision, the Supreme Court upheld the Partial-Birth Abortion Ban Act of 2003.[14]

On 3 September 1972, 200 members of the National Youth Pro-Life Coalition (NYPLC), youth affiliate of the NRLC, participated in an anti-abortion rally near the Lincoln Memorial at the close of their second annual convention. Fr. Richard John Neuhaus of Clergy and Laity Concerned About Vietnam (CALCAV), a leading antiwar organization, was one of the speakers, and messages of support were sent by civil rights leader Jesse Jackson and labor organizer Cesar Chavez. Describing their rally as the "Woodstock of the right-to-life movement," the young long-haired, antiwar and civil rights-supporting activists sang a version of John Lennon's "Give Peace a Chance"—"All We are Saying/Is Give Life a Chance." The rally closed with the burning of 2,000 birth certificates, a protest modeled quite self-consciously on the burning of draft cards by Vietnam War protesters.[15]

The anti-abortion movement is usually portrayed, for good reasons, as a manifestation of the New Right politics of backlash and the growing political power of evangelical Christians. But in important respects it was also a product of the radical climate of the 1960s. A number of the movement's founders were veterans of the civil rights and anti-Vietnam War struggles, and anti-abortion groups drew heavily on tactics pioneered by Sixties activists and justified their activism with reference to earlier struggles. As Richard L. Hughes has shown, the success of the anti-abortion movement during the 1970s and beyond was due in part to the ability of a small but influential number of its activists to adapt and co-opt modes of protest and approaches to activism that had come to the fore during the 1960s. Anti-abortionists, in short, were able to forge a "vibrant, effective, and controversial movement from the rich and complex legacy of American activism and the sixties."[16]

The link between Sixties activism and the anti-abortion struggle can be glimpsed in the lives of some of the movement's significant figures. Rachel McNair, who led numerous anti-abortion organizations, was a Quaker veteran of the peace movement.[17] Juli Loesch, a native of Erie, Pennsylvania, was an "ardent anti-war kid" who dropped out of Antioch College to work with the United Farm Workers in California. She later participated in a radical lesbian-feminist consciousness-raising group before becoming involved in the anti-abortion movement. In 1971 she organized Prolifers for Survival, which combined opposition to nuclear weapons with opposition to abortion. Loesch, a self-described "fetus-loving peacenik" engaged in civil disobedience at abortion clinics *and* nuclear facilities.[18]

Charles Fager exemplifies the links between 1960s protests and the anti-abortion activism of the 1970s. During the 1960s Fager was a "radical, dedicated to . . . reshaping society in some not very clear, but more peaceful and equalitarian manner." He worked for Martin Luther King's Southern Christian Leadership Conference (SCLC) during 1965-66, and was arrested three times for his civil rights activism. Later in the decade he became a conscientious objector and opposed the war in Vietnam. By the early 1970s he was an opponent of abortion, penning an anti-abortion article for the alternative *Real Paper* in Cambridge, Maryland, in January 1973. Fager explained, "if you think the unborn are human, it's no big jump to add them to the list of blacks, Vietnamese, women and so forth as an oppressed group deserving liberation and protection against undeserved violence." In the summer of 1974 Fager was invited to address a regional NYPLC meeting in Boston, where he promoted the idea of anti-abortion activists adopting King's nonviolent philosophy by engaging in civil disobedience at abortion clinics and demanding that "violence be visited upon me, not the unborn." Fager believed that nonviolent tactics would not only protect the woman and fetus but also help generate valuable publicity and wider support. The response to his ideas was enthusiastic, and Fager was asked to speak in November at the group's national convention and run a workshop on civil disobedience. Soon plans were being put in place for a sit-in. Like civil rights activists in the early 1960s, the young anti-abortionists planned their protest with great care: a detailed timetable was developed, roles were clearly assigned, and participants were trained in the nonviolent method through the use of "role-play."[19]

On 8 a.m. on 2 August 1975, the Sigma Reproductive Health Services Clinic in Rockville, Maryland, was targeted by a small group of protesters, including Tom Mooney, leader of NYPLC, and his wife Chris. While the men picketed outside, the women staged a sit-in that blocked the doors linking the waiting area to the operating rooms. The sit-in participants sang songs and prayed, while the picketers outside distributed literature. After a three-hour attempt to persuade the activists to leave peacefully, the police moved in making six arrests. While the case of the "Sigma Six" received almost no media coverage, it did indirectly have a longer term impact on the struggle: it inspired John O'Keefe to redouble his efforts at integrating civil disobedience into the anti-abortion movement.[20]

O'Keefe is widely "regarded as the father of the more activist wing of the movement"; and he certainly played a leading role in popularizing nonviolent direct action among the anti-abortion forces.[21] Raised in a devoutly Catholic household in Chevy Chase, Maryland, O'Keefe was "rail-thin, extraordinarily intense" and very bright—"he had the look of a nineteenth-century schoolteacher, perpetually lost in thought." On 6 February 1968 John's older brother, Roy, was killed in Vietnam while serving as a medic and platoon leader in an elite combat unit. John, by now a Harvard student, became an opponent of the war in Vietnam, volunteering at a draft counseling center run by the American Friends Service Committee and registering as a conscientious objector in the spring of 1970. O'Keefe became involved with the Charismatic Renewal movement among Catholics in the late 1960s; a movement that combined Pentecostal traditions with political engagement and social activism. After becoming interested in the abortion issue in the early 1970s, O'Keefe saw the potential of nonviolent direct action and worked hard to convince others. The Rockville protest cemented his conviction that the anti-abortion cause could be well served by civil disobedience. O'Keefe also knew that "he was no longer alone." Through the late 1970s and early 1980s he helped organize and sustain an anti-abortion sit-in movement in the Washington area.[22] His Pro-Life Nonviolent Action Project

(PNAP) drew heavily from the example of the civil rights movement—
O'Keefe produced picket signs with the phrase "Strength to Love" (from
the title of one of Martin Luther King's books) and protesters sang a
version of "We Shall Overcome" that included a specially tailored verse,
"You Must Save the Children." According to Richard Hughes, "King and
the civil rights movement became ubiquitous in PNAP's literature."[23]

John O'Keefe may have pioneered the use of nonviolent direct action
in the anti-abortion movement and emphasized parallels with the civil
rights movement, but it was Randall Terry's Operation Rescue that made
such strategies something of a national phenomenon. The group first
came to national prominence in 1988 when it launched a series of sit-ins
(which it renamed "rescues") in abortion clinics across New York City.
The first "rescue" took place at 8:00 a.m. on Monday 2 May, outside the
clinic of Herbert Schwartz; activists sat down outside and "began to read
prayers and sing hymns."[24] Over four days some 1,600 participants were
arrested.[25] In July, more than 1,000 were arrested in a series of protests at
abortion clinics in Atlanta, followed by demonstrations across 32 American cities, including San Francisco, on 28-29 October, which involved
more than 4,500 protesters (there were 2,600 arrests).[26]

Randall Terry justified the use of civil disobedience in a number of
ways. He quoted passages from both the Old and New Testaments, especially Proverbs 24:11—"Rescue those being led away to death; hold back
those staggering toward slaughter."[27] He also drew on a range of historical examples, including opposition to the Fugitive Slave Law in the 1850s
and resistance movements in Nazi-occupied Europe. But it was the civil
rights movement of the 1950s and 1960s that Terry emphasized most
heavily and sought to identify his organization with—in the winter of
1989, for example, he explained that "the civil-rights movement . . . has
been a tremendous source of inspiration for me."[28] Terry was particularly
struck by how the "peaceful, nonviolent, nonretaliatory suffering of the
black civil-rights activists, many of them Christians, helped win the hearts
of millions" and brought about political change. For Terry, the lesson
seemed clear—a willingness to "suffer and risk arrest in order to stand
for what" is right would create a "tension in the nation" that would force
politicians to take action. Indeed, he was "convinced that the American
people will begin to take the pro-life movement seriously when they see
good, decent citizens peacefully sitting around abortion mills, risking
arrest and prosecution as Martin Luther King, Jr. did."[29]

Thus activists protesting at Atlanta abortion clinics over 3-8 October
1988 were urged to go to jail. As an article in the September edition of
the Operation Rescue *Newsletter* explained, "As the nation sees hundreds
of decent, God-fearing Americans behind bars for fighting child-killing,
it will give more credence to our rhetoric. . . . The sight of hundreds of

blacks in jail for civil rights during the sixties helped their cause greatly. Our incarceration will also spur other activists to greater acts of courage."[30] A February 1989 edition of the *Newsletter* carried a cartoon with a silhouette of a heavily pregnant woman, watching "Operation Rescue" on television. A speech bubble coming from her belly contained the words, "We Shall Overcome."[31] In 1991 Operation Rescue used children in its protests at Baton Rouge and Wichita; a tactic that appeared to be modeled on the famous "Children's Crusade" in Birmingham of May 1963.[32] The link between Operation Rescue and the civil rights movement was not simply a matter of rhetoric and tactics. In 1989 Claude and Jeanne Nolen, activists with Operation Rescue, were jailed for 8 months for criminal trespass. A quarter of a century earlier they had been part of an interracial group that had entered the segregated Dixie Grill in Austin, Texas to test compliance with the Civil Rights Act.[33]

At first glance the comparisons anti-abortion protesters made with the civil rights movement seem convincing—staging sit-ins and pickets, willingly, even enthusiastically risking arrest, and singing "We Shall Overcome" certainly evoked memories of the black freedom struggle—as, for that matter, did Randall Terry's boast that his movement was ready to "fill the jails."[34] Many progressives wondered what anti-abortionists were "doing using our tactics?" But as a number of commentators have pointed out, there were some telling differences. A 1988 editorial in the *Atlanta Journal-Constitution* argued that "Civil rights demonstrators fought for rights. . . . The anti-abortion forces have a much narrower goal . . . to deny women their right to a legal medical procedure of the most personal sort" (though, of course, opponents of abortion believed fervently that they were fighting *for* the rights of the unborn).[35] As Philip Green pointed out in *The Nation*, civil rights protesters in the 1960s did not directly attack anybody's property or person. Instead, they "confronted white southerners with a choice: Either change your behavior or persecute the protesters and risk public obloquy."[36] The anti-abortion activists, in contrast, engaged in behavior that caused direct harm to women seeking abortions. Chicago leader Joseph Scheidler infamously hired a private detective to track down a woman who was planning to have an abortion, justifying this on the basis of the publicity it generated for his movement.[37] As Green explained, such harassment constituted an assault against women—"Forcing your way through a restrictive and abusive picket line while pregnant is not harmless; risking giving birth . . . is not harmless; changing your life to have an unwanted baby is not harmless." Green accused anti-abortion activists of "doing harm to some people so that a (supposedly) greater harm to others may be prevented."[38]

And whereas civil rights protesters had gone to great lengths to project an image of respectability, anti-abortion activists who engaged in civil disobedience were often "no friends of silent suffering." They "press their moral claims by shouting at incoming pregnant women . . . they give pseudonyms to the police; they throw up legal defenses in court by saying the harm associated with violating trespass laws is justified by the need to prevent the greater evil of abortion."[39] Julian Bond, a veteran of the civil rights movement who had participated in civil disobedience and helped found SNCC, explained that "civil rights demonstrators faced taunts and threats. Today's antiabortionists taunt and threaten those who brave their picket lines."[40] Perhaps the biggest difference was that in the anti-abortion protests it was not the "victims" of the supposedly unjust "system" that were being arrested, but adult surrogates, including men. This placed "limits on the movement's evocative capacity" and weakened the "connection between the disobedience and the evil [being] protested." Indeed, the lack of "sacrificial suffering" in the civil disobedience practiced by the anti-abortion movement undermined the usefulness of the nonviolent method; at times it even seemed counterproductive, projecting an image of "intolerance" and "self-righteousness" and thereby alienating potential supporters.[41] Bond accepted that anti-abortion leaders had "every right to use civil disobedience and mass demonstrations in their fight," but believed that attempts to claim solidarity with the civil rights movement were little more than a tactical ruse. In a November 1988 *New York Times* editorial he called on Operation Rescue to "Give us back our history . . . and make your own."[42]

The Sixties influence can also be seen in the adoption by anti-abortion activists of street theater, a tactic pioneered by New Left and antiwar activists who had sought to fuse political activism with the emerging counter-cultural sensibility. While creative, the street theater used by abortion opponents was often shocking. At the 1979 March for Life, for example, as the 60,000-strong crowd "exploded in a chant of 'No compromise, no compromise'," a "man in the front lines lifted a black cross on which a plastic baby doll had been nailed."[43] On 24 March 1982, several hundred opponents of abortion staged a "spirited" demonstration at the campus of the University of Florida in Gainesville. Organized by "Christians Care for Gainesville," a local anti-abortion group, the hour-long rally involved "singing, chanting, praying," and waving "colorful signs." Then the demonstrators marched past a nearby abortion clinic: "Led by four black-hooded pallbearers carrying a large black casket, the marchers shouted 'Down with abortion, up with life,' and 'Abortion is murder'." On top of the casket were a "barbed wire wreath, a few wilted flowers, and a banner proclaiming 'Moratorium on the Murder of Ten Million Babies'."[44]

Street theater-style protest was again in evidence at the 1992 March for Life—"some anti-abortion marchers carried large color photographs of late term aborted fetuses. One man was dressed as a doctor in a red-paint-spattered white coat."[45] The 300,000 abortion rights protesters who marched in Washington in April 1989 were met by counter-protesters—"several were dressed as babies, in bonnets and bloomers, shouting repeatedly 'What about the Babies?'"[46] Street theater was actually deployed by both sides. For instance a pro-choice demonstration in New York City on 22 January 1974 involved "crowning" a woman "pope" on the steps of St. Patrick's Cathedral, while at a NOW demonstration outside Senator Buckley's East Forty-Fifth Street office "some women were chained to symbolize what they call Senator Buckley's attempts to enslave women by unwanted childbirth."[47]

As historian Robert L. Hughes has shown, the struggle against the war in Vietnam constituted a vital part of the context in which the anti-abortion movement took shape.[48] Just as anti-abortion activists were influenced by civil rights protests of the early 1960s, so too did they draw on the example of the numerous antiwar protests that took place between 1965 and 1972. Nellie Gray, organizer of the March for Life demonstrations that began in 1974, recalled that the "first march was a circle of life, around and around and around the U.S. Capitol."[49] In June 1972, 2500 women and children had linked hands and encircled the Capitol during the "Ring Around Congress," an antiwar protest developed by folk singer Joan Baez and Cora Weiss of Another Mother for Peace.[50] Indeed the very name "March for Life" seemed intended to invite comparisons with the "March Against Death," the deeply moving demonstration of November 1969 in which, over a 40-hour period, the names of America's war dead had been read out in front of the White House.[51] Like that famous antiwar demonstration, the March for Life "included its share of coffins, crosses, grim reapers, and photos of the dead."[52] Moreover, in its use of symbolic cemeteries to memorialize those "lost" to abortion, the movement echoed peace protests of an earlier era (indeed, many activists viewed aborted fetuses as casualties of war).[53] On 9 April 1989 anti-abortion activists created a "cemetery of the innocents"—4,400 crosses set up in a corner of the Mall in Washington—to represent the daily rate of abortions in the United States.[54] In June, raw eggs and maple syrup were poured over surgical instruments at the Summit Women's Center in West Hartford, Connecticut. The protest mirrored that of Philip Berrigan and other radical pacifists who, in October 1967, had poured blood over draft files in Baltimore.[55]

While he would later adopt a pro-choice position, Rev. Jesse Jackson was an opponent of abortion in the late 1970s. In a January 1977 article, "How We Respect Life Is the Over-Riding Moral Issue," Jackson outlined the moral arguments that were grounded in his Christian faith and drew on theories then fashionable in black radical circles that population control was a tool of white supremacy. "It is strange," he wrote, that "they choose to start talking about population control at the same time that black people in America and people of color around the world are demanding their rightful place as human citizens and their rightful share of the material wealth in the world." But Jackson also drew directly on America's recent experiences in Vietnam—a war the charismatic young civil rights leader had opposed. "When American soldiers can drop bombs on Vietnam and melt the faces and hands of children into a hunk of rolling protoplasm and in their minds say they have not maimed or killed a fellow human being," he explained, "something terribly wrong and sick has gone on in that mind." Similarly, those "advocates of taking life prior to birth do not call it killing or murder, they call it abortion." "Fetus," he explained, "sounds less than human and therefore [abortion] can be justified."[56]

Peace organizations such as Women Strike for Peace (WSP) and Another Mother for Peace had sought to raise awareness of the Vietnam War and foster opposition to it among American women. In July 1965 members of WSP had met with Vietnamese women in Indonesia and learned first-hand of the damage that American weapons, particularly fragmentation bombs, were capable of causing; Another Mother for Peace sold antiwar cards containing the slogan "War Is Not Healthy for Children and Other Living Things."[57] The antiwar movement also used signs with pictures of dead or injured children, and Nick Ut's Pulitzer-prize winning photograph of a naked nine-year-old Kim Phuc, her body badly burned by napalm, became an iconic image of the conflict.[58] There can be little doubt that the peace movement's symbolic use of motherhood and children influenced the anti-abortion movement.[59] Anti-abortion activists began carrying pictures of aborted fetuses at demonstrations in an attempt to shock the public into reevaluating their stance on abortion. Particularly infamous was the "bucket shot," a "picture of a late term aborted fetus that a pathologist had removed from a plastic container in a hospital lab and, to enhance the effect of a baby discarded like trash, placed in a metal bucket."[60] Such images served the same symbolic purpose as images of injured, maimed or killed Vietnamese did for antiwar forces. Furthermore, anti-abortion protesters drew on a well-established Sixties idiom in presenting the aborted fetus as a victim.[61]

The connections with the Catholic Left and 1960s protest traditions were ultimately eclipsed in the 1980s when the anti-abortion movement became dominated by conservative evangelical Protestants. But a residual influence remained—in something of an irony anti-abortion leaders now sought to legitimize their own activism by drawing on the example of Sixties protest movements. The Moral Majority, for example, justified the involvement of Christians in politics by appropriating the example of Martin Luther King,—"It is certainly the right of any group or organization, including Christians, to participate in the political process of this nation. That is the strength of America. In the early 1960s, religious leaders such as Martin Luther King, Jr. organized rallies and actively marched for civil rights. However, no protest was ever made concerning their involvement in politics."[62] Another Moral Majority architect, Texan Richard Viguerie—veteran of the Goldwater campaign and undisputed king of direct-mail fundraising—understood very well that the New Right was, in may ways, borrowing ideas, styles, and rhetoric from the New Left.[63]

The anti-abortion movement also copied 1960s radical movements in emphasizing grassroots organizing. With its emphasis on participatory democracy and building political movements at the local level, the New Left and civil rights movements had sought to empower ordinary people and encourage political engagement to effect change. The New Right adopted similar tactics to great effect—as pro-choice strategist Jean Weinberg explained, they "by gosh, get them out to vote and . . . get the bucks."[64] Indeed, both the Goldwater campaign of 1964 and George Wallace's challenge in 1968 were testament to the ability of conservatives to mobilize and organize at the local level, and Ralph Reed's assertion that "real power flows upward from the precinct" would not have sounded out of place at a Students for a Democratic Society organizing workshop.[65] Phyllis Schlafly, for example, worked hard to empower conservative women—encouraging them to recognize their latent leadership potential and talent by conducting workshops on how to testify at a public hearing and how to debate, using their femininity and social and cultural conservatism to their advantage.[66] Operation Rescue's leaders explained that their organization was "truly a grass-roots *movement*." "We are *not*," they stated, "asking *you* to send *us* money so that *we* can fight and win the war." Instead, ordinary people who opposed abortion were asked to contribute time and energy to the struggle "to save mothers and children in your community. . . . You could volunteer at a pregnancy center, picket, sidewalk counsel, recruit, rescue and lobby in your local community."[67] For anti-abortion activists, emphasis on local organizing was made all the more attractive given the relatively low prospects for success at the national level. As Judie Brown explained, "I've learned that once you involve people in their *communities* and you teach them how to be effective in politics, with the media, at the abortion clinics and everywhere else, what you have is victory after victory. Whereas, if you concentrate all your effort in Washington, D.C., you have one defeat after another."[68] Anti-abortion activists often sought not just to generate national publicity and create pressure for political change in Washington, but to bring about specific local results—whether closing a particular abortion clinic, or passing laws that restricted abortion at the state level.

One of the weaknesses of the anti-abortion movement was its negative portrayal in much of the mainstream media and apparent unpopularity with large numbers of ordinary Americans. Indeed, despite all the activism and organizing (perhaps, in some cases, because of it) opinion polls continued to register significant levels of support for abortion.[69] Nevertheless the movement attempted to build popular support for its cause, and as part of its efforts it sought to style itself as a patriotic movement, working to implement and restore "American" values. As we shall see, numerous anti-abortion leaders, activists, and organizations—along with their New Right allies—sought to present opposition to abortion as a form of patriotic protest.[70]

Phyllis Schlafly, the "Boadicea of social conservatism," played a leading role in the reemergence of the American right during the second half of the twentieth century, and the Catholic mother-of-six was a firm opponent of abortion. Born in 1924, Schlafly rose to national prominence in 1964 when she published *A Choice, Not an Echo* in praise of conservative Republican Barry Goldwater. The lawyer and two-time congressional candidate was a supremely talented political operator and grassroots organizer. In 1972 she launched STOP ERA, a national network of activists that worked successfully to prevent ratification of the Equal Rights Amendment. Three years later she founded the Eagle Forum, a Washington-based organization to promote conservative principles, which claimed a membership of 60,000.[71] The Eagle Forum's patriotism was represented in its appropriation of America's national symbol, perched atop Old Glory, and in its description of itself as an organization for those who "believe in God, Home, and Country, and are determined to defend the values that have made America the greatest nation in the world."[72] Like many conservatives, Schlafly combined a belief in the moral codes laid down in Scripture with the Declaration of Independence's "fundamental doctrine that we owe our existence to a Creator who has endowed each of us with inalienable rights."[73]

Through her monthly *Phyllis Schlafly Report*, the "Sweetheart of the Silent Majority" communicated directly with thousands of followers and presented reports from local chapters alongside analyses of national and international events and opinion pieces. In making the anti-abortion argument Schlafly sought to emphasize the Christian principles on which she claimed the United States was founded. Writing during the bicentennial year of 1976, Schlafly argued that abortion, along with homosexuality and pornography, was part of a bigger problem of moral decay that threatened the Republic's very foundations: "As we take our Bicentennial moral inventory, we should heed the advice of the great French commentator, Alexis de Tocqueville, who wrote in the last century: 'America is great because America is good. And if America ever ceases to be good, America will cease to be great'."[74] Indeed arguments that drew on the Republic's Christian heritage, emphasized its founding values, and invited comparison with celebrated episodes from its past were a staple of the anti-abortion movement. When a 28-minute anti-abortion film, *The Silent Scream*, began to generate publicity during the mid-1980s, for example, it was claimed that "The 'Shot Heard Round the World' at Concord, New Hampshire, in defense of freedom and liberty has again been heard in defense of unborn children."[75]

Appeals to American values and attempts to identify the movement with patriotism characterized the annual March for Life, held in Washington on the anniversary of *Roe v. Wade*, where appeals to the Declaration of Independence and patriotic songs, such as the "Battle Hymn of the Republic" were typical. On 22 January 1976 more than 60,000 demonstrators, some from as far as Texas and Arizona, braved Washington's "bitter cold weather" to protest abortion. As a "dozen legislators, many hatless and coatless, addressed the crowd" they found themselves "interrupted by repeated chants of 'No compromise, no compromise',," as the exhilarated demonstrators loudly condemned the 1973 Supreme Court decision and "held aloft red roses and scores of signs that proclaimed 'abortion is murder,' 'choose life, stop abortion'." Former California governor Ronald Reagan, who had announced his decision to challenge President Gerald R. Ford for the Republican presidential nomination back in November, sent a telegram of support read out by North Carolina's Senator Jesse Helms.[76] Reagan, the darling of American conservatives, asserted that the "right to life belongs to all human beings, born and unborn." Addressing the crowd, New York senator James L. Buckley described the "truly magnificent turnout" as a "wonderful birthday present for our country" in its bicentenary year. Insisting that "respect for life" constituted "opposition to tyranny," Buckley asserted that those who opposed abortion represented "the great truth that Thomas Jefferson wrote into the Declaration of Independence: that each human being is endowed—not by government, not by the courts—but by his Creator with the inalienable right to life." Senator Richard Stone, a Florida Democrat, picked up on this theme, telling the protesters that "the time is past due for the right to life in the Bill of Rights to be recognized for individuals not yet born."[77]

Patriotic protest also characterized the Moral Majority's opposition to abortion—in fact New Right organizations presented their broader project (opposition to feminism, "special rights" for homosexuals, pornography, sex education; support for low taxes and a strong foreign policy against Soviet-led Communism) as a return to the Republic's founding ideals and moral code. The Moral Majority was founded in 1979 by the Rev. Jerry Falwell and political operator Paul Weyrich. Falwell—an "ambitious and shrewd" minister from Lynchburg, Virginia, whose *Old Time Gospel Hour* had an audience of 1.5 million—symbolized the extraordinary evangelical outpouring of the 1970s, a decade in which some 50 million Americans claimed to be born-again. Weyrich, described by one historian as having the demeanor of a "formal, slightly constipated owl," had dedicated his career to building a new conservative dominance in Washington by out-lobbying, out-organizing, and out-maneuvering liberals. To this end he founded a host of conservative organizations and institutes, most famously the Heritage Foundation in 1973 and the Committee for the Survival of a Free Congress in 1974. The immediate impulse behind the Moral Majority was the furious reaction among conservatives to the Carter administration's 1978 decision to withdraw tax-exempt status from private, religious schools. The group quickly became a formidable political force: it played a key role in Reagan's quest for the GOP presidential nomination in 1980 and helped mobilize conservative voters, not least by registering some 2.5 million of them in its first ten years.[78]

Falwell was an uncompromising opponent of abortion, which he viewed not only as a sin against God but as a violation of "the very first principle on which America was founded"—the dignity of human life. In May 1981 he called on "Jews, Catholics, Protestants, Mormons, Fundamentalists, and all Americans who share a belief in traditional values" to "join hands to restore the great American dream. It can be done. It must be done."[79] The following year, he wrote of his belief that "the overwhelming majority of Americans are sick and tired of the way amoral liberals are trying to corrupt our nation from its commitment to freedom, democracy, traditional morality, and the free enterprise system . . . I believe that the majority of Americans agree upon the basic moral values which this nation was founded upon over 200 years ago."[80]

The American Life League, an offshoot of the NRLC, was founded by Judie and Paul Brown, with the help of Paul Weyrich, in order to "move closer to the New Right and a more activist religious stance."[81] The organization emphasized that, in opposing abortion, Americans would be standing up for the true meaning of their country. In the fall of 1987, for instance, the organization urged activists around the nation to persuade their mayor to sign an anti-abortion proclamation that quoted the Declaration of Independence's assertion of the "inalienable right" to "life, liberty, and the pursuit of happiness." The proclamation stated further that, in defining "innocent pre-born human beings as less than human," abortion denied them the "protection of federal, state and local laws."[82] In a fundraising letter for the organization, New Hampshire Republican senator Gordon J. Humphrey explained that the United States was "founded on a sacred principle—that men and women possess the irrevocable right to life"; a principle that he claimed was under threat from abortion—"the greatest evil in modern history." Believing that abortion threatened America's survival, the senator explained that "it is horrifying to realize that a nation committed to life, liberty and justice allows the legal wholesale slaughter of its most precious resource—children."[83] The following year the organization newsletter carried an article about John Monaghan, a fifteen-year-old member of Teen American Life League who had written an anti-abortion essay for school. Monaghan, from New Hope, Kentucky, argued that "as at Gettysburg . . . we are engaged in a great struggle over what the Declaration of Independence stands for." "This time," he claimed, "the great issue is not liberty or equality, but the right to life."[84]

Operation Rescue not only adopted tactics that had been deployed by the civil rights movement, it also sought, as had the black freedom struggle thirty years before, to ground its demands in the distinctive values of Americanism. During the protests in Manahattan on 2 May 1988, for example, teams of protesters were led to the clinic of Dr. Herbert Schwartz at 154 East Eighty-Fifth Street by "guides holding American flags."[85] In planning a National Day of Rescue for 29 April 1989, the group pointed out that the date for the protest was the "382nd anniversary of the first settlers arriving at Cape Henry, Virginia. When they arrived they planted a large wooden cross in the sand, then knelt and prayed. Let's take the challenge that is inspired by that historic moment by rededicating ourselves and our land back to God by rescuing future generations from death on 29 April."[86] As conceived by Operation Rescue, the anti-abortion movement was not just about defending the rights of the unborn, it was also a battle for "*your* freedom, and perhaps the very survival of America." Where Martin Luther King had talked of redeeming the soul of America, Operation Rescue's leaders spoke of "not only saving children, but perhaps our very nation."[87] But Operation Rescue's relationship with Americanism was a complex one. As they sought to ground their activism firmly within the founding ideals of the Republic, the group's organizers simultaneously believed that the nation had become corrupted—that secularism and moral decline had weakened the United States and incurred the wrath of God. They thus also urged Americans to "ignore the false god of the 'American Dream',," a dream which they believed had "become the god of convenience who exacts a terrible toll from those who defy him."[88]

Placing the anti-abortion movement within the story of the rise of American conservatism is a difficult task. The argument that evangelical Christians, enraged by *Roe v. Wade*, turned to social activism and political mobilization and thus effected a political realignment might be attractive, but it does not stand up particularly well to critical analysis. For one thing, it is quite clear that the conservative revival pre-dated abortion's emergence as a significant issue. Although at the time Lyndon Johnson's 1964 landslide victory over Barry Goldwater seemed like a disaster for conservatives, it in fact signaled their growing strength. Conservatives had exercised decisive influence within the GOP and shown that there was a significant core base of support for conservatism. Running against an incumbent, renowned for his formidable political skills, Goldwater still won 40% of the vote. Meanwhile the relatively strong showing of Alabama's segregationist governor in that year's Democratic primaries in Wisconsin, Indiana and Maryland—where his attacks on the "godless" Supreme Court and open housing went down particularly well among blue collar ethnics—indicated that the political winds might be beginning to blow in a new direction. Moreover, the Goldwater campaign itself was a formative experience for a new generation of conservative activists and leaders, including William Rehnquist, Pat Buchanan, and Richard Viguerie. Two years after Goldwater's defeat a growing revulsion with urban race riots, and white hostility at measures to combat residential segregation, helped deliver the GOP massive gains: they picked up 47 seats in the House and 3 in the Senate.[89]

Conservatives, to be sure, put forward a set of ideas that large numbers of Americans found attractive, calling for a smaller government and emphasizing individual freedom, a strong national defense, and traditional moral values. But the right was also able to profit from, and exploit, a growing sense of discontent among many voters with liberalism and its perceived consequences. Indeed conservatives emphasized a range of issues—race, urban riots, welfare dependency, the counterculture, campus protests, and demonstrations against the war in Vietnam—in constructing this politics of "backlash." In effect, they attempted to run against everything that the 1960s appeared to stand for.

One of the first to benefit from this new political algorithm was Ronald Reagan. A former liberal Democrat and supporter of FDR, Reagan had moved to the right in opposition to communism. He became a hero to many conservatives after a powerful televised speech in support of Barry Goldwater during the 1964 election. In California's 1966 gubernatorial race Reagan won much support for his pledge to send "the welfare bums back to work" and to "clean up the mess at Berkeley," the scene of numerous student protests.[90] In capturing the governor's mansion he defeated the liberal incumbent, Edmund G. "Pat" Brown, by almost 1 million votes. During the 1968 presidential election both Richard Nixon for the Republicans and George Wallace, running as an independent, attempted to win support by exploiting growing fears and discontent among significant portions of the electorate who felt that their country was falling apart. Nixon, for example, appealed to the "non-shouters, the non-demonstrators . . . those who do not break the law, people who pay their taxes and go to work, who send their children to school, who go to their churches . . . people who love this country and cry out . . . 'that is enough, let's get some new leadership'." Wallace, meanwhile, had great fun attacking pointy-headed bureaucrats and intellectual elites who were, he claimed, incapable of parking a bicycle straight. He also threatened to run over any antiwar protester foolish enough to lie in the path of the presidential motorcade were he to be elected to the White House.

The essence of this "backlash" politics was encapsulated nicely in a speech made by vice-president Spiro Agnew in Harrisburg, Pennsylvania, in October 1969, almost a year after Nixon's narrow victory over Hubert Humphrey in the presidential election. "It is time," declared Agnew, "for the preponderant majority, the responsible citizens of this country, to assert *their* rights. It is time to stop dignifying the immature actions of an arrogant, reckless, inexperienced element within our society . . . their tantrums are insidiously destroying the fabric of American democracy."[91] In fact so successful was this strategy that conservatives continued to denounce the Sixties long after the decade's fiery radicalism had waned. Interviewed in the *Christian American* in the spring of 1993, former Nixon administration "evil genius" Charles Colson—now a born again Christian and conservative commentator—explained that the "values of the 1960s which rejected authority, rejected God, rejected absolute standards" had now become mainstream. "Look at the values of the 60s," he said, "and you will understand what's wrong with America today."[92]

It is also clear that abortion was not the catalyst for the political mobilization of evangelical Christians during the 1970s. Indeed *Roe v. Wade* seems initially to have merely confirmed many Christians' belief that they should avoid politics and its corrupting influence. Paul Weyrich explained, "I had discussions with all the leading lights of the [evangelical] movement in the late 1970s and early 1980s, post *Roe v. Wade*, and they were all arguing that the decision was one more reason why Christians had to isolate themselves from the rest of the world." The decisive factor triggering evangelical political engagement was the Internal Revenue Service decision, in August 1978, to challenge the charitable status—and associated tax-exemptions—of independent Christian schools. As Edward G. Dobson, a pastor from Grand Rapids, Michigan, explained, "all of a sudden, the larger secular world was having an impact" on Christian communities that had sought isolation. This tied in with long-standing conservative attacks on powerful, intrusive, "big" government, to help forge a new political coalition—the New Right. Recalling the founding of the Moral Majority in 1979, Dobson explained that "I frankly do not remember abortion ever being mentioned as a reason why we ought to do something." Instead, "there was a perceived threat . . . of what the government was going to do to Christian schools that prompted the activism."[93] The IRS received more than 120,000 letters of protest, and in 1979 Congress blocked implementation of the new guidelines. But the damage had been done—the IRS decision seemed to confirm growing suspicions that both liberalism and the federal government were hostile toward conservative Christianity, and they resolved to enter the political fray in order to reverse what they viewed as a period of serious moral decline and associated deterioration in the nation's vitality.

All this is not to argue that abortion was unimportant to either the religious right or the conservative movement. The issue certainly reso- nated strongly with many conservative Christians, encouraging them to become politically active and to engage in protest. Abortion also served as a broader symbol of alleged "liberal excess"—sexual permissiveness, an intrusive government that impinged on personal freedoms, the power of secular elites, and a decline in traditional morality that threatened both the family and the nation. Opposition to abortion, then, offered a rela- tively smooth path into the broader panoply of conservative politics— indeed, New Right leaders sought actively to place the abortion issue within this wider context. An early sign of this approach can be found in Phyllis Schlafly's unsuccessful congressional campaign of 1970. Schlafly not only made clear her opposition to abortion; she also attacked the recently released report of the President's Commission on Pornography for not taking a strong enough stand, and denounced 1960s radicals— condemning those who "curse America and desecrate the flag. Instead of Old Glory, they wave the black flag of anarchy, the clenched fist of hate, the Viet Cong flag of oppression."[94] Five years later Schlafly used the opportunity of the vacancy on the Supreme Court caused by the retirement of William O. Douglas to link together a host of conservative issues. "President Ford's appointee to fill the Douglas vacancy should be asked fundamental questions about the major moral and constitutional issues that have come before the Supreme Court in recent years," she stated. These major questions included not only abortion—"what is his position on the alleged right of a woman to kill her unborn baby?"—but also the right of communists to teach in public schools, the constitu- tionality of voluntary prayer in public schools, and whether "children must be bused across town away from their neighborhood schools in order to satisfy racial quotas arbitrarily decreed by the bureaucrats?"[95] For Baptist preacher and conservative activist Tim LaHaye, the "wide- spread acceptance of easy divorce, abortion-on-demand, gay rights, mili- tant feminism . . . and leniency towards pornography, prostitution and crime" showed that, unless Christians took action, America was heading the way of Sodom and Gomorrah.[96]

The broader strategy was summarized by Paul Weyrich in an August 1979 article for the *Conservative Digest.* He sought to increase support for the GOP among working-class blue collar voters in socially conservative parts of the country, such as the Midwest and the South, by attacking liberals' support for abortion, welfare, gun control, and other hot-button issues. Weyrich believed that opposition to abortion and other "pro-family" issues could play a critical role in bringing about a wider political realignment—"what the right-to-life movement has managed to put together on the abortion issue is only a sample of what is to come when the full range of family and educational issues becomes the focus of debate in the 1980s." He warned that the "homosexual rights advocates, genetic engineers and militant secular humanists who insist on their religion in the schools" had "better understand what is happening." In short, Weyrich and other conservative strategists believed that "the family will be to the decade of the 1980s" what "the Vietnam War was to the 1960s"—an issue that served to raise consciousness about an array of conservative concerns and illustrated the (moral, economic, intellectual and political) bankruptcy of liberalism.[97] With the "crisis in the American family" a topic of mainstream concern during the 1970s—fueled by "anxieties about a culture of moral permissiveness, the consequences of the sexual revolution" and the women's and gay rights movements, as well as economic concerns relating to stagflation and malaise—such a strategy made a good deal of sense.[98]

There was, in fact, evidence to believe that Weyrich's strategy might reap significant electoral rewards. During the 1972 Nebraska Democratic primary, abortion had become a controversial election issue after a group called Citizens Concerned for the Preservation of Life took out a half-page ad in a state newspaper quoting from syndicated conservative columnists Rowland Evans and Robert Novak that "the people don't know [George] McGovern is for amnesty, abortion, and legalization of pot." Spooked, the McGovern campaign denied that they supported any federal abortion law and condemned the "scarecrows . . . trotted out" by a "cowardly" opposition.[99] It was a sign of things to come: McGovern's heavy defeat in 1972 was due, in part, to the successful attempt by Republicans to brand the World War II hero, history professor, and son of a rural fundamentalist minister as a dangerous, unpatriotic radical.[100] Six years later activists in Minnesota, where there was a strong grassroots anti-abortion movement, claimed success in derailing Democratic representative Donald Fraser's bid for the Senate seat once held by Hubert Humphrey.[101]

Ronald Reagan's quest for the presidency in 1980 offered the New Right an opportunity to demonstrate its new found power. Indeed the "right-to-life movement, the religious-schools movement, the prayer-in-school movement, the antipornography movement, and the evangelical Christians who are motivated by a cluster of moral issues including homosexuality," proved important in Reagan's critical victories in the New Hampshire and Illinois primaries. Evangelical activists also helped shape a Republican party platform that reflected many of their key concerns on social issues.[102] The Gipper actually made a concerted effort to woo the evangelical vote in the general election, telling assembled evangelicals in Dallas on 22 August that "I endorse you and what you are doing."[103] In November, just six years after Watergate's dramatic dénouement had seemingly discredited both conservatism and the Party of Lincoln, conservatives won a comprehensive victory. Ronald Reagan buried President Jimmy Carter in a landslide, winning more than 90 percent of the Electoral College. The Republicans also won 33 seats in the House and, spectacularly, 12 in the Senate, seizing control of the upper chamber for the first time since 1952. Among those defeated were liberal icons George McGovern, Birch Bayh, and Frank Church. The Moral Majority, which, in the words of Jerry Falwell, had attempted to get people "out of the pew and into the precinct," appears to have made an important contribution to Reagan's triumph. Its "pro-life, pro-family, pro-moral, and pro-American" platform is credited with helping switch some 6 million evangelicals from the Democrats to the Republicans, providing crucial votes for Reagan in the South (below the Mason-Dixon line Jimmy Carter, the region's native son, won only his home state of Georgia). Phyllis Schlafly went so far as to claim that Reagan harnessed the support of "the Pro-Family Movement and the Conservative Movement" and "rode them into the White House."[104]

If the New Right provided Reagan with a decisive triumph—and it should be pointed out that Reagan, the "Great Communicator," had the good fortune to be running against an incumbent with low popularity ratings against the wider backdrop of stagflation and the Iranian hostage crisis—they did not enjoy power. There were some victories, most notably the controversial appointment of C. Everett Koop, an opponent of abortion, as surgeon general in 1981, and a 1982 decision to prohibit the distribution of contraceptives to minors without parental consent. But the "Reagan Revolution," if it existed at all, certainly did not satisfy the demands of the Christian Right. The administration focused on tax cuts at home and fighting communism abroad rather than "social issues," leaving anti-abortion activists to make do with the politics of symbolism.[105] After the January 1981 March for Life, for example, the president met with seven anti-abortion leaders in the Oval Office, and three years later Reagan addressed the rally by telephone (a clever ruse that enabled him to speak to the crowd while avoiding being pictured there), declaring that "I feel a great sense of solidarity with all of you. The momentum is with us."[106] In March 1983 Reagan gave a heavily publicized speech at the convention of the National Association of Evangelicals, in which he declared that "Human life legislation" ending the "tragedy" of "abortion on demand" would "some day pass the Congress, and you and I must never rest until it does." Reagan also argued that until it could be proved that "the unborn child is not a living entity" its "right to life, liberty, and the pursuit of happiness must be protected."[107]

But Reagan never showed any inclination to spend political capital on the abortion issue and Christian conservatives and the New Right quickly became frustrated. The nomination of Sandra Day O'Connor to the Supreme Court in 1981 was particularly unpopular among opponents of abortion as earlier in her career she had supported a Family Planning law in Arizona.[108] In January 1982 Weyrich claimed that the "Administration has been getting the image of not caring about some of the Middle-American voters who elected them."[109] One major problem for the anti-abortion forces was that, while abortion had become a symbolic issue that divided liberals from conservatives (and, increasingly, Democrats from Republicans), by itself it did not promise significant electoral reward. As a *New York Times*/CBS poll in 1984 showed, only a tiny minority of voters (around 4 percent) said they would change their vote based solely on candidates' stance on abortion, and those who did view "abortion as the single overriding issue" were "evenly divided between those who want to outlaw it and those who do not." Indeed, polls showed that more than three-quarters of Americans supported a woman's right to choose.[110] The Republican Party, then, had little to gain, and perhaps a good deal to lose, by taking a tough stand on abortion. After all, GOP leaders knew that they could take opponents of abortion for granted—it was inconceivable that they would vote for Walter Mondale or Michael Dukakis.[111] If the raw arithmetic was not enough, the turn to violence among some abortion opponents, which hit the headlines in late 1984 and drew condemnation from the White House, further underlined how politically unproductive it could be to make abortion a priority.[112] In many ways less successful than the anti-busing movement and the tax revolt when it came to achieving its central goal (though, of course, the struggle to overturn *Roe v. Wade* continues), the anti-abortion movement's real importance lay in its wider contribution to the "culture wars" of the 1980s and 1990s and the rise of the Religious Right as a force in electoral politics.[113]

Conclusion

The popular interpretation of the 1960s stresses the youthful idealism and initial optimism of the civil rights and student movements, as well as activists' commitment to nonviolence and participatory democracy. But as the decade wore on, we are told, protesters became consumed by bitterness and violence, and the various movements that they sustained (civil rights, New Left, anti-Vietnam War) succumbed to disillusion, factionalism and the rise of identity politics. As the "years of hope" gave way to "days of rage," the New Left and its allies were rendered helpless in the face of a growing New Right backlash in which conservatives generated valuable political traction by positioning themselves as the antithesis of everything that Sixties protesters stood for.[1] While compelling and in many ways instructive, this dominant "rise and fall" narrative obscures an important historical continuity: namely the persistence of quintessentially "Sixties" ideas and styles of protest into the 1970s and beyond and their enthusiastic adoption by those involved in a range of conservative causes. Americans of varying political stripes, active in social movements during the 1970s, 1980s and 1990s, lived in a world that had been shaped profoundly by the radical convulsions of the 1960s.

The women's and gay rights movements provide perhaps the most striking examples of the continuation of the tradition of Sixties protest and ideology among progressives. Engaging in a range of direct action protests, displaying a deep dedication to local organizing and the building of alternative institutions (such as bookstores, health clinics and community centers), and insisting that the personal was political, these movements have sought to pressure the government (local, state, and federal) and the courts to eliminate discrimination, guarantee basic citizenship rights, and help to deliver a greater measure of equality. At the same time, as Stephen Tuck has shown, the black freedom struggle during the 1970s saw the persistence and proliferation of protest as activists built upon the achievements of, and drew inspiration from the tactics used by, the movements of the 1960s even as many of them were simultaneously attracted to elements of Black Power.[2]

In their enthusiasm for direct action (including sit-ins, mass marches and rallies) and their willingness to engage in guerilla theater and countercultural protest, activists involved in the anti-busing struggle, the tax revolt, and the anti-abortion movement can reasonably be considered "children of the Sixties" too; indeed many conservatives drew quite self-consciously on the civil rights and antiwar movements in seeking to legitimate their own activism. It was not simply a matter of appropriating or aping Sixties forms of protest, though: conservative activists, like the radicals they so often denounced, worked hard to organize at the neighborhood and precinct level (often, it might be added, much more successfully than the New Left had), called for government to be made more responsive to the wishes and needs of ordinary people, demanded their "rights," and, in focusing on issues such as neighborhood schools and abortion, embraced too the idea that traditional boundaries between the "personal' and the "political," the public and private spheres, should be reconfigured. In short, during the last decades of the twentieth century, direct action was woven into the tapestry of political protest, once controversial ideas about the personal being political moved to the mainstream, and the language of "rights" became ubiquitous.

In citing passages from the Declaration of Independence and the Constitution, invoking the ideals of the Founding Fathers, expropriating patriotic symbols, and dressing up as the Statue of Liberty or as soldiers from the Revolutionary War, activists in the black freedom struggle, the gay rights movement, the women's rights movement, the anti-busing struggle, the tax revolt, and the anti-abortion movement have all made extensive use of patriotic protest and sought to craft a language and style of dissent rooted firmly in Americanism. The recourse to patriotism was fortified during the 1970s by the nation's celebration of its Bicentennial (something that, as we have seen, a number of activists were keen to exploit).[3] Patriotic protest was not just deployed in the service of a range of very different causes (in the case of the women's movement and the anti-abortion movement, causes that often defined one another as the "enemy")—it was also constructed in markedly different ways. The Black Panthers, for instance, were keen to emphasize the right to overthrow unjust and despotic government—a right articulated very clearly in the Declaration of Independence—while many other black activists adopted elements of the new Black Power style while continuing to demand the enforcement of their constitutional rights and laying claim to the nation's promise of equality. Tax protesters and those opposed to "forced" busing preferred to highlight the importance of individual rights vis-à-vis the state, dwell on the Founders' fears of an overbearing and tyrannical central authority, and call for a return to the values of small-town America. While the anti-abortion movement drew repeated attention to the Declaration of Independence's guarantee of the "right to life," women and gay rights activists trumpeted that same document's avowal of the rights to "liberty" and the "pursuit of happiness." More generally, while progressives sought to urge the United States to do more to live up to its lofty ideals of equality and freedom and close the gap between rhetoric and reality, conservatives both celebrated the nation's past achievements and called for a return to the traditional religious and moral values on which, they claimed, the Republic had been founded.

Rather than helping to cement a shared, consensual language of public debate and establish common ground upon which Americans could, in good faith, debate one another and disagree, the use of patriotic protest by activists from across the political spectrum probably contributed instead to some of the sharp divisions that have characterized recent American politics—seen in the so-called "culture wars" of the 1980s and 1990s and the "red states" versus "blue states" rhetoric that emerged during the presidency of George W. Bush, for example.[4] In taking matters of policy and making them fundamental questions about the meaning of the nation, the political stakes and the passions of participants were raised, and the scope for pragmatic compromise reduced. The language of patriotism may also have encouraged politicians, commentators, and activists to play fast and loose with charges of "anti-American" and "un-American," thereby stoking further animosity.

Sixties activists were convinced that ordinary people had, in the words of Bettina Aptheker, "the collective strength to change the course of human events." While debate will doubtless continue about the relative success, or otherwise, of the various "people's movements" of the 1960s, it is clear that, in the years since the election of Richard Nixon, social movements—and the activism of ordinary people that sustains them—have become critically important actors on the American political scene. While the decisions of elected politicians, court rulings, and the actions of bureaucrats should be neither underestimated nor dismissed, social movements have helped to make policy and shape the wider political discourse. The staunch opposition to busing at the grassroots level, for instance, ultimately encouraged both public officials and judges to retreat from policies designed to bring about the widespread integration of the nation's public schools; the tax revolt has helped to set the economic agenda of the Republican Party since Ronald Reagan captured the White House; and the activism of gay and women's rights campaigners has helped make the United States a more tolerant and more equal society and pushed debates about gender and sexuality to the center-stage of public discourse.

Historians of postwar America have done a good job of describing and analyzing the rise and fall of the so-called New Deal Order and explaining how, during the late 1960s, the liberal consensus (in which conservatives accommodated themselves to the welfare state and liberals embraced anti-communism and containment) unraveled. During the four decades that followed Richard Nixon's victory over Hubert Humphrey, conservative politicians tended to prosper and support for liberalism fell. By the 1990s there was little public appetite for, and fewer votes to be gained by advocating, publicly funded government welfare programs that were once the hallmark of American liberalism—indeed, the word "liberal" had become something of a dirty word in the nation's politics.[5] But while the political center of gravity in America clearly shifted to the right during the 1970s and 1980s, a new political consensus remained elusive. Writing at the end of the 1980s, Steve Fraser and Gary Gerstle accepted that the old liberal order was "dead," but argued that "nothing with the same combination of programmatic coherence, ideological credibility, and mass political appeal" as liberalism had "arisen to take its place." We live, they claimed, "inside a political parenthesis."[6]

A new political consensus may have proved elusive, but by the end of the twentieth century a well-established model of protest was in place—a model to which activists on both sides of the American political spectrum often subscribed. As we have seen, those involved in numerous social movements during the 1970s, 1980s, and 1990s drew heavily on the example of the civil rights, New Left, and anti-Vietnam War movements as they filed lawsuits, engaged in direct action protests, participated in guerrilla theater, and demanded their "rights." And protesters sought consistently to portray their particular struggle as congruent with the ideals and traditions of their nation by deploying strategies of patriotic protest—quoting from the Declaration of Independence and Constitution, claiming the support of the Founding Fathers, invoking the Republic's symbolic association with equality, liberty and freedom, and waving the flag.

In the spring of 2009 conservatives, incensed by Barack Obama's victory over John McCain in the 2008 presidential election and opposed to his plans to use large amounts of taxpayers' money to combat the deepening economic crisis, launched a day of nationwide "Tax Day Tea Parties."[7] On 15 April (the deadline for filing income tax returns) protesters in Washington's Lafayette Park sang the national anthem, carried signs that stated "America: Of the People, By the People, For the People," and wore tea bags "hanging from umbrellas or eyeglasses."[8] In San Francisco's Civic Center, protesters—many carrying American flags—echoed the Vietnam demonstrations of an earlier era by chanting "our time to say hell no!" and appealed to patriotic values—one demonstrator carried a placard that read "Give me Liberty not Tyranny."[9] In Houston, Texas, 2,000 assembled in Jesse H. Jones Plaza, where those calling for the Lone Star Sate to secede from the Union were joined by "anti-abortion activists, Libertarians and fiscally conservative Republicans." Many of the protesters carried American flags, and others waved "hand-painted placards that bore messages like 'Abolish the I.R.S.,' 'Less Government More Free Enterprise,' [and] 'We Miss Reagan.'"[10] In the "Cradle of Liberty" itself, several hundred gathered on Boston Common, some wearing colonial-era costume. Despite the sunshine, one of the participants, Jo Ouimete from Northampton, Massachusetts, carried an umbrella that featured "an American flag pattern" with "a tea pot on top and Red Rose tea bags hanging from it." She explained that "The American taxpayers are really getting pressed too hard. We can't live like this, and our kids can't live like this." Meanwhile in a separate action across town at Boston Harbor, gay rights activists—some sporting tricorner hats and colonial dress—staged a reenactment of the Boston Tea Party. Several dozen activists "threw boxes of tea, labeled '1040EZ' and 'Tax Forms'" into the sea and chanted "Equal taxes, equal rights" to protest the fact that, despite same-sex marriage being legal in Massachusetts, married same-sex couples were unable to file joint federal tax returns.[11]

Notes

Introduction

1   Lena Williams, "200,000 March in Capital to Seek Gay Rights and Money for AIDS," "Memorial Quilt Rolled Out," *New York Times*, 12 October 1987, A1, D11; "National March on Washington for Lesbian and Gay Rights, October 11, 1987," Documentary Film, Gay Cable Network; http://www.aidsquilt.org/about.htm, accessed 29 January 2009.

2   Lena Williams, "600 in Gay Demonstration Arrested at Supreme Court," *New York Times*, 14 October 1987, B8.

3   Maurice Isserman and Michael Kazin, "The Contradictory Legacy of the Sixties," in Robert Griffith and Paula Baker, eds., *Major Problems in American History Since 1945*, 2nd ed. (Boston: Houghton Mifflin, 2001), 345.

4   Christopher Lasch, 1970, quoted in David S. Brown, *Beyond the Frontier: The Midwestern Voice in American Historical Writing* (Chicago: University of Chicago Press, 2009), 149.

5   Carl Oglesby, "Notes on a Decade Ready for the Dustbin," *Liberation* 14, 5–6 (August–September 1969): 5–19.

6   Godfrey Hodgson, *The World Turned Right Side Up: A History of the Conservative Ascendancy in America* (Boston: Houghton Mifflin, 1996), 118; Van Gosse, "Postmodern America: A New Democratic Order in the Second Gilded Age," in Van Gosse and Richard Moser, eds., *The World the Sixties Made: Politics and Culture in Recent America* (Philadelphia: Temple University Press, 2003), 24.

7   Alexander Bloom, "Why Read About the 1960s at the Turn of the Twenty-First Century?" in Bloom, ed., *Long Time Gone: Sixties America Then and Now* (Oxford: Oxford University Press, 2001), 4.

8   Quoted in M. J. Heale, "The Sixties as History: A Review of the Political Historiography," *Reviews in American History* 33 (2005): 134.

9   Gosse, "Postmodern America," 5.

10   Godfrey Hodgson, *More Equal Than Others: America from Nixon to the New Century* (Princeton, N.J.: Princeton University Press, 2004), 9.

11   For the rise of the New Right and the end of New Deal order, see Steve Fraser and Gary Gerstle, eds., *The Rise and Fall of the New Deal Order, 1930–1980*

(Princeton, N.J.: Princeton University Press, 1989). See also Earl Black and Merle Black, *The Rise of Southern Republicans* (Cambridge, Mass.: Belknap Press of Harvard University Press, 2002); Dan T. Carter, *The Politics of Rage: George Wallace, the Origins of the New Conservatism, and the Transformation of American Politics* (Baton Rouge: Louisiana State University Press, 2000); Gareth Davies, *From Opportunity to Entitlement: The Transformation and Decline of Great Society Liberalism* (Lawrence: University Press of Kansas, 1999); Hodgson, *The World Turned Right Side Up*; Thomas Byrne Edsall with Mary D. Edsall, *Chain Reaction: The Impact of Race, Rights, and Taxes on American Politics* (New York: Norton, 1991); Allan J. Matusow, *The Unraveling of America: A History of Liberalism in the 1960s* (New York: Harper and Row, 1984).

12   Letter, Cur Furr to Sam J, Ervin, Jr., 18 June 1968, Folder 669, Box 204, Legislative Files, Samuel J. Ervin Papers, Southern History Collection, University of North Carolina-Chapel Hill, quoted in Michael W. Flamm, "The Politics of "Law and Order" in David Farber and Jeff Roche, eds., *The Conservative Sixties* (New York: Peter Lang, 2003), 152.

13   See Joan Hoff, *Nixon Reconsidered* (New York: Basic Books, 1995).

14   Hodgson, *The World Turned Right Side Up*, 251; on the "Reagan Revolution" see 248–52. On the persistence of "big government" liberalism see, for example, Gareth Davies, *See Government Grow: Education Politics from Johnson to Reagan* (Lawrence: University Press of Kansas, 2007).

15   See "Introduction," in John D'Emilio, William B. Turner, and Urvashi Vaid, eds., *Creating Change: Sexuality, Public Policy, and Civil Rights* (New York: St. Martin's, 2000), ix.

16   Highlander was particularly important to the civil rights movement, and the SWP was a driving force in the Student Mobilization Committee to End the War in Vietnam. Although historians have traditionally presented the New Left as constituting a "decisive break" from the labor-based Left of the 1930s and 1940s, more recently revisionists have sought to emphasize the continuities. Andrew Hunt has been particularly vociferous in arguing that historians of the 1960s "have overemphasized the discontinuity between the new wave of radicalism and its predecessors." See Hunt, "How New Was the New Left?" in John McMillan and Paul Buhle, eds., *The New Left Revisited* (Philadelphia: Temple University Press, 2003). On the relationship between the Old and New Lefts see, for example, Michael Denning, *The Cultural Front: The Laboring of American Culture in the Twentieth Century* (London: Verso, 1998), esp. 110–14; John Patrick Diggins, *The Rise and Fall of the American Left* (New York: Norton, 1992); Maurice Isserman, *If I Had a Hammer...The Death of the Old Left and the Birth of the New Left* (New York: Basic Books, 1987); Doug Rossinow, *The Politics of Authenticity: Liberalism, Christianity, and the New Left in America* (New York: Columbia University Press, 1998).

17   American radicals and protest movements also exercised a significant influence internationally. On "the Sixties" in Europe see, for example, Tony Judt, *Postwar: A History of Europe Since 1945* (London: Heinemann, 2005), chaps. xii, xiii; Michael Kenny, *The First New Left: British Intellectuals After Stalin* (London: Lawrence and Wishart, 1995); Martin Klimke and Joachim Scarloth, eds., *1968 in Europe: A History of Protest and Activism, 1956–1977* (New York: Palgrave Macmillan, 2008); Arthur Marwick, *The Sixties: Cultural Revolution in Britain, France, Italy, and the United States, c. 1958–c. 1974* (Oxford: Oxford University Press, 1998); and Dominic Sandbrook, *White Heat: A History of Britain in the Swinging Sixties* (London: Little, Brown, 2006), 491–515.

18   Drawing on the work of the sociologist C. Wright Mills, early members of SDS sought to erase what they viewed as the artificial distinction made between the "public" and "private" spheres. They argued (and organized on the basis) that what were traditionally viewed as "personal" issues—such as dormitory rules, the role played by sororities and fraternities on university campuses, and the lack of student influence on curricula—were, in fact, political. The idea that the "personal was political" was popularized by second-wave feminists. See, for example, Alice Echols, "Women's Liberation and Sixties Radicalism," in Griffith and Baker, eds., *Major Problems in American History Since 1945*, 409.

19   Participatory democracy, as championed by SNCC and the early New Left, was based on the idea that people should have a say in all of the decisions that affect them. On the importance of grassroots organizing to the New Left see, in particular, Jennifer Frost, *An Interracial Movement of the Poor: Community Organizing and the New Left in the 1960s* (New York: New York University Press, 2005).

20   See in particular Sara M. Evans, *Personal Politics: The Roots of Women's Liberation in the Civil Rights Movement and The New Left* (New York: Vintage, 1980); John D'Emilio, *Sexual Politics, Sexual Communities: The Making of a Homosexual Minority in the United States, 1940–1970* (Chicago: University of Chicago Press, 1983); Ronald P. Formisano, *Boston Against Busing: Race, Class, and Ethnicity in the 1960s and 1970s* (Chapel Hill: University of North Carolina Press, 1991); Richard L. Hughes, "Burning Birth Certificates and Atomic Tupperware Parties: Creating the Antiabortion Movement in the Shadow of the Vietnam War," *The Historian* 68, 3 (Fall 2006); and Hughes, "'The Civil Rights Movement of the 1990s?': The Anti-Abortion Movement and the Struggle for Racial Justice," *Oral History Review* 33, 2 (2006).

21   See Heale, "The Sixties as History" and Richard Moser, "Was It the End or Just a Beginning? American Storytelling and the History of the Sixties," in Gosse and Moser, eds., *The World the Sixties Made*; and Stephen Tuck, "Introduction: Reconsidering the 1970s—The 1960s to a Disco Beat?" *Journal of Contemporary History* 43, 4 (October 2008).

22   John D'Emilio, "Placing Gay in the Sixties," in Bloom, ed., *Long Time Gone*, 211. For examples of this approach see Matusow, *The Unraveling of America*; Todd Gitlin, *The Sixties: Years of Hope, Days of Rage* (New York: Bantam, 1993); and James Miller, *Democracy is in the Streets: From Port Huron to the Siege of Chicago* (Cambridge, Mass.: Harvard University Press, 1994).

23   Robert O. Self, *American Babylon: Race and the Struggle for Postwar Oakland* (Princeton, N.J.: Princeton University Press, 2003), 330–31.

24   D'Emilio, "Placing Gay in the Sixties," 211. Robert Self's book on the black struggle in postwar Oakland, for instance, demonstrates how the traditional interpretation of the 1960s "implicitly dismisses the enormous flowering of black political movements after 1965 across the nation and ignores the fundamental urban story of the period between 1965 and the middle 1970s: the rise of African American urban political power in dozens of American cities." Self, *American Babylon*, 331. For valuable discussions of the vibrancy of black protest after the end of the "classic" civil rights movement see, for example, Mark Newman, *Divine Agitators: The Delta Ministry and Civil Rights in Mississippi* (Athens: University of Georgia Press, 2004) and Stephen Tuck, *We Ain't What We Ought to Be: The Black Freedom Struggle from Emancipation to Obama* (Cambridge, Mass.: Belknap Press of Harvard University Press, 2010).

25   For this see, for instance, Mary Brennan, *Turning Right in the Sixties: The Conservative Capture of the GOP* (Chapel Hill: University of North Carolina Press, 2007); Lisa McGirr, *Suburban Warriors: The Origins of the New American Right* (Princeton, N.J.: Princeton University Press, 2001); and Farber and Roche, eds., *The Conservative Sixties.*

26   Jim Cullen, *The American Dream: A Short History of an Idea That Shaped a Nation* (Oxford: Oxford University Press, 2003), 117. Swedish sociologist Gunnar Myrdal used the phrase "national creed."

27   Cullen, *The American Dream*, 38, 87. See also Michael Kazin and Joseph A. McCartin, "Introduction," in Kazin and McCartin, eds., *Americanism: New Perspectives on the History of an Ideal* (Chapel Hill: University of North Carolina Press, 2006), 1, and George Packer, "Introduction: Living Up to It," in Packer, ed., *The Fight Is for Democracy: Winning the War of Ideas in America and the World* (New York: Perennial, 2003), 14.

28   Todd Gitlin, "Varieties of Patriotic Experience," in Packer, ed., *The Fight Is for Democracy*, 116.

29   Kazin and McCartin, "Introduction," 3 and Michael Kazin, "A Patriotic Left," *Dissent* (Fall 2002): 1. See also Woden Teachout, *Capture the Flag: A Political History of American Patriotism* (New York: Basic Books, 2009).

30   Mark Naison, *Communists in Harlem During the Depression* (Urbana: University of Illinois Press, 2005), 169–70, see also chap. 12; Diggins, *The Rise and Fall of the American Left*, 174. For a good, recent analysis of the Popular Front see Doug Rossinow, *Visions of Progress: The Left-Liberal Tradition in America* (Philadelphia: University of Pennsylvania Press, 2008), chap. 4 and Michael Denning, *The Cultural Front: The Laboring of American Culture in the Twentieth Century* (London: Verso, 1998), esp. 4–21.

31   "Statement submitted by the Student Nonviolent Coordinating Committee to the Platform Committee of the National Democratic Convention, Thursday Morning, July 7, 1960, Los Angeles," 1–8, in *The Bayard Rustin Papers*, intro. John H. Bracey and August Meier, Guide compiled by Nanette Dobrosky (Frederick, Md.: University Publications of America, 1988), reel 1, frame 554–62.

32   Gitlin, "Varieties of Patriotic Experience," 119; Kazin, "A Patriotic Left," 2.

33   Gitlin, "Varieties of Patriotic Experience," 121; Kazin, "A Patriotic Left," 3. Woden Teachout's history of American patriotism, for instance, offers no examples of leftist struggles that used patriotic protest after the civil rights movement. She focuses on the "hard-hat" supporters of the Vietnam War during the 1970s, and then the co-optation of patriotism by supporters of the so-called war on terror. See Teachout, *Capture the Flag.*

34   Richard Stengel, "America's New Patriotism," *Time*, 14 July 2008, 31. See also Andrew O'Hehir, "Is the Homeland Where America's Heart Is?," *Salon*, 28 September 2006 (www.salon.com), 5 and Phyllis Schlafly fundraising letter, 1970, in Schlafly for Congress Committee, Box 17-1, Folder 2156, Hall-Hoag.

35   The latter tendency seems peculiarly American. It is hard to imagine an English politician—or social movement activist—claiming to have the support of Alfred the Great.

36   Stengel, "America's New Patriotism." See also O'Hehir, "Is the Homeland Where America's Heart Is?"; Schlafly fundraising letter, 1970.

37   Thomas Bender, "Wholes and Parts: The Need for Synthesis in American History," *JAH* 73, 1 (June 1986): 128.

38   Ibid., 123.

39   David Oshinsky, "The Humpty Dumpty of Scholarship: American History Has Broken in Pieces. Can It Be Put Together Again?" *New York Times*, 26 August 2000.

40   In this I have been influenced in particular by the work of Rebecca Klatch and Eric Foner. Klatch's *A Generation Divided: The New Left, the New Right, and the 1960s* (Berkeley: University of California Press, 1999)—which emphasized the shared experiences, language and sometimes political positions, of YAF (Young Americans for Freedom) and SDSers, encouraged me to think about the common ground upon which both progressive and conservative activists might stand. Eric Foner's *The Story of American Freedom* (New York: Norton, 1999) suggested that patriotism might well be a key part of that shared terrain.

41   John Higham, "Beyond Consensus: The Historian as Moral Critic," *American Historical Review* 67, 3 (April 1962): 616.

42   Richard Hofstadter, *The American Political Tradition and the Men Who Made It* (New York: Vintage, 1974), xxix (from the Preface).

Chapter 1. Patriotism, Protest, and the 1960s

1   Marisa Chappell, Jenny Hutchinson, and Brian Ward, "'Dress modestly, neatly . . . as if you were going to church': Respectability, Class, and Gender in the Montgomery Bus Boycott and the Early Civil Rights Movement," in Peter J. Long and Sharon Moneith, eds., *Gender in the Civil Rights Movement* (New York: Garland, 1999), 73.

2   Ibid., 73.

3   See "Speech by Martin Luther King, Jr., at Holt Street Baptist Church," in Clayborne Carson et al., eds., *The Eyes on the Prize Civil Rights Reader: Documents, Speeches, and Firsthand Accounts from the Black Freedom Struggle* (New York: Penguin, 1991), 48–51.

4   Jim Cullen, *The American Dream: A Short History of an Idea That Shaped a Nation* (Oxford: Oxford University Press, 2003), 126.

5   David J. Garrow, *Bearing the Cross: Martin Luther King, Jr., and The Southern Christian Leadership Conference* (1986; London: Vintage, 1993), 283.

6   See, for example, Mary Dudziak, *Cold War Civil Rights: Race and the Image of American Democracy* (Princeton, N.J.: Princeton University Press, 2000) and Azza Salama Layton, *International Politics and Civil Rights Policies in the United States, 1941–1960* (Cambridge: Cambridge University Press, 2000).

7   Letter from William H. Oliver, Co-Director Fair Practices and Anti-Discrimination, writing on behalf of the United Automobile Workers (UAW) regarding the March on Washington to Bayard Rustin, in *The Bayard Rustin Papers*, Intro. John H. Bracey and August Meier, Guide compiled by Nanette Dobrosky (Frederick, Md.: University Publications of America, 1988), reel 7, frames 536–44.

8   James Reston, "I Have a Dream," *New York Times*, 29 August 1963, 1.

9   SNCC statement to the Platform Committee of the National Democratic Convention, 7 July 1960, Los Angeles, California, quoted in *Bayard Rustin Papers*, reel 1, frame 554.

10   John Lewis, "Wake Up America," 28 August 1963, in Alexander Bloom and Wini Breines, eds., *"Takin' it to the streets": A Sixties Reader* (New York: Oxford University Press, 1995), 33–34.

11   "Remarks of Mrs. Fannie Lou Hamer," 22 August 1964, in ibid., 40–43.

12   Roy Wilkins, letter to NAACP Special Contribution Fund supporters, 17 October 1966, in NAACP Records Part IV, Box A18—NAACP Administration, 1966–; General Office File, Folder "Black Power 1966–69."

13   Thomas A. Johnson, "NAACP Fight Begins over a Wilkins Successor," *New York Times*, 6 January 1976, 18.

14   Port Huron Statement, in Bloom and Breines, *"Takin' it to the streets"*, 61–74.

15   Tom Hayden, "The Politics of 'The Movement,'" 1966, in ibid., 91–96.

16   See Staughton Lynd, "Coalition Politics or Nonviolent Revolution," *Liberation*, June/July 1965; Simon Hall, *Peace and Freedom: The Civil Rights and Antiwar Movements in the 1960s* (Philadelphia: University of Pennsylvania Press, 2005), 30–31. Although Hayden's "The Politics of 'the Movement'" appeared in 1966, Lynd acknowledged Hayden's idea for a second "Continental Congress" in the summer of 1965.

17   For a brief history of the relationship between patriotism and opposition to U.S. foreign policy, see Alan McPherson, "Americanism Against American Empire" in Michael Kazin and Joseph A. McCartin, eds., *Americanism: New Perspectives on the History of an Ideal* (Chapel Hill: University of North Carolina Press, 2006), 169–91.

18   Hall, *Peace and Freedom*, 35–36.

19   Carl Oglesby, "Trapped in a System" (27 November 1965), in Bloom and Breines, eds., *"Takin' it to the streets"*, 220–25.

20   Statement, Washington Mobilization Committee to End the War in Vietnam, 1966, in ARC, Part 1. I am grateful to Noel Heath for bringing this source to my attention.

21   Hall, *Peace and Freedom*, 80–81.

22   Martin Luther King, "A Time to Break Silence," in James Melvin Washington, *A Testament of Hope: The Essential Writings and Speeches of Martin Luther King, Jr.* (New York: HarperOne, 1990), 231–45; see also McPherson, "Americanism Against American Empire," 184–85.

23   Hall, *Peace and Freedom*, 8–9.

24   Robert D. Johnson, "The Progressive Dissent: Ernest Gruening and Vietnam," and Thomas J. Knock, "'Come Home, America': The Story of George McGovern," in Randall B. Woods, ed., *Vietnam and the American Political Tradition: The Politics of Dissent* (Cambridge: Cambridge University Press, 2003), 58, 72; 93–94, 117–18.

25   Johnson, "The Progressive Dissent," 79.

26   Raymond Mungo, "The Road to Liberation (A Letter to What Used to Be His Draft Board)," *Resist*, April 1968, reprinted in Massimo Teodori, ed., *The New Left: A Documentary History* (Indianapolis: Bobbs-Merrill, 1969), 351.

27   William L. Van Deburg, *New Day in Babylon: The Black Power Movement and American Culture, 1965–1975* (Chicago: University of Chicago Press, 1993), 32 and Adam Fairclough, *Better Day Coming: Blacks and Equality, 1890–2000* (New York: Penguin, 2002), 315.

28   "Max Stanford Calls for Independent Black Nation," 17 April 1968 press release, in John H. Bracey, August Meier, and Elliot Rudwick, eds., *Black Nationalism in America* (1971), 514–15; David Barber, *A Hard Rain Fell: SDS and Why It Failed* (Jackson: University Press of Mississippi, 2008), 18, 19.

29   McKissick quoted in Van Deburg, *New Day in Babylon*, 12.

30   Michael Kazin, "A Patriotic Left," *Dissent* (Fall 2002), 2.

31   Todd Gitlin, "Varieties of Patriotic Experience' in George Packer, ed., *The Fight Is for Democracy: Winning the War of Ideas in America and the World* (New York: Perennial, 2003), 121, and Kazin, "A Patriotic Left," 3. Woden Teachout's recent history of American patriotism, for instance, offers no examples of leftist struggles that used patriotic protest after the civil rights movement. She focuses on the "hard-hat" supporters of the Vietnam War during the 1970s, and then the co-optation of patriotism by supporters of the so-called war on terror. See Woden Teachout, *Capture the Flag: A Political History of American Patriotism* (New York: Basic Books, 2009).

32   Milton S. Katz, "Peace Liberals and Vietnam: SANE and the Politics of 'Responsible' Protest," *Peace and Change* 9 (Summer 1983): 21.

33   See Nathan Blumberg, "Misreporting the Peace Movement," *Columbia Journalism Review* 9 (Winter 1970–71); Herbert Gans, *Deciding What's News: A Study of CBS Evening News, NBC Nightly News, Newsweek and Time* (London: Constable, 1980); Todd Gitlin, *The Whole World Is Watching: Mass Media in the Making and Unmaking of the New Left* (Berkeley: University of California Press, 1980); and Melvin Small, *Covering Dissent: The Media and the Anti-Vietnam War Movement* (New Brunswick, N.J.: Rutgers University Press, 1994). See also "Youth Witness," *New Republic*, 4 November 1967, 6.

34   Resistance, "We Refuse to Serve," April 1967, reprinted in Teodori, *The New Left*, 297–29.

35   Tom Wells, *The War Within: America's Battle over Vietnam* (Berkeley: University of California Press, 1994), 139.

36   For histories of the VVAW, see Andrew Hunt, *The Turning: A History of Vietnam Veterans Against the War* (New York: New York University Press, 1999) and Richard Stacewicz, *Winter Soldiers: An Oral History of the Vietnam Veterans Against the War* (Chicago: Haymarket Books, 2008).

37   On the Winter Soldier Investigation see VVAW, *The Winter Soldier Investigation: An Inquiry into American War Crimes* (Boston: Beacon Press, 1972).

38   John Kerry, "Vietnam Veterans Against the War Testimony to the U.S. Senate Foreign Relations Committee," 22 April 1971, in Van Gosse, *The Movements of the New Left, 1950–1975: A Brief History with Documents* (Boston: Bedford/St. Martin's, 2005), 165–69.

39   Eugenia Kaledin, "Vietnam Comes to Lexington: Memorial Day, 1971," in Mary Susannah Robbins, ed., *Against the Vietnam War: Writings by Activists*, rev. ed. (Lanham, Md.: Rowman and Littlefield, 2007); Juan M. Vasquez, "Memorial Day Observed Traditionally and by Protests on War," *New York Times*, 1 June 1971, 1, 21; http://en.wikipedia.org/wiki/Vietnam_Veterans_Against_the_War; http://www.lexingtonbattlegreen1971.com/files/ homepagegui.swf; both accessed 14 January 2010.

40   Robert D. McFadden, "War Foes Seize Statue of Liberty," *New York Times*, 27 December 1971, 1, 21; Michael T. Kaufman, "15 Veterans Leave the Statue of Liberty, Claiming a Victory in Take-Over," *New York Times*, 29 December 1971, 32. VVAW would take over the statue again in 1976 to demand better treatment for veterans.

41   "'Got to Fight to Live,' Says Seale in Prison," *Philadelphia Sunday Bulletin*, 6 September 1970, RH WL Eph 2761, folder 40, Wilcox Collection.

42   "Serve The People Body and Soul"—c. 1971, Flier—The Black Panther Intercommunal News Service, RH WL Eph 898, Folder 2, Wilcox Collection; "Message to America, Delivered on the 107th Anniversary of the Emancipation Proclamation at Washington, D.C. Capitol of Babylon, World Racism, and

Imperialism, June 19, 1970 By the Black Panther Party," special four-page newspaper, c. June/July 1970, RH WL Eph 898, Wilcox Collection.

43 *Black Panther*, 17 January 1970, 1; Eldridge Cleaver, "To My Black Brothers in Viet Nam" (written 4 January 1970), Black Panther, RH WL Eph 2761, Folder 35, Wilcox Collection.

44 Bridgette Baldwin, "In the Shadow of the Gun: The Black Panther Party, the Ninth Amendment, and Discourses of Self-Defense" in Jama Lazerow and Yohuru Williams, eds., *In Search of the Black Panther Party: New Perspectives on a Revolutionary Movement* (Durham, N.C.: Duke University Press, 2006), 69. Baldwin appears to be on less firm ground when she argues that the Panthers' "language and approach to armed self-defense" was "rooted in the language and history of the Ninth amendment." Indeed, Baldwin herself concedes that this approach may well have been "unintentional"—and there appears to be scant evidence that the BPP leadership ever gave serious consideration to the importance/ relevance of the Ninth Amendment. 76.

45 *The Black Panther*, 10 January 1970, 3; "Huey P. Newton Speaks to the People," Message to the Revolutionary Peoples' Constitutional Convention, Plenary Session, 5 September 1970, Philadelphia, in *WE The People! The Revolutionary People's Constitutional Convention* (published by Rising Up Angry), 10, RH WIL Eph 2761, folder 45, Wilcox Collection.

46 Black Panther Party Platform and Program, "What We Want, What We Believe," October 1966, RH WL Eph 2761, folder 29, Wilcox Collection; Black Panther Party, Harlem Branch, press release "Beware of the Pig," 25 May 1969 in Black Panther, RH WL Eph 2761, folder 28, Wilcox Collection. The Panthers claimed that the 14th amendment guaranteed the right to be tried by "a jury of one's peers." This phrase is not found in the American Constitution, but has its roots in Magna Carta and English Common Law. See, for example, http://www.crfc.org/americanjury/jury_peers.html, accessed 17 December 2008. See also Bobby Seale, *Seize the Time: The Story of the Black Panther Party and Huey P. Newton* (New York: Vintage, 1970), 87, 89, 97.

47 Clayborne Carson, "Foreword," in Philip S. Foner, ed., *The Black Panthers Speak* (Cambridge, Mass.: Da Capo Press, 2002), x–xi.

48 Candy, "Pigs-Panthers," *Black Panther*, 22 November 1969, reprinted in Foner, ed., *The Black Panthers Speak*, 34–37. See also Baldwin, "In the Shadow of the Gun," 80. The slogan "All Power to the People" was also reflective of the ideology of participatory democracy that was fashionable among the New Left, and the Panthers sometimes described themselves as "working to establish a society in which every man will be free to determine his own destiny." See "Pigs-Panthers," 36.

49 *Black Panther*, 10 January 1970, 4, in RH WL G58, Wilcox Collection.

50 "Panthers Seeking New Constitution," *New York Times*, 20 June 1970, 15. King had used the words "But one hundred years later, the Negro still is not free." See Martin Luther King, "I Have a Dream," in Washington, *A Testament of Hope*, 217.

51 "Message to America, Delivered on the 107th Anniversary of the Emancipation Proclamation."

52 Peniel Joseph, *Waiting 'Til The Midnight Hour: A Narrative History of Black Power in America* (New York: Henry Holt, 2006), 254.

53 Ibid., 176–18, 212–13; "'He Was a Symbol': Eldridge Cleaver Dies at 62," CNN, 1 May 1998, http://www.cnn.com/US/9805/01/cleaver.late.obit/, accessed 17 December 2008.

54   Eldridge Cleaver, "On The Constitution," special four-page newspaper, c. June/July 1970, RH WL Eph 898, Wilcox Collection.

55   Mike Ellis, "The Constitution Talks About Equality on Paper Like It's Going Out of Style," *Black Panther*, 11 July 1970, 9.

56   Zaslow quoted in "Los Angeles Planning Session for the Revolutionary People's Constitutional Convention," *Black Panther*, 17 October 1970, 3.

57   Afeni Shakur, "We Will Have a New Constitution and Liberty or Revolutionary Suicide and Liberation," *Black Panther*, 15 August 1970, 11.

58   James Mott, "The Death of an Ideology of the Constitution of the U.S.A.," *Black Panther*, 15 August 1970, 10.

59   "Panthers Seeking New Constitution," *New York Times*, 20 June 1970, 15.

60   "Not to Believe in a New World After Philadelphia Is a Dereliction of the Human Spirit," *Black Panther*, 26 September 1970, 19.

61   Paul Delaney, "Panthers Weigh New Constitution," *New York Times*, 7 September 1970, 13.

62   Robert W. Cottroll, "The Philadelphia Story: Peaceful Black Panthers," *New York Amsterdam News*, 12 September 1970, 1.

63   George Katsiaficas, "Organization and Movement: The Case of the Black Panther Party and the Revolutionary People's Constitutional Convention of 1970," in Kathleen Cleaver and George Katsiaficas, eds., *Liberation, Imagination, and the Black Panther Party: A New Look at the Panthers and Their Legacy* (New York: Routledge, 2001), 148, 153; Joseph, *Midnight Hour*, 254. See also "Not to Believe in a New World After Philadelphia Is a Dereliction of the Human Spirit," *Black Panther*, September 26, 1970, 20. According to David Hilliard, Newton believed the RPCC was "a nonsense" that was the product of Eldridge Cleaver's grandiosity. See David Hilliard and Lewis Cole, *This Side of Glory: The Autobiography of David Hilliard and the Story of the Black Panther Party* (Boston: BackBay Books, 1993), 302–3, 308.

64   "Not to Believe in a New World After Philadelphia," 19.

65   Katsiaficas, "Organization and Movement," 148; Joseph, *Midnight Hour*, 254. See also Hilliard and Cole, *This Side of Glory*, 313.

66   "Huey's Message to the Revolutionary People's Constitutional Convention, Plenary Session, September 5, 1970, Philadelphia, PA," *Black Panther*, 12 September 1970, 10.

67   Kitsi Burkhart and J. Regan Kerney, "Newton Keynotes Panther Parley, Calls for Socialism in America," *Philadelphia Sunday Bulletin*, 6 September 1970, in RH WL Eph 2761, folder 40, Wilcox Collection; "Huey P. Newton Speaks to the People," Message to the Revolutionary Peoples' Constitutional Convention, Plenary Session, 5 September 1970, Philadelphia, in *WE The People! The Revolutionary People's Constitutional Convention* (published by Rising Up Angry), 10, RH WIL Eph 2761, Folder 45, Wilcox Collection.

68   "The People and the People Alone Were the Motive Force in the Making of History of the People's Revolutionary Constitutional Plenary Session!," *Black Panther*, 12 September 1970, 3.

69   Paul Delaney, "Panthers Weigh New Constitution," *New York Times*, 7 September 1970, 13.

70   Ibid.

71   Paul Delaney, "Panthers to Reconvene in Capital to Ratify Their Constitution," *New York Times*, 8 September 1970, 57.

72   Ibid.; "Panthers Give Up Convention Plan," *New York Times*, 29 November 1970, 34; Katsiaficas, "Organization and Movement," 154.

73 "Black Student Union: Platform and Program," quoted in *Radical's Digest* 1, 2 (May 1969) (New York, edited by Joe Dubovy), in ARC, Part 3, "Black Liberation Movement," reel 122.

74 Trinka Cline, "New Black Era Forseen," *Michigan State News*, Welcome Week, September 1969, C10; "Shop Sells Records at Low Cost," *MSN*, 2 November 1970, "Black Students Force Cafeteria Shutdown," *MSN*, 22 October 1969; Jeanne Sanddler, "BAA Changes Emphasis," *MSN*, 25 September 1969; "Umaoja Committee Hosts Night of African Culture," *MSN*, 7 December 1969; in ARC, Part 3, "Michigan State University: BLF," reel 168.

75 "Rights" (author—BLF chairman), *The Insurrection* 1, 1 (n.d., c. 1971): 1, 3, in ARC, Part 3, "Michigan State University: BLF," reel 168.

76 Keynote Address of Roy Wilkins, 1–2 in NAACP Records, Part IV, Box A3, NAACP Admin, 1966–, Annual Conference File, Folder "Speeches, 1966," LC; and letter, Gloster Current to Virna Canson, NAACP field director, 24 February 1969 in *Papers NAACP, C*, reel 8, Group IV, Series C, Branch Department Files cont., Regional File cont., West Coast Regional Office, Virna M. Canson, Correspondence and Memoranda, 1968–1970. Using branch newsletters as a basis of analysis, the vast majority of "supportive" articles relating to Black Power come from branches in the north and west, with a striking lack of similar pieces in newsletters produced by southern branches. An article written for the July–August 1972 edition of the Norwalk, Connecticut, branch of the NAACP concluded that "Both integrationists and separatists, by quarrelling with each other, are likely to forget that we are presently in no position to choose either course" and that "Most blacks are integrationists *and* separatist—all at the same time—, and (I almost forgot)—pluralists, too." See "All Together?? (or: What DIDN'T Happen in Gary," *Norwalk News Bulletin* July–August 1972, 2, in *Papers NAACP B*, reel 2, Group VI, Series C, Branch Department Files cont. Newsletters Cont., Group VI, Box C-176, Connecticut [Norwalk], 1972. For a full discussion of the NAACP's response to Black Power see Simon Hall, "The NAACP, Black Power, and the African American Freedom Struggle, 1966–1969." *The Historian* (2007).

77 *NAACP News* (Mid-Manhattan Branch) 5, no. 1 (January 1972): 1, 3, in *Papers NAACP B*, reel 3, Group VI, Series C, Branch Department Files, Newsletters, New York [New York City Department of Social Services, Mid-Manhattan, Greenwich Village-Chelsea, Williamsbridge, Albany, Central Long Island, New York City Housing Authority, Auburn-Cayuga, Far Rockaway-Inwood], 1972.

78 *The Plain Truth* (Davenport NAACP newsletter), February–March 1968, 1, 3, in *Papers NAACP B*, reel 1, Group VI, Series C, Branch Department Files, Newsletters, Iowa [Davenport, Fort Madison], 1968. The front cover of the April 1968 edition of *The Plain Truth* was peppered with patriotic slogans, including "All Men Are Created Equal," "With Liberty and Justice for All," and "Certain Inalienable Rights." The cover of the October edition featured a ballot paper and the slogan "Ballot Power, Black Power, Vote Baby Vote!"—reel 1, Group VI, Series C, Branch Department Files, Newsletters, Group VI, Box C-174, Iowa [Davenport, Fort Madison], 1968.

79 *The Plain Truth*, February–March 1968, 4, 5.

80 *NAACP Newsletter* (Oakland Branch), 1, 4 (February 1967): 2, 3, in *Papers NAACP C*, reel 1, Group IV, Series J, Printed Matter, Branches—Newsletters and Other Material, Group IV, Box J-4, California, "A"–"O" [Beverly Hills-Hollywood, Compton, Los Angeles Metropolitan Council, Merced, Monterey Peninsula, Oakland], 1966–1969.

81   *NAACP Newsletter* (Oakland Branch) 1, 3 (January 1967): 2.

82   Andrew Feffer, "Show Down in Center City: Staging Redevelopment and Citizenship in Bicentennial Philadelphia, 1974–1977," *Journal of Urban History* 30, 6 (2004): 810–11.

83   John Kifner, "2 Counterrallies in Philadelphia," *New York Times*, 5 July 1976, 14. Interestingly, while Roy Wilkins was happy to sign on to the National Committee for the Bicentennial Era's aspiration to celebrate the nation's founding ideals in a "profound sense of renewal and dedication" there was, reported the *New York Times*, "no reference to the 200th anniversary of the United States" during the NAACP 67th annual convention—see Michael T. Kaufman, "Bicentennial Goal: 'Back to Fundamentals'," *New York Times*, 21 February 1975, 28; Thomas A. Johnson, "Few Blacks Inspired by Bicentennial," *New York Times*, 8 July 1976, 47.

Chapter 2. The Struggle for Gay Rights

1   Robin Toner, "A Gay Rights Rally over Gains and Goals," *New York Times*, 1 May 2000, 14. See Matthew Shepard Foundation, http://www.matthewshepard.org/site/PageServer?pagename=mat_Matthews_Life, accessed 18 April 2008.

2   Walter L. Williams and Yolanda Retter, eds., *Gay and Lesbian Rights in the United States: A Documentary History* (Westport, Conn.: Greenwood Press, 2003), 282–83.

3   Ibid., 283.

4   John D'Emilio, *Sexual Politics, Sexual Communities: The Making of a Homosexual Minority in the United States, 1940–1970* (Chicago: University of Chicago Press, 1983), 23–39.

5   Marc Stein, ed., *Encyclopedia of Lesbian, Gay, Bisexual, and Transgender History in America* (New York: Scribner, 2004), 235; Immanuel Ness, ed., *Encyclopedia of American Social Movements*, vol. 4 (Armonk, N.Y.: Sharpe, 2004), 1335.

6   Stein, ed., *Encyclopedia*, 235; Ness, ed., *Encyclopedia of American Social Movements*, 1335–36.

7   Information on Lucas and Call from D'Emilio, *Sexual Politics, Sexual Communities*, 89; Ness, ed., *Encyclopedia of American Social Movements*, 1336. See also Martin Meeker, "Behind the Mask of Respectability: Reconsidering the Mattachine Society and Male Homophile Practice, 1950s and 1960s," *Journal of the History of Sexuality* 10, 1 (January 2001): 91–99.

8   Ness, ed., *Encyclopedia of American Social Movements*, 1337, 1339; Stein, ed., *Encyclopedia*, 236.

9   D'Emilio, *Sexual Politics, Sexual Communities*, 150.

10   Ness, ed., *Encyclopedia of American Social Movements*, 1340.

11   Cited in D'Emilio, *Sexual Politics, Sexual Communties*, 164.

12   Ibid., 161–64, 168–73; "Frank Kameny—The Pioneer," in Jeff Kisseloff, *Generation on Fire: Voices of Protest from the 1960s* (Lexington: University Press of Kentucky, 2007), 190.

13   The election, in which radical candidate Julian Hodges defeated conservative David Goldberger in the presidential contest, may well have been fraudulent. Some ballot papers were apparently tampered with the night before the count, to ensure the radicals' victory. See Martin L. Duberman, *Stonewall* (New York: Dutton, 1993), 108–9.

14   For the organization's cultural activities see, for example, MSNY, Series 2, Topical File, Box 3, Folder 22 "Drama Group 1965," reel 9.

15   See "Mattachine" leaflet, esp. 2, 4 in MSNY, Series 2, Topical File, Box 3, Folder 15 "Community Affairs Committee 1966," reel 9.

16   Stein, *City of Sisterly and Brotherly Loves: Lesbian and Gay Philadelphia, 1945–1972* (Chicago: University of Chicago Press, 2000), 245–46.

17   Memorandum, 7 March 1965, "Report on February 10, 1965, Mattachine Meeting Panel and Audience Discussion," 2, in MSNY, Series 2, Topical File, Box 4, Folder 14 "Mattachine Newsletter Scripts," reel 12.

18   Dick Leitsch and Warren D. Adkins, "Homosexuals Picket the White House and the United Nations," n.d., c. spring 1965, 4, in MSNY, Series 2, Topical File, Box 4, Folder 14 "Mattachine Newsletter Scripts," reel 12.

19   On the civil rights movement and "respectability" see in particular Marisa Chappell, Jenny Hutchinson and Brian Ward, "'Dress modestly, neatly . . . as if you were going to church': Respectability, Class and Gender in the Montgomery Bus Boycott and the Early Civil Rights Movement," in Peter Ling and Sharon Monteith, eds., *Gender in the Civil Rights Movement* (New York: Garland, 1999); Simon Hall, "Marching on Washington: The Civil Rights and Anti-War Movements of the 1960s," in Matthias Reiss, ed., *The Street as Stage: Public Demonstrations and Protest Marches Since the Nineteenth Century* (Oxford: Oxford University Press, 2007).

20   D'Emilio, *Sexual Politics, Sexual Communities*, 161, 158–68.

21   Committee on Picketing and Lawful Demonstrations, "Rules for Picketing," in MSNY, Series 2, Topical File, Box 3, Folder 21, "Demonstrations 1965–1966," reel 9.

22   For the Mattachine as radical, see Meeker, "Behind the Mask of Respectability."

23   August Meier, "On the Role of Martin Luther King," in Meier and Elliott M. Rudwick, *Along the Color Line: Explorations in the Black Experience* (Urbana: University of Illinois Press, 1976), 180.

24   Letter, Frank Kameny to Dick Leitsch, 12 July 1965, 3, in MSNY, Series 3, Gay Organizations, Box 8, Folder 5, "Washington, D.C., Mattachine Society of (1957–1968)," reel 18.

25   "War Role Sought for Homosexuals," *New York Times*, 17 April 1966, 10 in MSNY, Series 2, Topical File, Box 3, Folder 2 "Armed Forces Day Protest (1966)," reel 8.

26   D'Emilio, *Sexual Politics, Sexual Communities*, 206.

27   Letter, Dick Leitsch to Del Martin, 15 April 1966 and Clark Polak memorandum, 4 April 1966 in MSNY, Series 2, Topical File, Box 3, Folder 2, "Armed Forces Day Protest (1966)," reel 8.

28   David Eisenbach, *Gay Power: An American Revolution* (New York: Carroll and Graf, 2006), 20–21.

29   Mattachine Society of Washington, "Statement of Purpose," in MSNY, Series 2, Topical File, Box 3, Folder 21, "Demonstrations 1965–1966," reel 9.

30   "Introductory Address, as given by Mattachine Midwest, President Robert Sloane, at the First Open Meeting of Mattachine Midwest, July, 1965," 1–2, in MSNY, Series 3, Gay Organizations, Box 7, Folder 21, Midwest Mattachine, 1965–1972, reel 17.

31   See Leitsch and Atkins, "Homosexuals Picket the White House and the United Nations."

32   Mattachine Society of Washington, Information Bulletin, in MSNY, Series 3, Gay Organizations, Box 8, Folder 5, Washington, D.C., Mattachine Society of (1957–1968), reel 18.

33   "Pickets Demand Fair Treatment for Homosexuals," *Washington Sunday Star*, 30 May 1965, in MSNY, Series 2, Topical File, Box 3, Folder 21, "Demonstrations 1965–1966," reel 9.

34   R. Cafiero, undated and untitled report, in MSNY, Series 2, Topical File, Box 4, Folder 11,"Mattachine Newsletter" (July 1965), reel 12.

35   Mattachine Society of Washington, News Release, 24 June 1965 in MSNY, Series 2, Topical File, Box 3, Folder 21 "Demonstrations 1965–1966," reel 9; Mattachine Society of Washington, Information Bulletin, in MSNY, Series 3, Gay Organizations, Box 8, Folder 5 "Washington, D.C., Mattachine Society of Washington (1957–1968)," reel 18.

36   Mattachine Society of Washington, Information Bulletin, 3, in MSNY, Series 2, Topical File, Box 3, Folder 21,"Demonstrations 1965–1966," reel 9.

37   See "Why Are Homosexual American Citizens Picketing the Pentagon?" MSNY, Series 2, Topical File, Box 3, Folder 21, "Demonstrations 1965–1966," reel 9.

38   Mattachine Society of Washington, Information Bulletin.

39   "Craig L. Rodwell, 52, Pioneer for Gay Rights," *New York Times*, 20 June 1993, 38; Eisenbach, *Gay Power*, 40.

40   Stein, *City of Sisterly and Brotherly Loves*, 248.

41   ECHO, "Announcement," in MSNY, Series 2, Topical File, Box 3, Folder 21,"Demonstrations 1965–1966," reel 9.

42   Frank Kameny for Dick Leitsch, telephone call, 30 June 1965, 7:15 p.m., message recorded by R. W. Bracken, in MSNY, Series 2, Topical File, Box 3, Folder 21,"Demonstrations 1965–1966," reel 9; "Philadelphia Demonstration" in MSNY, Series 2, Topical File, Box 4, Folder 11,"Mattachine Newsletter" (July 1965), reel 12.

43   Stein, *City of Sisterly and Brotherly Loves*, 249.

44   Ibid., 248.

45   "2nd Annual Reminder" flyer in MSNY, Series 2, Topical File, Box 3, Folder 21,"Demonstrations 1965–1966," reel 9.

46   Stein, *City of Sisterly and Brotherly Loves*, 289, 272–73.

47   D'Emilio, *Sexual Politics, Sexual Communities*, 173, 174.

48   Ibid., 190–91, 197, 199—the 15 groups that had existed in 1966 had become 50 by summer 1969; "Frank Kameny—The Pioneer," 189.

49   Duberman, *Stonewall*, 181–82.

50   Ibid., xv; Terence Kissack, "Freaking Fag Revolutionaries: New York's Gay Liberation Front, 1969–1971," *Radical History Review* 62 (Spring 1995): 105. One of the defining accounts of the Stonewall Riot and its aftermath is David Carter, *Stonewall: The Riots That Sparked the Gay Revolution* (New York: St. Martin's Griffin, 2005). See also Stein, ed., *Encyclopedia*, 155–59. On gay liberation movements globally see Aart Hendriks, Rob Tielman, and Evert van der Veer, eds., *The Third Pink Book: A Global View of Lesbian and Gay Liberation and Oppression* (New York: Prometheus, 1993); Julian Jackson, *Living in Arcadia: Homosexuality, Politics, and Morality in France from the Liberation to AIDS* (Chicago: University of Chicago Press, 2010); Arthur Marwick, *The Sixties: Cultural Revolution in Britain, France, Italy, and the United States, c. 1958–c. 1974* (Oxford: Oxford University Press, 1998), 725–32; Lisa Power, *No Bath But Plenty of Bubbles: Stories from the London Gay Liberation Front, 1970–73* (London: Continuum International, 1995); Michael Sibalis, "The Spirit

of May '68 and the Origins of the Gay Liberation Movement in France," in Leslie Joe Frazier and Deborah Cohen, eds., *Gender and Sexuality in 1968: Transformative Politics in the Cultural Imagination* (New York: Palgrave Macmillan, 2009), 235–54; Aubrey Walter, *Come Together: The Years of Gay Liberation, 1970–1973* (London: Heretic Books, 1981), esp. 7–11 for the influence of Stonewall and the New York GLF on the British movement.

51   *Village Voice* report quoted in D'Emilio, *Sexual Politics, Sexual Communities*, 231–32.

52   Craig Rodwell quoted in Duberman, *Stonewall*, 197.

53   Duberman, *Stonewall*, 198, 199–202.

54   Ibid., 202–5; D'Emilio, *Sexual Politics, Sexual Communities*, 232.

55   Stein, *City of Sisterly and Brotherly Loves*, 289.

56   John D'Emilio, "After Stonewall," in *Making Trouble: Essays on Gay History, Politics, and the University* (New York: Routledge, 1992), 241.

57   For the growth in campus activism see in particular "Homosexuals Defy Campus Taboos," *Berkshire Eagle* (Pittsfield, Mass.), 8 January 1972 in GAA, Series 4, Printed Ephemera, Box 22A, Folder 3 "Sorted Press Clippings, Massachusetts-New Hampshire," reel 19.

58   D'Emilio, "After Stonewall," 241–44; D'Emilio, *Sexual Politics, Sexual Communities*, 232–39.

59   D'Emilio, *Sexual Politics, Sexual Communities*, 232.

60   D'Emilio, "After Stonewall," 242.

61   Dudley Clendinen and Adam Nagourney, *Out for Good: The Struggle to Build a Gay Rights Movement in America* (New York: Touchstone, 1999), 41.

62   D'Emilio, "After Stonewall," 242, 36–37.

63   D'Emilio, *Sexual Politics, Sexual Communities*, 233–34; Kissack, "Freaking Fag Revolutionaries" esp. 108, 113, 115; Stein, ed., *Encyclopedia*, 439.

64   Statement of 31 July 1969, quoted in D'Emilio, *Sexual Politics, Sexual Communities*, 234.

65   See Simon Hall, *Peace and Freedom: The Civil Rights and Antiwar Movements in the 1960s* (Philadelphia: University of Pennsylvania Press, 2005).

66   Lindsy Van Gelder, "'Gay Bill of Rights' Makes Progress," *New York Post*, 5 November 1970, 16, in GAA Records, Series 4, Printed Ephemera, Box 22A, Folder 5 "Sorted Press Clippings, New York," reel 19.

67   "Darers Go First," *The Furies—lesbian/feminist monthly* 1, 5 (June–July 1972): 5, 13 in GAA Records, Series 4, Printed Ephemera, Box 22, Folder 15 "Miscellaneous Newsletters and Periodicals," reel 18.

68   See Martha Shelley, "Gay Is Good" (1970) in Mark Blasius and Shane Phelan, eds., *We Are Everywhere: A Historical Sourcebook of Gay and Lesbian Politics* (New York: Routledge, 1997), 391.

69   "The Militant Homosexual," *Newsweek*, 23 August 1971, 47 in GAA Records, Series 4, Printed Ephemera, Box 22A, Folder 1 "Sorted Press Clippings, Alabama-D.C.," reel 19. See also Dudley Clendinen and Adam Nagourney, *Out for Good: The Struggle to Build a Gay Rights Movement in America* (New York: Touchstone, 1999), 72.

70   See, for instance, Sara M. Evans, *Personal Politics: The Roots of Women's Liberation in the Civil Rights Movement and the New Left* (New York: Vintage, 1980); Doug Rossinow, *The Politics of Authenticity: Liberalism, Christianity, and the New Left in America* (New York: Columbia University Press, 1998).

71   D'Emilio, *Sexual Politics, Sexual Communities*, 235.

72   Carl Wittman, "A Gay Manifesto" (1969) quoted in Williams and Retter, eds., *Gay and Lesbian Rights in the United States*, 116.

73   Clendinen and Nagourney, *Out for Good*, 26, 30.

74   Eisenbach, *Gay Power*, 131.

75   Stein, *City of Sisterly and Brotherly Loves*, 315–16.

76   Ibid., 322.

77   "Harmonyville Music Festival" flyer, n.d., in Wilbur Collection; Stein, *City of Sisterly and Brotherly Loves*, 315.

78   Ortez Alderson, "The "Disease" Fights Back," *Gay Flames: A Bulletin of the Homofire Movement* 6, 24 October 1970, 1, in Wilbur Collection, Box 3, "Gay Liberation."

79   "Love Is All You Need" flyer, http://www.lib.neu.edu/archives/voices/gl_pride2.htm, accessed 11 April 2008.

80   Civil Action, *GLF v. University of Kansas*—"Verified Complaint," 4–5, in Queers and Allies, Series 67/66, Box 1, Folder "1970/71," UKA.

81   See Beth Bailey, *Sex in the Heartland* (Cambridge, Mass.: Harvard University Press, 1999), 178–81 and Civil Action, *GLF v. University of Kansas*—"Verified Complaint," 6–8.

82   Bailey, *Sex in the Heartland*, 181–82; Emily Winerock, "Gay Civil Rights: The Gay, Lesbian, and Bisexual Student Organization of the University of Kansas's Fight for Funding," 3–7, in Queers and Allies, Series 67/66, Box 1, UKA.

83   Gay Services of Kansas, flyer, 1981, 2 in David D. Barney, Gay and Lesbian History at the University of Kansas: Lawrence Gay Liberation Front: 1971–1975; Gay Services of Kansas: 1976–1980 (The Historical Records Project, June 1992), 121, in Queers and Allies, Series 67/66, Box 1, UKA.

84   Winerock, "Gay Civil Rights," in Queers and Allies, Series 67/66, Box 1, UKA.

85   Jan Hyatt, "Area Gay Group No Longer Political," *University Daily Kansan*, 6 February 1975, 3, UKA.

86   Bailey, *Sex in the Heartland*, 184–85.

87   Ibid., 176.

88   Barney, Gay and Lesbian History, 9, in Queers and Allies, Series No 67/66, Box 1.

89   GLF statement (n.d.) in Queers and Allies, Series 67/61, Box 1, Folder "Artificial, n.d."

90   *Lawrence GLF News* 1 (10 March 1972), 2, in Queers and Allies, Series 67/61, Box 1.

91   Gay Services of Kansas flyer, 1981, 1, in Barney, Gay and Lesbian History, 121.

92   Rob MacRae, "Struggle for Social Issues Inherently in Lawrence," *University Daily Kansan*, n.d., October 1997, in Queers and Allies, Box 4, Folder "Scrapbook, 1997/98." The abolitionist influence can be seen today: the Sunflower State's premier gay and lesbian magazine, available in many Lawrence coffee shops and bars, is called *Liberty Press*.

93   Gerard Koskovich, "The History of Homosexuality at Stanford University: A Brief Chronology," Gay and Lesbian Alliance at Stanford, 1985 GALA Week Program Book—for "Gay and Lesbian Awareness Week" (5–11 May 1985), 7, and GALA Week 1984 programme, 8, in Gay and Lesbian Alliance at Stanford, Wilcox Collection.

94   Eisenbach, *Gay Power*, 141–42.

95   Stein, ed., *Encyclopedia*, 427–28.

96   "A Glimpse at Gay Liberation on GAA's 2nd Anniversary" in GAA Records, Series 2, Topical File, Box 18, Folder 11, "Gay Activist (Newsheet)," reel 11.

97   Cendinen and Nagourney, *Out for Good*, 51.

98   Dennis Altman quoted in Neil Miller, *Out of the Past: Gay and Lesbian History from 1869 to the Present* (New York: alyson books, 2006), 342.

99   Stein, ed., *Encyclopedia*, 440.

100   See Maurice Isserman and Michael Kazin, *America Divided: The Civil War of the 1960s* (New York: Oxford University Press, 2000), 147–64; Jonah Raskin, *For the Hell of It: The Life and Times of Abbie Hoffman* (Berkeley: University of California Press, 1997); Tom Wells, *The War Within: America's Battle over Vietnam* (Berkeley: University of California Press, 1994), 175; David Burner, *Making Peace with the 60s* (Princeton, N.J.: Princeton University Press, 1996), 206.

101   Raskin, *For the Hell of It*, 118.

102   Eisenbach, *Gay Power*, 120.

103   Ibid., 119.

104   Stein, ed., *Encyclopedia*, 428–29.

105   Clendinen and Nagourney, *Out for Good*, 66.

106   See Finding Aid to GAA Records.

107   Clendinen and Nagourney, *Out for Good*, 54, 67, 66. In August 1968, for example, following a raid on the Patch, a gay bar in L.A., a group of activists marched to a flower shop, purchased "all the gladioli, mums, carnations, roses, and daisies (but not pansies)" and delivered several huge bouquets to officers at the nearby police station. See Lillian Faderman and Stuart Timmons, *Gay L.A.: A History of Sexual Outlaws, Power Politics, and Lipstick Lesbians* (New York: Basic Books, 2006), 157–58.

108   Governor Nelson Rockefeller and Carol Greitzer, Greenwich Village councilwoman, were among the targets of GAA zaps. See Timothy Farris, "A 'Gay' Sit-In at GOP HQ," *New York Times*, 25 June 1970, 11; "5 Gay Activists Arrested in Sit-In," *GAY* #23, 13 July 1970, in GAA Records, Series 4, Printed Ephemera, Box 23, Folder 2 "Unsorted Press Clippings," reel 20; Clendinen and Nagourney, *Out for Good*, 54.

109   Clendinen and Nagourney, *Out for Good*, 52–53.

110   "GAA Confronts Lindsay at Channel 5," *GAY* #14, 11 May 1970; Sandra Vaughn, "Lindsay and Homosexuals: An Edited Encounter," *Village Voice*, 23 April 1970, 8, in GAA Records, Series 4, Printed Ephemera, Box 23, Folder 2 "Unsorted Press Clippings," reel 20.

111   "N.Y. Gay Activists Disrupt Lindsay's Campaign Fund Raiser at Music Hall," *Variety*, 26 January 1972, 1, in GAA Records, Series 4, Printed Ephemera, Box 22A, Folder 1 "Sorted Press Clippings, Alabama-D.C.," reel 19.

112   GAA News Release, "Slepian Trial for Harassment March 8," in GAA Records, Series 1, Committee Files, Box 17, Folder 10 "News and Media Relations Press Releases," reel 8.

113   GAA, News Committee Release, 12 September 1970 and c. 15 October 1970 in GAA Records, Series 1, Committee Files, Box 17, Folder 10 "News and Media Relations Press Releases," reel 8.

114   GAA News Release, 24 October 1970 in GAA Records, Series 1, Committee Files, Box 17, Folder 10 "News and Media Relations Press Releases," reel 8.

115   "Lindsay Orders City Protection for Homosexuals in Jobs, Hiring," 8 February 1972, in GAA Records, Series 4, Printed Ephemera, Box 22A, Folder 4 "Sorted Press Clippings, New York," reel 19.

116   Susan Fogg, "Homosexuals Take Rights Fight to Demo Convention," *Oregonian*, 13 June 1972, in GAA Records, Series 4, Box 24, Folder 5 "Unsorted Press Clippings," reel 21.

117   "GOP Platform Leader Criticizes McGovern," *Detroit News*, 7 June 1972 in GAA Records, Series 1, Box 22A, Folder 3 "Sorted Press Clippings, Massachusetts-New Hampshire," reel 19.

118   Williams and Retter, eds., *Gay and Lesbian Rights in the United States*, 127; Clendinen and Nagourney, *Out for Good*, 132–36.

119   Williams and Retter, eds., *Gay and Lesbian Rights in the United States*, 158.

120   Eisenbach, *Gay Power*, 147, 149–50; for Evans see 127, 144. Clive James, "Dick Cavett: The Secret Art of the Talk Show Host," *Slate*, 9 February 2007, www.slate.com/ id/2159367, accessed 11 April 2008.

121   See, for instance, GAA News Release, "Slepian Trial for Harrassment March 8."

122   Eisenbach, *Gay Power*, 154–56, 163–64, 173–74; "Lindsay Orders City Protection for Homosexuals in Jobs, Hiring," 8 February 1972, in GAA Records, Series 4, Printed Ephemera, Box 22A, Folder 4 "Sorted Press Clippings, New York," reel 19.

123   On final passage of the bill see Clendinen and Nagourney, *Out for Good*, 526–30.

124   "Equal Rights for Gay People," pamphlet (produced by GAA/Coalition in support of a New York Gay Civil Rights Bill), n.d. c. summer 1975, 1, in Wilbur Collection, Box 3, "Gay Liberation 2." See also "March on St. Patrick's For Gay Rights! Sat., July 12," flyer, c. June/July 1975 in Wilbur Collection, Box 3, "Gay Liberation 2."

125   Stein, *City of Sisterly and Brotherly Loves*, 381–82.

126   D'Emilio, *Sexual Politics, Sexual Communities*, 238; D'Emilio, "After Stonewall," 249–50.

127   Chris Bull and John Gallagher, *Perfect Enemies: The Religious Right, the Gay Movement, and the Politics of the 1990s* (New York: Crown, 1996), 16.

128   Clendinen and Nagourney, *Out for Good*, 295.

129   For an account of the Miami, Dade County campaign see ibid., 291–311.

130   Williams and Retter, eds., *Gay and Lesbian Rights in the United States*, xl, 144; Bull and Gallagher, *Perfect Enemies*, 18; Clendinen and Nagourney, *Out for Good*, 377–90.

131   Tom Foley, "Anti-Gay Rights Drive Will Be Started Here," *Capital Times*, 28 April 1978 in UR, Box 1, Folder 4, WHS.

132   "Local Coalition Is Backing Homosexuals' Civil Rights," *Wisconsin State-Journal*, 12 May 1978 in UR, Box 1 Folder 1, WHS; The United, Press Release, 5 February 1979, UR, Box 1, Folder 1, WHS.

133   "Ohio Parish Can't Forget Dillabaugh," Madison Press Connection, 23 May 1978 in The United Records, 1977–1981, Box 1, Folder 2, WHS.

134   "Local Coalition Is Backing Homosexuals' Civil Rights"; Doug Mobe, "The Rev, the Dangle, the Lawyer," *Capital Times*, 22 March 2005, 2A.

135   Mike Stone, "Dillabaugh Sets Three-Day 'God and Decency' Drive," *Capital Times*, 22 June 1978 in UR, Box 1, Folder 4, WHS.

136   "Ohio Parish Can't Forget Dillabaugh." Although he was found not guilty in June 1978, the charge echoed concerns expressed in his previous parish. Eric Wardle, headmaster of the Indian Hills Christian School who fell out with Dillabaugh, believed excessive discipline was used under Dillabaugh's watch.

137 Virginia Mayo, "Groups Join to Save Equal Rights Ordinance," *Capital Times*, 11 May 1978 in UR, Box 1, Folder 1, WHS.

138 Information from the Finding Aid, UR, WHS.

139 Mayo, "Groups Join to Save Equal Rights Ordinance."

140 Lauren Dohr, "United Trying to Give Gays More 'Breathing Room,'" *Daily Cardinal*, 30 January 1979 in UR, Box 1, Folder 1; also "The United, Political Program" [n.d.] in UR, Box 1, Folder 1, WHS.

141 Virginia Mayo, "Groups Join to Save Equal Rights Ordinance," *Capital Times*, 11 May 1978 in UR, Box 1, Folder 1, WHS.

142 "Madison Gay Group Lashes Out at 2 Ministers for Sex Crusade," Madison Press Connection, 14 February 1979 in UR, Box 1, Folder 4, WHS.

143 Bill Christofferson, "Equal Opportunity Law Attacked," Madison Press Connection, 17 June 1978, in UR, Box 1, Folder 4, WHS.

144 United press release, n.d. (summer 1978?) in UR, 1977–1981, Box 1, Folder 2, WHS; "Farewell to Rev. Pritchard," *Capital Times*, 1 July 1992, 9A; "People of Note," *Wisconsin State Journal*, 2 April 2006.

145 Dan Allegretti, "Gay Rights Law Is Pritchard Target," *Capital Times*, 23 October 1978 in UR, Box 1, Folder 4, WHS.

146 "Reader Connection: Pritchard on Gays," Madison Press Connection, 8 June 1978 in UR, Box 1, Folder 2, WHS.

147 Timothy B. Tyson, "Cries of War," *Raleigh News and Observer*, 9 November 2003, G4.

148 http://psoglin.typepad.com/about.html, accessed 1 November 2006.

149 http://badgerherald.com/news/2005/04/28/history_of_the_miffl.php, accessed 1 November 2006.

150 http://psoglin.typepad.com/about.html, accessed 1 November 2006.

151 Joint Meeting, MCRC and United Steering Committees, 24 October 1978, 11:30 a.m., minutes, 3 in UR, Box 1, Folder 1, WHS.

152 Letter, David E. Clarenbach to Madison City Council, 3 November 1978 in UR, Box 1, Folder 4, WHS.

153 Stuart Levitan, "Candidates Shun Pritchard," Madison Press Connection, 24 June 1978 in UR, Box 1, Folder 4; The United, Press Release, 5 February 1979 in UR, 1977–1981, Box 1, Folder 1, WHS.

154 Karen A. Foss, "Harvey Milk: 'You Have to Give Them Hope' ," *Journal of the West* 27, 2 (1988), esp. 78–80.

155 Williams and Retter, eds., *Gay and Lesbian Rights in the United States*, 146–48.

156 Bull and Gallagher, *Perfect Enemies*, 19.

157 Ibid., 149.

158 Ibid., 150.

159 See http://www.aidsquilt.org, accessed 5 May 2008; Christopher Capozzola, "A Very American Epidemic: Memory, Politics and Identity Politics in the AIDS Memorial Quilt, 1985–1993," *Radical History Review* 82 (Winter 2002): 91–109.

160 See GLAD Questionnaire, September 1983, in Gay and Lesbian Advocates and Defenders, Folder 1, Wilcox Collection; Letter, David Jean and Don Babets, 7 December 1987, in Gay and Lesbian Advocates and Defenders, Folder 3, Wilcox Collection.

161 "San Francisco: Prop 8 Goes to Federal Court," *Time*, 25 January 2010, 12; see also http://www.marriageequality.org/, accessed 24 January 2010.

162   John D'Emilio, "Placing Gay in the Sixties," in Alexander Bloom, ed., *Long Time Gone: Sixties America Then and Now* (Oxford: Oxford University Press, 2001), 213, 214, 224.

163   Todd Gitlin, "Varieties of Patriotic Experience," in George Packer, ed., *The Fight Is for Democracy: Winning the War of Ideas in America and the World* (New York: Perennial, 2003), 119, 121; Michael Kazin, "A Patriotic Left," *Dissent* (Fall 2002), 2.

164   D'Emilio, "After Stonewall," 242; Carl Wittman, "A Gay Manifesto," in Blasius and Phelan, eds., *We Are Everywhere*, 382.

165   Kissack, "Freaking Fag Revolutionaries," 109.

Chapter 3. Women's Rights—The Second Wave

1   Linda Charlton, "Women March Down Fifth in Equality Drive," *New York Times*, 27 August 1970, 1, 30; Judy Klemesrud, "It Was a Great Day for Women on the March," *New York Times*, 31 August 1970, 125.

2   On the international dimension of the women's movement see, for example, Drude Dahlerup, ed., *The New Women's Movement: Feminism and Political Power in Europe and the USA* (London: Sage, 1986); Robin Morgan, ed., *Sisterhood Is Global: The International Women's Movement Anthology* (New York: Anchor, 1984); Leila Rupp, *Worlds of Women: The Making of an International Women's Movement* (Princeton, N.J.: Princeton University Press, 1997); Kristina Schulz, "The Women's Movement," in Martin Klimke and Joachim Scarloth, eds., *1968 in Europe: A History of Protest and Activism, 1956–1977* (New York: Palgrave Macmillan, 2008), 281–93; and Bonnie G. Smith, ed., *Global Feminisms Since 1945* (London: Routledge, 2000).

3   Sara M. Evans, *Tidal Wave: How Women Changed America at Century's End* (New York: Free Press, 2002), 4, 3; Josh Zeitz, "Rejecting the Center: Radical Grassroots Politics in the 1970s—Second-Wave Feminism as a Case Study," *Journal of Contemporary History* 43, 4 (October 2008): 676.

4   See, for example, Evans, *Tidal Wave*, 28–38; Alice Echols, *Daring to Be Bad: Radical Feminism in America, 1967–1975* (Minneapolis: University of Minnesota Press, 1989, 2003), 51–65.

5   NOW Statement of Purpose (adopted at the organizing conference, Washington, D.C., 29 October 1966), 1, Box 39-3X, Folder 3054, Hall-Hoag.

6   Echols, *Daring to Be Bad*, 16, 168–69, 212–13.

7   Tricia Tunstall and Callie Kenady, "What Happened to the Radical Women's Movement?" *Sister* 1, 7 (June 1974), 5, Box 39-3, Folder 322/1/1, Hall-Hoag.

8   Echols, *Daring to Be Bad*, 388; Alexander Bloom and Wini Breines, eds., "*Takin' it to the streets*": A Sixties Reader (New York: Oxford University Press, 1995), 486.

9   Evans, *Tidal Wave*, 55.

10   Untitled article by Ginny Berson, *The furies* (lesbian/feminist monthly) 1 (January 1972): 1 and Charlotte Bunch, "Lesbians in Revolt," *The furies* 1 (January 1972): 8. For more on the Furies see Echols, *Daring to Be Bad*, 228–38; for a useful discussion of a wide range of radical feminist groups see chap. 2. For a general introduction to the women's movement see Kathleen C. Berkeley, *The Women's Liberation Movement in America* (Westport, Conn.: Greenwood Press, 1999). See also Ruth Rosen, *The World Split Open: How the Modern Women's Movement Changed America* (New York: Viking, 2000). For a good example of the radical wing of the

movement see "Who We Are" (1970), in Dawn Keetley and John Pettigrew, eds., *Public Women, Public Words: A Documentary History of American Feminism*, vol. 3, *1960 to the Present* (Lanham, Md.: Rowman and Littlefield, 2005), 38–39, originally in *Siren: A Journal of Anarcho-Feminism*, 1970.

11   Stephanie Gilmore, "The Dynamics of Second-Wave Feminist Activism in Memphis, 1971–1982: Rethinking the Liberal/Radical Divide," *NWSA Journal* 15, 1 (Spring 2003): 94–117.

12   Evans, *Tidal Wave*, 42–43, 56–57.

13   Ibid., 119.

14   For a more detailed discussion see, for example, Anne M. Valk, *Radical Sisters: Second-Wave Feminism and Black Liberation in Washington, D.C.* (Urbana: University of Illinois Press, 2008).

15   Evans, *Tidal Wave*, 115.

16   Kay Mills, *This Little Light of Mine: The Life of Fannie Lou Hamer* (Lexington: University Press of Kentucky, 2007), 274.

17   Evans, *Tidal Wave*, 115.

18   Frances Beale, "Double Jeopardy: To Be Black and Female," in Bloom and Breines, eds., *"Takin' it to the streets"*, 529.

19   Evans, *Tidal Wave*, 76–77. See also Toni Morrison, "What the Black Woman Thinks About Women's Lib," *New York Times*, 22 August 1971, SM14, 63, 66; "Blacks v. Feminists," *Time*, 26 March 1973; Barbara Campbell, "Black Feminists Form Group Here," *New York Times*, 16 August 1973, 36. On the tensions between black and white feminists see, for example, Patricia Robinson, "Poor Black Women" (1968), Charlayne Hunter, "Many Blacks Wary of 'Women's Liberation' Movement" (1970), Toni Morrison, "What the Black Woman Thinks About Women's Lib" (1971), and Combahee River Collective, "A Black Feminist Statement" (1977), all in Keetley and Pettigrew, eds., *Public Women, Public Words*.

20   Zeitz, "Rejecting the Center"; William H. Chafe, *The Unfinished Journey: America Since World War II* (New York: Oxford University Press, 2006), chap. 14; Evans, *Tidal Wave*, 63–70, 84–85. See also "Great Changes, New Chances, Tough Choices," *Time*, 5 January 1976.

21   Evans, *Tidal Wave*, 129–30, 168–69. On the founding of the National Women's Studies Association see also Gene I. Maeroff, "The Growing Women's Studies Movement Gets Organized," *New York Times*, 18 January 1977, 41.

22   Evans, *Tidal Wave*, 113.

23   Ibid., 171–78; Rosen, *The World Split Open*, 331–32. On the history of the ERA see, for instance, Jane J. Mansbridge, *Why We Lost the ERA* (Chicago: University of Chicago Press, 1986); Mary Frances Berry, *Why ERA Failed: Politics, Women's Rights, and the Amending Process of the Constitution* (Bloomington: Indiana University Press, 1986); Donald Mathews and Jane De Hart, *Sex, Gender and the Politics of ERA: A State and the Nation* (New York: Oxford University Press, 1990). See also "ERA Dies," *Time*, 5 July 1982; Anastasia Troufexis, "What Killed Equal Rights?" *Time*, 12 July 1982.

24   Evans, *Tidal Wave*, 190–201; Rosen, *The World Split Open*, 339; Sara M. Evans, "American Women in the Twentieth Century," in Harvard Sitkoff, ed., *Perspectives on Modern America: Making Sense of the Twentieth Century* (New York: Oxford University Press, 2001), 172.

25   Structural changes—particularly deindustrialization and the economic crisis of the 1970s—also help explain some of the dramatic changes that affected millions of American women. See Beth Bailey, "She 'Can Bring Home the Bacon': Negotiating Gender in Seventies America," in Bailey and David Farber,

eds., *America in the Seventies* (Lawrence: University Press of Kansas, 2004), 108–9; for the influence of the women's movement on Americans' understanding of gender, and the ways ideas could move from "radical collectives" see 108, 116.

26   Rosen, *The World Split Open*, 337–38.

27   Alice Echols, "Nothing Distant About It: Women's Liberation and Sixties Radicalism," in Farber, ed., *The Sixties: From Memory to History*, 151.

28   Jo Freeman, "The Origins of the Women's Liberation Movement," *American Journal of Sociology* 78, 4 (January 1973): 797–98.

29   NOW Statement of Purpose, 3; NOW Origins: A Chronology of NOW 1966–1985 (leaflet), both Box 39-3X, Folder 3054, Hall-Hoag. On Howard W. Smith see Rosen, *The World Split Open*, 71.

30   Freeman, "The Origins of the Women's Liberation Movement," 798–99.

31   NOW Statement of Purpose, 1.

32   Ibid., 1, 3.

33   The most influential exponent of the thesis that women's liberation was shaped decisively by the activism of the civil rights and New Left movements is Sara M. Evans. See, in particular, her hugely influential *Personal Politics: The Roots of Women's Liberation in the Civil Rights Movement and the New Left* (New York: Vintage, 1980). On the links between the New Left, civil rights movement, and feminism see also Echols, *Daring to Be Bad*, 23–50.

34   David Barber, *A Hard Rain Fell: SDS and Why It Failed* (Jackson: University Press of Mississippi, 2008), 108, 118, 132.

35   SNCC Founding Statement, April 1960, in Bloom and Breines, eds., *"Takin' it to the streets"*, 24.

36   SDS Port Huron Statement, in ibid., 67–68.

37   SNCC Position Paper: Women in the Movement, in ibid., 45–47.

38   Evans, *Personal Politics*, 76; Jean Wiley interview with Judy Richardson, February 2007, http://www.crmvet.org/nars/judyrich.htm.

39   Quoted in Jack E. Davis, *The Civil Rights Movement* (New York: Wiley-Blackwell, 2000), 149.

40   Tom Wells, *The War Within: America's Battle over Vietnam* (Berkeley: University of California Press, 1994), 115–16; http://currents.ucsc.edu/06-07/10-23/aptheker.asp, accessed 20 May 2009. For more see Bettina Aptheker, *Intimate Politics: How I Grew Up Red, Fought for Free Speech, and Became a Feminist Rebel* (Emeryville, Calif.: Seal Press, 2006).

41   Bettina Aptheker, "The Business of Breaking Silence," *New Women's Times*, June 1982, 10 in Box 39-3, Folder 1102, Hall-Hoag.

42   Rebecca Klatch, *A Generation Divided: The New Left, the New Right, and the 1960s* (Berkeley: University of California Press, 1999), 165; the deep-rooted sexism of the movement is revealed in the comments of one male SDS organizer at a meeting at the University of Washington in Seattle during winter 1967: he explained that by "balling a chick together" a sense of rapport could be forged among the poor whites with whom he had been organizing. See Freeman, "The Origins of the Women's Liberation Movement," 801.

43   Klatch, *A Generation Divided*, 167–68.

44   Ibid., 168. See also "Marilyn Salzman Webb—The Feminist," in Jeff Kisseloff, *Generation on Fire: Voices of Protest from the 1960s* (Lexington: University Press of Kentucky, 2007), 172–73.

45   Klatch, *A Generation Divided*, 167–69, 170.

46   Amy Kesselman, "Women's Liberation and the Left in New Haven, Connecticut, 1968–1972," *Radical History Review* 81 (Fall 2001): 17–18, 22. On

sexism in the New Left see also Anne Koedt, "Women and the Radical Movement" (originally in *Notes from the First Year*, June 1968) and Robin Morgan, "Goodbye to All That" (originally in *Rat: Subterranean News*, 6 February 1970), both in Keetley and Pettigrew, eds., *Public Women, Public Words*, 18–20, 33–38.

47   Casey Hayden and Mary King, "Sex and Caste: A Kind of Memo' in Bloom and Breines, *"Takin' it to the streets"*, 47–51.

48   Jill Severn, "Women and Draft Resistance: Revolution in the Revolution" (April 1968), in Keetley and Pettegrew, eds., *Public Women, Public Words*, 486.

49   Evans, *Personal Politics*, 189–92.

50   Barber, *A Hard Rain Fell*, 111.

51   Evans, *Personal Politics*, 197–200. For more on the NCNP see Simon Hall, *"On the Tail of the Panther*: Black Power and the 1967 Convention of the National Conference for New Politics," *Journal of American Studies* 37, 1 (April 2003).

52   Barber, *A Hard Rain Fell*, 118.

53   "Marilyn Salzman Webb—The Feminist," 170–71, 172–73, 177–78. See also Barber, *A Hard Rain Fell*, 137. On the hostile response of male New Leftists to issues of women's equality see also Echols, *Daring to Be Bad*, 120–24.

54   The U.S. experience was not unique. At a September 1968 conference of Germany's SDS (Sozialistischer Deutscher Studentenbund), for example, one woman threw tomatoes at the podium to protest the group's failure to take the "women's question" seriously. See Schulz, "The Women's Movement," 288.

55   Klatch, *A Generation Divided*, 172.

56   Jean Wiley interview with Judy Richardson, February 2007, http://www.crmvet.org/ nars/judyrich.htm.

57   Barber, *A Hard Rain Fell*, 97, 98.

58   Aptheker, "The Business of Breaking Silence."

59   Hayden and Mary King, "Sex and Caste."

60   Klatch, *A Generation Divided*, 183. See also Todd Gitlin, *The Sixties: Years of Hope, Days of Rage* (New York: Bantam 1993); Evans, *Personal Politics*; and James Miller, *Democracy Is in the Streets: From Port Huron to the Siege of Chicago* (Cambridge, Mass.: Harvard University Press, 1994).

61   Jane Ciabattari, "To Be a Woman: How Other Women Gave Me the Courage to Change," *Redbook*, November 1973, reprinted in Robert Griffith and Paula Baker, eds., *Major Problems in American History Since 1945* (Boston: Houghton Mifflin, 2001), 381, 383.

62   *It Ain't Me Babe* (Berkeley Women's Liberation Newspaper) 1, 1, 15 January 1971, back page, in Box 39-3X, Folder 1352, Hall-Hoag.

63   Kesselman, "Women's Liberation and the Left," 22–23.

64   In March 1971, 150 women's liberation activists seized a building on Harvard University campus, which they renamed a "women's center." See "Harvard Gets Court Order Against Seizure of Building," *New York Times*, 19 March 1971, 26.

65   NOW Origins: A Chronology.

66   Rosen, *The World Split Open*, 300–301; Grace Lichtenstein, "Feminists Demand "Liberation" in Ladies' Home Journal Sit-In," *New York Times*, 19 March 1970, 51; "Ladies Journal Has 'Lib' Section," *New York Times*, 28 July 1970, 13.

67   Nancy Moran, "9 Women Arrested in 5-Hour Sit-in at Grove Press," *New York Times*, 14 April 1970, 55.

68   Joanna Dyl, "Women's Liberation: Origins and Development of the Movement," www.shapingsf.org/ezine/womens/1960s/main.html, viewed 9

June 2009; ARC, Part 3, Michigan State University: Women's Liberation Teach-In, March 7, 1970, Reel 168.

69   Marijean Suelzle, "Outgoing President's Remarks—The Year in Review," NOW Berkeley *Newsletter,* January 1971, 6, RH WL D2794, Wilcox Collection.

70   *It Ain't Me Babe* 1, 1 (15 January 1970); "Coeds at Berkeley Demonstrate Against All-Male Karate Class," *New York Times,* 9 January 1970, 38; Marijean Suelzle, "Outgoing President's Remarks—The Year in Review," NOW Berkeley *Newsletter,* January 1971, 6, RH WL D2794, Wilcox Collection.

71   "Yale University: Milestones in the Education of Women at Yale," http:// www.yale.edu/ oir/book_numbers_updated/A9_Milestones_for_Yale_Women. pdf, accessed 19 May 2009; "Woman and Man at Yale," *Time,* 20 March 1972, www.time.com, accessed 19 May 2009.

72   "Woman and Man at Yale"; Roberta Smith, "Anne Coffin Hanson, 82; Yale Professor of Art History," *New York Times,* 4 September 2004.

73   Kesselman, "Women's Liberation and the Left," 24–25.

74   Bruce J. Schulman, *The Seventies: The Great Shift in American Culture, Society, and Politics* (New York: Da Capo Press, 2002), 161.

75   "Yale Women Strip to Protest a Lack of Crew's Showers," *New York Times,* 4 March 1976, 65; for information on Ernst see, for example, http://www.wwhp. org/News/ Newsletters/ 00fall.html accessed 19 May 2009.

76   "Yale's Women Crew to Get Locker Room," *New York Times,* 11 March 1976, 41; Marc Wortman, "Women Athletes Take the Spotlight," *Yale Alumni Magazine,* November 1993.

77   Laurie Johnston, "'Women Power' Protests 'Male Domination' of Wall St.," *New York Times,* 24 August 1973, 39.

78   Charlotte Curtis, "Miss America Pageant Is Picketed by 100 Women," *New York Times,* 8 September 1968, 81; Alice Echols, "Women's Liberation and Sixties Radicalism," in Griffith and Baker, eds., *Major Problems in American History Since 1945,* 400–401.

79   Echols, *Daring to Be Bad,* 96–98.

80   "Who's Come a Long Way, Baby?" *Time,* 31 August 1970.

81   "Coeds Throw Pills at Rally," *New York Times,* 23 April 1970, 30; Elizabeth Kolbert, "In the Air," *New Yorker,* 27 April 2009, http://www.newyorker.com/talk/comment/2009/04/ 27/090427taco_talk_kolbert, accessed 23 June 2009.

82   Evans, *Tidal Wave,* 41.

83   Mark Alden Branch, "A Very Special Saloon," *Yale Alumni Magazine,* April 1999; www.yalealumnimagazine.com/issues/99_04/morys.html, accessed 19 May 2009.

84   Ibid.; Mark W. Foster, Letters, *Yale Alumni Magazine,* November/December 2008; www.yalealumnimagazine.com/issues/2008_11/letters.html, accessed 19 May 2009.

85   Kesselman, "Women's Liberation and the Left," 24; photograph details at Manuscripts and Archives Digital Images Database, Yale University Library. After a class action suit filed by Anne Coffin Hanson, a Yale professor of art history, led to the revocation of Mory's liquor license, the famous establishment's Board of Governors relented in 1972 and changed the bylaws to permit women members; see Roberta Smith, "Anne Coffin Hanson, 82; Yale Professor of Art History," *New York Times,* 4 September 2004; "A Brief History," http://www.morysclub.org/history.php, accessed 19 May 2009.

86   Michael Knight, "Yale's Bar Gives In," *New York Times,* 30 March 1974, 1.

87   Judy Klemesrud, "Can Feminists Upstage Miss America?" *New York Times*, 8 September 1974, 58; Carlo M. Sardella, "'Miss America' Faces Ms.," *New York Times*, 1 September 1974, 47.

88   "GNHWPC," *Sister* (New Haven's women's liberation newsletter), 2, 10, October 1973, 3, Box 39-3, Folder 322, Hall-Hoag.

89   *ACT NOW*, vol. 3, 6, July 1971, 4, RH WL D1758, Wilcox Collection.

90   "Women's Credit Union: Economic Self Help," *Sister*, 1, 7 (June 1974): 1, Box 39-3, Folder 322/1/1, Hall-Hoag; Michael Knight, "Feminists Open Own Credit Union," *New York Times*, 27 August 1974, 37; Echols, "Nothing Distant About It," 160; Echols, *Daring to Be Bad*, 269–76.

91   ALFA flier—n.d. (after 1979—mentions 1979 March on Washington), Atlanta Lesbian Feminist Alliance, RH WL Eph 594, Wilcox Collection.

92   Kesselman, "Women's Liberation and the Left in New Haven," 24.

93   Abigail Adams to John Adams, 31 March 1776, in Mary Beth Norton and Ruth Alexander, eds., *Major Problems in American Women's History*, 3rd ed. (Boston: Houghton Mifflin, 2002), 70.

94   "The Declaration of Sentiments of the Seneca Falls Convention, 1848," reprinted in ibid. See also http://www.fordham.edu/halsall/mod/senecafalls.html, accessed 15 January 2010.

95   See, for example, http://memory.loc.gov/cgi-bin/query/I?suffrg:2:./temp/~ammem_ yvwd::displayType=1:m856sd=cph:m856sf=3g05585:@@@; http://memory.loc.gov/cgi-bin/query/I?suffrg:1:./temp/~ammem_yvwd::displayType=1:m856sd=cph:m856sf=3a23348 :@@@. Victoria Woodhull, the nation's first female presidential candidate, also drew extensively on America's founding ideals in her rhetoric. See, for example, "And the Truth Shall Make You Free: A Speech on the Principles of Social Freedom," 20 November 1871. During the nation's centennial year the National Woman Suffrage Association engaged extensively in patriotic protest. See Kathryn Kish Sklar and Thomas Dublin *Women and Social Movements in the United States, 1600–2000* (Alexandria, Va.: Alexander Street Press), database.

96   Evans, *Tidal Wave*, 76–77.

97   Letter from Norma Ojeman, president of Springfield, Ill., NOW, *off our backs: a women's news journal*, March 1972, 28, Box 39-3, Folder HH560, Hall-Hoag.

98   ARC, Part 3, "Michigan State University: Women Students," reel 168.

99   Evans, *Tidal Wave*, 42.

100   "Dinner Drama: Women's Liberation Acts," *Yale Daily News*, 25 February 1970, 1; Thomas Kent, "Women's Lib Meets," *Yale Daily News*, 26 February 1970. Kate Millet and Naomi Weisstein were keynote speakers.

101   "Dinner Drama: Women's Liberation Acts," 1.

102   Kent, "Women's Lib Meets."

103   Letter from Patricia H. Durgin, Syracuse, N.Y., *off our backs*, March 1972, 29, Box 39-3, Folder 560, Hall Hoag. In February NOW President Wilma Scott Heide had mooted the possibility of launching a tax protest to highlight the political status of America's women which, she said, amounted to "taxation without representation." See Laurie Johnston, "Women's Tax Rebellion Urged to Achieve Political Equality," *New York Times*, 13 February 1972, 32.

104   Klemesrud, "Can Feminists Upstage Miss America?" 58.

105   NOW Statement of Purpose.

106   NOW Legal Defense and Education Fund leaflet, "If you woke up tomorrow and discovered that you were a (boy)(girl), how would your life be different?" (1983), 4, Box 39-3, Folder 1124, Hall-Hoag.

107   "From the President Kathe Rauch," *NOW York Woman*, September 1979, 3 RH WL G1076, Wilcox Collection.

108   "Position paper—re: Forming a Harlem Branch," 1, Women for Racial and Economic Equality, Box 12, Folder 25, "Newspapers and Media," RH WL MS16, Wilcox Collection.

109   Pamphlet, "a proposal for a WOMEN'S BILL OF RIGHTS," Women for Racial and Economic Equality, Box 9, Folder "WBR: Women's Bill of Rights," RH WL MS16, Wilcox Collection.

110   "Jobs and Affirmative Action" (n.d., early 1980s), Women for Racial & Economic Equality, Box 7, Folder "Position Papers," RH WL MS16, Wilcox Collection.

111   In the month America celebrated its 200th birthday, some 35 women's magazines published special issues dedicated to the ERA. See Bailey, "She 'Can Bring Home the Bacon,'" 113, 122.

112   Grace Lichtenstein, "McSorley's Admits Women Under a New City Law," *New York Times*, 11 August 1970, 23.

113   ERAmerica pamphlet, "For full and permanent equality . . . The Equal Rights Amendment" (n.d.—late 1970s), Women for Racial and Economic Equality, Box 4, Folder "Equal Rights Amendment" and Flyer—American Association of University Women—supporting the ERA, WREE, Box 4, Folder 7, "Equal Rights Amendment," RH WL MS16, Wilcox Collection.

114   Gilmore, "The Dynamics of Second-Wave Feminist Activism," 101. Tennessee had become the 10th state to ratify, in April 1972 with votes of 70-0 in the House and 25-5 in the Senate. See "Tennessee Is 10th to Ratify Equal Rights Amendment," *New York Times*, 5 April 1972, 42.

115   Krska's response was to joke, "Maybe we shouldn't have given you the vote"; see "ERA Marches on to Another Loss," *Time*, 26 May 1980.

116   In his "I have a dream" speech, King had used the metaphor of the promissory note. See Martin Luther King, "I Have a Dream," in James Melvin Washington, *A Testament of Hope: The Essential Writings and Speeches of Martin Luther King, Jr.* (New York: HarperOne, 1990), 217.

117   New York Coalition for Equal Rights, "Equal Rights Amendment flier," 1975 in WREE, Box 4, Folder "ERA," RH WL MS16, Wilcox Collection.

118   Letty Cottin Pogrebin, "Sexism Rampant," *New York Times*, 19 March 1976, 32.

119   On the conference see, for example, Ellen Pratt Fout, "'A Miracle Occurred!': The Houston Committee of International Women's Year, Houston, 1977," *Houston Review of History and Culture* 1, Part 1 (2003): 4–11; and Marjorie J. Spruill, "Gender and America's Right Turn," in Schulman and Zelizer, eds., *Rightward Bound.*

120   Rosen, *The World Split Open*, 291–92; "Women March on Houston," *Time*, 28 November 1977; National Commission on the Observance of International Women's Year, Washington, D.C., *The Spirit of Houston: The First National Women's Conference: An Official Report to the President, the Congress and the People of the United States, March 1978*, 10.

121   Rosen, *The World Split Open*, 292; see also Evans, *Tidal Wave*, 140.

122   "Women March on Houston," *Time*, 5 December 1977.

123   Jennifer Dunning, "Women at Albany Meeting Vote to Support Abortion," *New York Times*, 11 July 1977, 24.

124   Joan Cook, "Delegates Are Preparing for Women's Conference," *New York Times*, 20 July 1977, 41.

125   Caroline Bird, "State Meetings: Every Woman Her Say," *The Spirit of Houston*, 99.

126   "Selection of Women's Conference Delegates Assailed," *New York Times*, 16 September 1977, 51; *Spirit of Houston*, 119.

127   See "The Torch Relay," *Spirit of Houston*, 193–203; "Women Relay the Movement's Torch from Seneca Falls to Houston," *New York Times*, 7 October 1977, 53; Judy Klemsrud, "At Houston Meeting, "A Kaleidoscope of American Womenhood"," *New York Times*, 19 November 1977, 47.

128   Rosen, *The World Split Open*, 291–93; see also photo by Diana Mary Henry.

129   "Women March on Houston" and "What Next for U.S. Women," *Time*, 5 December 1977.

130   Klemsrud, "At Houston Meeting," 22.

131   *Spirit of Houston*, 119.

132   "What Next for U.S. Women," *Time*, 5 December 1977.

133   Ibid.; Rosen, *The World Split Open*, 293–94; Anna Quindlen, "Women's Conference Approves Planks on Abortion and Rights for Homosexuals," *New York Times*, 21 November 1977, 44.

134   "What Next for U.S. Women," *Time*, 5 December 1977; Anna Quindlen, "Women's Conference: The Follow-Up Is Next," *New York Times*, 23 November 1977, 14.

135   "What Next for U.S. Women," *Time*, 5 December 1977. See also Evans, *Tidal Wave*, 142. Eleanor Smeal, president of NOW, described the Houston conference as a "rite of passage."

136   *Spirit of Houston*, 16, 195.

137   Ibid., 217; biographical information 248.

138   Donald R. Martin and Vicky Gordon Martin, "Barbara Jordan's Symbolic Use of Language in the Keynote Address to the National Women's Conference," *Southern Speech Communication Journal* 49, 3 (Spring 1984): 321, 325.

139   *Spirit of Houston*, 52.

140   Ibid., 149, 129, 133.

141   Ibid., 129; the question of the confidence on show at the conference is also discussed in "What Next for U.S. Women."

142   "Women March on Houston."

143   "What Next for U.S. Women"; Evans, *Tidal Wave*, 142.

144   Rosen, *The World Split Open*, 294.

Chapter 4. The Battles over Busing

1   John Kifner, "Violence Mars Busing in Boston," *New York Times*, 13 September 1974, 1, 16. In the following weeks, buses traveling into South Boston would be greeted with roadside signs stating "Nigger Go Home," "Boneheads," and "This Is Klan Country." See John Kifner, "South Boston, a 'Town' of Irishmen, Feels as if It's a Persecuted Belfast," *New York Times*, 21 September 1974, 40.

2   Robert Reinhold, "Boston Is Fearful in Busing Dispute," *New York Times*, 15 September 1974, 21.

3   Ibid.

4   Kifner, "Violence Mars Busing in Boston," 16.

5   In the fall of 1966, only 14 percent of black children attended predominantly white schools. By the end of 1968 more than 200 school districts had had their federal funding cut off by HEW. See Walter G. Stephan and Joe R. Feagin, eds., *School Desegregation: Past, Present, and Future* (New York: Plenum Press, 1980), 18.

6   J. Harvie Wilkinson, III, *From Brown to Bakke: The Supreme Court and School Integration, 1954–1978* (New York: Oxford University Press, 1978), 116.

7   Richard A. Pride, *The Political Uses of Racial Narratives: School Desegregation in Mobile, Alabama, 1954–1997* (Urbana: University of Illinois Press, 2002), 107.

8   "A Bad Day in Lamar," *Newsweek*, 16 March 1970, 26.

9   "Busing and Strikes: Schools in Turmoil," *Time*, 15 September 1975.

10   Wilkinson, *From Brown to Bakke*, 131. See, for example, James T. Wooten, "Parents in Charlotte, Even Those Who Favor Integration, Deeply Resent Racial Busing," *New York Times*, 7 October 1970, 34.

11   See Ronald P. Formisano, *Boston Against Busing: Race, Class, and Ethnicity in the 1960s and 1970s* (Chapel Hill: University of North Carolina Press, 1991), 7; Kifner, "South Boston, a "Town" of Irishmen," *New York Times*, 21 September 1974, 40; Ed Magnuson, "The Pleasure of Hating," *Time*, 21 March 1977; and Kifner, "A Tense, Troubled City," *New York Times*, 11 October 1974, 1, 46.

12   Wilkinson, *From Brown to Bakke*, 203; Formisano, *Boston Against Busing*, 44, 46; "Southie Fights On," *Time*, 23 September 1974.

13   Formisano, *Boston Against Busing*, 70; Louis P. Masur, *The Soiling of Old Glory: The Story of a Photograph That Shocked America* (New York: Bloomsbury, 2008), 39–41.

14   Wilkinson, *From Brown to Bakke*, 203.

15   Opinion polls regularly showed white opposition to busing running at around 80 percent. See James Bolner and Robert Shanley, *Busing: The Political and Judicial Process* (New York: Praeger, 1974), 238–41. A September 1973 Gallup poll indicated that a large majority of Americans supported integration, but only 5 percent supported busing; see Wilkinson, *From Brown to Bakke*, 202. There is a debate about the extent to which white opposition to busing was shaped by self-interest. Some scholars have concluded that "it is apparently the *symbolism* evoked by the prospect of *any* white children's forced intimate contact with blacks, rather than the *reality* of one's *own* children's contact, that triggers opposition to busing." See David O. Sears, Carl P. Hensler, and Leslie K. Speer, "Whites' Opposition to 'Busing': Self-Interest or Symbolic Politics?" *American Political Science Review* 73, 2 (June 1979): 382. Nevertheless, self-interest was much more important in predicting active involvement in the anti-busing movement. See Donald Philip Green and Jonathan A. Cowden, "Who Protests: Self-Interest and White Opposition to Busing," *Journal of Politics* 54, 2 (May 1992).

16   For one-way busing see Matthew D. Lassiter, "The Suburban Origins of 'Color-Blind' Conservatism: Middle-Class Consciousness in the Charlotte Busing Crisis," *Journal of Urban History* 30, 4 (May 2004): 557.

17   "The Busing Dilemma," *Time*, 22 September 1975. As Roy Wilkins pointed out in September 1972, of the 20 million students who were bused to school, only about 3 percent were bused for the purpose of effecting desegregation. See letter, Roy Wilkins to Senator Claiborne Pell, 19 September 1972, in Davison M. Douglas, ed., *School Busing: Constitutional and Political Developments*, vol. 2, *The Public Debate over Busing and Attempts to Restrict Its Use* (New York: Garland, 1994), 229.

18   "Southie Fights On."

19   One Gallup poll indicated that 60 percent of busing opponents based their position on their support for neighborhood schools. See Bolner and Shanley, 239.

20   Pride, *The Political Use of Racial Narratives*, 70.

21   Lassiter, "The Suburban Origins of 'Color-Blind' Conservatism," 550. See also comments of Charlotte resident Mrs. Reynolds—"It's just horrible all of this. My husband and I have worked for everything we have. Why do you think we moved to this neighborhood? Because of the schools so close, that's why." Quoted in James T. Wooten, "Parents in Charlotte, Even Those Who Favor Integration, Deeply Resent Racial Busing," *New York Times*, 7 October 1970, 34.

22   John Kifner, "Kennedy Jeered on Boston Busing," *New York Times*, 10 September 1974, 30.

23   Formisano, *Boston Against Busing*, 115.

24   Lassiter, "The Suburban Origins of 'Color-Blind' Conservatism," 571; Formisano, *Boston Against Busing*, 106. Anti-busing protesters in Louisville, Kentucky, wore t-shirts bearing the slogan "Oppose Tyranny" during September 1975; see "Busing and Strikes: Schools in Turmoil," *Time*, 15 September 1975.

25   Lassiter, "The Suburban Origins of 'Color-Blind' Conservatism," 562.

26   Formisano, *Boston Against Busing*, 192. Lassiter cites one Richmond parent and navy veteran who, having fought during World War II, was prepared to fight for "freedom . . . in my own country if I have to." Matthew D. Lassiter, *The Silent Majority: Suburban Politics in the Sunbelt South* (Princeton, N.J.: Princeton University Press, 2006), 19.

27   Wilkinson, *From* Brown *to* Bakke, 209–10.

28   SDS, Port Huron Statement, 1962, in Massimo Teodori, ed., *The New Left: A Documentary History* (Indianapolis: Bobbs-Merrill, 1969).

29   See David Farber and Jeff Roche, "Introduction," in Farber and Roche, eds., *The Conservative Sixties* (New York: Peter Lang, 2003), 9.

30   Formisano, *Boston Against Busing*, 3, 172, 190.

31   Jonathan Rieder, *Canarsie: The Jews and Italians of Brooklyn Against Liberalism* (Cambridge, Mass.: Harvard University Press, 1985), 205.

32   Boston activist Rosamond Tutela quoted in Joseph Rosenbloom, "They Came in Buses to Oppose Imbalance Law," *Boston Globe*, 2 March 1973, 12.

33   Pride, *The Political Use of Racial Narratives*, 85.

34   Richard A. Pride and J. David Woodard, *The Burden of Busing: The Politics of Desegregation in Nashville, Tennessee* (Knoxville: University of Tennessee Press, 1985), 71.

35   Lassiter, "The Suburban Origins of 'Color-Blind' Conservatism," 562.

36   Ben A. Franklin, "Impact of White Boycott Unclear as Charlotte Schools Begin Busing," *New York Times*, 10 September 1970, 18; Lassiter, *The Silent Majority*, 167.

37   "9 Students Hurt in Pontiac Clash," *New York Times*, 9 September 1971, 21. McCabe's picket of the Fisher body plant resulted in the closing of the car assembly plant, also in Pontiac, after it ran out of car bodies to work on. See Jerry M. Flint, "Antibusing Pickets Close 2 Car Plants," *New York Times*, 15 September 1971, 22.

38   Patricia Zacharias, "Irene McCabe and Her Battle Against Busing," *Detroit News*; http://apps.detnews.com/apps/history/index.php?id=161, accessed 15 January 2010.

39   McCabe always denied that she and her group were racist—though they did accept the support of Dearborn Mayor Orville Hubbard, a long-time opponent of open housing. "Busing Protesters Reach Hills Midway on March to Capital," *New York Times*, 2 April 1972, 23 and Zacharias, "Irene McCabe and Her Battle Against Busing."

40   "Michigan Women Hike 620 Miles to Urge Congress to Ban Busing," *New York Times*, 28 April 1972, 9. The women had apparently been hoping for a crowd of 30,000; see Zacharias, "Irene McCabe and Her Battle Against Busing."

41   Masur, *The Soiling of Old Glory*, 2.

42   Formisano, *Boston Against Busing*, 150–51.

43   Kerrigan description from *New York Times*, 4 April 1974, 37.

44   Formisano, *Boston Against Busing*, 76, Kifner, "Kennedy Jeered on Boston Busing," 1, 30; Alan Lupo, *Liberty's Chosen Home: The Politics of Violence in Boston* (Boston: Little, Brown, 1977), 200–205; "Southie Fights On."

45   James S. Kunen, "Who Are These People?" *Boston Magazine*, November 1974, 51.

46   Kifner, "Kennedy Jeered on Boston Busing," 30.

47   http://bioguide.congress.gov/scripts/biodisplay.pl?index=H000566; Mark Feeney, "Louise Day Hicks, Icon of Tumult, Dies," *Boston Globe*, 22 October 2003; Formisano, *Boston Against Busing*, 2.

48   Ibid., 30.

49   John Kifner, "3d Week of Boston Busing Ends in Protest March," *New York Times*, 5 October 1974, 14.

50   Formisano, *Boston Against Busing*, 156.

51   J. Anthony Lukas, "Who Owns 1776?" *New York Times Sunday Magazine*, 18 May 1975, 39.

52   *Boston News Digest*, March 1976, 19, in ROAR materials, Box 76.46-7, Folder 3763, Hall-Hoag. The cartoon was protesting the implementation of the latest phase of Judge Garrity's desegregation plan.

53   John Kifner, "6,000 in Boston Protest Busing," *New York Times*, 16 December 1974, 19.

54   Lukas, "Who Owns 1776?" 40–41.

55   Formisano, *Boston Against Busing*, 105.

56   John Kifner, "Guardsmen in Boston for Busing Today," *New York Times*, 8 September 1975, 1. An anonymous postcard, distributed in the fall of 1974, which urged civil disobedience, was signed "Patricia Henry." See Lupo, *Liberty's Chosen Home*, 173. See also Leaflet, "Let It Be Known to All: Freedom Was Born Here, We Shall Not Let It Die Here," undated, in STOP materials, Box 76.46-8, Folder 3360, Hall-Hoag (this leaflet compared Louise Day Hicks to George Washington and her followers to latter-day Winter Soldiers); and Louise Day Hicks, "From the National ROAR Office," *Boston News Digest*, February 1976, 8, in ROAR materials, Box 76.46-7, Folder 3763, Hall-Hoag.

57   Louise Day Hicks, testimony before Subcommittee No. 5, House Judiciary Committee, 24 May 1972, in Douglas, ed., *School Busing*, 216, 218–19.

58   Jeffrey A. Raffel and Barry R. Morstain, "Wilmington, Delaware: Merging City and Suburban School Systems" in Charles V. Willie and Susan L. Greenblatt, eds., *Community Politics and Educational Change: Ten School Systems Under Court Order* (New York: Longman, 1981), 103.

59   Letter, Roy Wilkins to Senator Claiborne Pell, 19 September 1972, in Douglas, ed., *School Busing*, 229. See also Lukas, "Who Owns 1776?"

60   John Kifner, "2 Boston Rallies at Odds on Busing," *New York Times*, 19 May 1975, 19.

61   Masur, *The Soiling of Old Glory*, 1, 4, 19 (biographical information 1–19). See also "Boston Heats Up Once Again," *Time*, 3 May 1976; Formisano, *Boston Against Busing*, 150.

62   Formisano, *Boston Against Busing*, 17, 19, 121, 158, x.

63   Ibid., 66, xi.

64   Ibid., 69, 140.

65   Ibid., 155, 53.

66   Ibid., 156.

67   Ibid., 190; Rieder, *Canarsie*, 1, 203.

68   Formisano, *Boston Against Busing*, 138.

69   Lassiter, "The Suburban Origins of 'Color-Blind' Conservatism," 561, 558.

70   Sal Giarratani, "City Scene: The Bus Stops in '78?" *Regional Review*, 11 January 1978, 4, in STOP materials, Box 76.46-8, Folder 3360, Hall-Hoag.

71   Formisano, *Boston Against Busing*, 142. The "Patricia Henry" postcard mentioned above noted that Martin Luther King, Jr., had risen to prominence "fundamentally because he taught his followers to resort to civil disobedience, that is, to refuse to honor or obey laws they considered to be unfair, unreasonable, etc." Quoted in Lupo, *Liberty's Chosen Home*, 173. John Kerrigan may well have had King in mind when he urged his fellow activists to be "so non-violent that we will win the Nobel Peace Prize." Formisano, *Boston Against Busing*, 75.

72   Lassiter, *The Silent Majority*, 285–86. Anti-busing activists in Canarsie, New York, spoke of the need to win "rights" for white ethnics and to follow the example of other groups, particularly black civil rights organizations, by organizing and mobilizing. See Rieder, *Canarsie*, 203–6.

73   See Rieder, *Canarsie*, 203–6.

74   Formisano, *Boston Against Busing*, 141; Lassiter, "The Suburban Origins of 'Color-Blind' Conservatism," 562.

75   See, for example, Joyce Miller Lutcovich and Elaine Clyburn, "Erie, Pennsylvania: The Effect of State Initiative"; Raffel and Morstain, "Wilmington, Delaware: Merging City and Suburban School Systems"; and Amelia Cirilo-Medina and Ross Purdy, "The South and Southwest: Corpus Christi, Texas: A Tri-Ethnic Approach," all in Willie and Greenblatt, eds., *Community Politics and Educational Change*.

76   Formisano, *Boston Against Busing*, 141.

77   Alan Lupo in Henry Hampton and Steve Fayer, eds., *Voices of Freedom: An Oral History of the Civil Rights Movement from the 1950s Through the 1980s* (New York: Bantam, 1990), 611–12.

78   Pride, *The Political Use of Racial Narratives*, 104.

79   John Kifner, "Blacks Urged to Attend Boston Schools," *New York Times*, 16 September 1974, 14. A 2-mile convoy was held 14 October 1974. See Wayne King, "Whites in Boston Score Democrats," *New York Times*, 15 October 1974, 15.

80   Masur, *The Soiling of Old Glory*, 48; Lukas, "Who Owns 1776?"

81   Kifner, "South Boston, a 'Town' of Irishmen," 40. See also Formisano, *Boston Against Busing*, 139–40. The chant "Hell, no! We won't go" was also used.

82   "Busing and Strikes: Schools in Turmoil," *Time*, 15 September 1975; Lupo, *Liberty's Chosen Home*, 204.

83   Lupo in Hampton and Fayer, eds., *Voices of Freedom*, 612.

84   "To The Editors," *Time*, 13 October 1975.

85   Kunen, "Who Are These People?" 86.

86   Formisano, *Boston Against Busing*, 190, 236. See also Steve Fraser and Gary Gerstle, eds., *The Rise and Fall of the New Deal Order, 1930–1980* (Princeton, N.J.: Princeton University Press, 1989).

87   Nixon quoted in Lassiter, *The Silent Majority*, 5.

88   Dean Kotlowski, *Nixon's Civil Rights: Politics, Principle, and Policy* (Cambridge, Mass.: Harvard University Press, 2002), 32–33.

89   Richard Nixon, "School Desegregation: A Free and Open Society" (24 March 1970), in Douglas, ed., *School Busing*, 129, 135.

90   Lawrence J. McAndrews, "The Politics of Principle: Richard Nixon and School Desegregation," *Journal of Negro History* 83, 3 (Summer 1998): 190; Bolner and Shanley, *Busing*, 156; Dan T. Carter, *The Politics of Rage: George Wallace, the Origins of the New Conservatism, and the Transformation of American Politics* (Baton Rouge: Louisiana State University Press, 2000), 425.

91   Carter, *The Politics of Rage*, 426.

92   Ibid., 423.

93   Donald Critchlow, "Conservatism Reconsidered: Phyllis Schlafly and Grassroots Conservatism," in Farber and Roche, eds., *The Conservative Sixties*, 125.

94   Quoted in Kurt Schuparr, "'A Great White Light': The Political Emergence of Ronald Reagan," in Farber and Roche, eds., *The Conservative Sixties*, 106.

95   Quoted in Lassiter, *The Silent Majority*, 211.

96   Second 1980 Presidential Debate, 28 October 1980; http://www.pbs.org/newshour/ debatingourdestiny/80debates/cart4.html, accessed 9 March 2009.

97   "Michigan Women Hike 620 Miles," 9.

98   Lassiter, *The Silent Majority*, 3, 6; Lassiter, "The Suburban Origins of 'Color-Blind' Conservatism," 551. See Lisa McGirr, *Suburban Warriors: The Origins of the New American Right* (Princeton, N.J.: Princeton University Press, 2001); Donald Critchlow, *Phyllis Schlafly and Grassroots Conservatism: A Woman's Crusade* (Princeton, N.J.: Princeton University Press, 2005).

99   Lassiter, "The Suburban Origins of 'Color-Blind' Conservatism," 550, 552.

100   See Lillian B. Rubin, *Busing and Backlash: White Against White in a California School District* (Berkeley: University of California Press, 1972), 78, 168–83; Rieder, *Canarsie*, 231; Lutcovich and Clyburn, "Erie, Pennsylvania,", 74.

101   See ROAR materials, Box 76.46-7, Folder 3763, Hall-Hoag. The *Boston News Digest* opposed the ERA in October 1976.

102   STOP leaflet, November–December 1977 in STOP materials, Box 76.46-8, Folder "3360,.

103   See http://www.conservativeusa.org/whoweare.htm, accessed 14 May 2007.

104   "'Impossible' Is Not in Their Vocabulary," *Conservative Digest*, February 1976; Conservative Caucus recruitment letter from Governor Meldrim Thomson, Jr., 1975, 3, both in Box 76.49-5, Folder 1750, Hall-Hoag.

105   "'Impossible' Is Not in Their Vocabulary."

106   Conservative Caucus recruitment letter.

107   Ibid., 1.

108   Rubin, *Busing and Backlash*, 148.

109   Rieder, *Canarsie*, 237, 238, 240.

110   Formisano, *Boston Against Busing*, 195–96.

111 Flynn governed from the center—his administration had a good record in hiring minorities, and he offered support to limited efforts to end housing segregation.

112 Formisano, *Boston Against Busing*, 200–202.

113 Ibid., 194.

114 Rieder, *Canarsie*, 243–63.

115 Formisano, *Boston Against Busing*, 198–99, 200.

Chapter 5. The Tax Revolt

1 Isaac William Martin, *The Permanent Tax Revolt: How the Property Tax Transformed American Politics* (Stanford, Calif.: Stanford University Press, 2008), 50; "SM County Group Burns Tax Assessment Notices," *Palo Alto Times*, 20 April 1977, MEJ Records, Box 18, Folder 3.

2 Martin, *The Permanent Tax Revolt*, 101; "Sound and Fury over Taxes," *Time*, 19 June 1978.

3 "Sound and Fury over Taxes"; Clarence Y. H. Lo, *Small Property Versus Big Government: Social Origins of the Property Tax Revolt* (Berkeley: University of California Press, 1990), 1; Howard Jarvis with Robert Pack, *I'm Mad as Hell: The Exclusive Story of the Tax Revolt and Its Leader* (New York: Times Books, 1979), 13, 15.

4 Martin, *The Permanent Tax Revolt*, 2, 3; Lo, *Small Property Versus Big Government*, 1, 2.

5 Ideas promoted by high-profile economists Milton Friedman, Arthur Laffer, Jude Wanniski, and Robert Mundell.

6 Martin, *The Permanent Tax Revolt*, 126.

7 Bruce J. Schulman, *The Seventies: The Great Shift in American Culture, Society, and Politics* (New York: Da Capo Press, 2002), 205.

8 Lo, *Small Property Versus Big Government*, 141.

9 Schulman, *The Seventies*, 205.

10 Ibid., 205–6; Martin, *The Permanent Tax Revolt*, 44–45; Robert Kuttner, *Revolt of the Haves: Tax Rebellions and Hard Times* (New York: Simon and Schuster, 1980), 31.

11 Martin, *The Permanent Tax Revolt*, 6, 9.

12 See, for example, Richard D. Pomp, "The Victims of Property-Tax Reform," *New York Times*, 15 June 1980, CN18. For a history of the property tax and the attempts to reform it, see Kuttner, *Revolt of the Haves*, 109–46.

13 Martin, *The Permanent Tax Revolt*, 60.

14 Schulman, *The Seventies*, 206.

15 Ibid., 206–7; Jarvis, *I'm Mad as Hell*, 32, 36, 39; David O. Sears and Jack Citrin, *Tax Revolt: Something for Nothing in California* (Cambridge, Mass.: Harvard University Press, 1982), 20.

16 Lo, *Small Property Versus Big Government*, 13–15; Sears and Citrin, *Tax Revolt*, 21, 22; Jarvis, *I'm Mad as Hell*.

17 Previous two paragraphs from Jarvis, *I'm Mad as Hell*, chap. 8. Robert Kuttner is one of those to describe Jarvis as a "crank" and a "nut"—see Kuttner, *Revolt of the Haves*, 36–37.

18 "Maniac or Messiah?" *Time*, 19 June 1978; Jarvis, *I'm Mad as Hell*, 75. See also William Safire, "Taxpayers' Revolt," *New York Times*, 27 February 1978, A19

and "Generals of a Rebellion by California Taxpayers: Howard Arnold Jarvis and Paul Gann," *New York Times*, 8 June 1978, A25.

19   Jarvis, *I'm Mad as Hell*, 40, 43, 47, 53; Martin, *The Permanent Tax Revolt*, 101–3.

20   Martin, *The Permanent Tax Revolt*, 104.

21   Lo, *Small Property Versus Big Government*, 106.

22   Jarvis, *I'm Mad as Hell*, 112, 55, 88. Big business feared that shortfalls in revenue caused by a curtailed property tax would result in the tax burden being shifted onto corporations.

23   Schulman, *The Seventies*, 210–11.

24   Martin, *The Permanent Tax Revolt*, 104.

25   Jarvis, *I'm Mad as Hell*, 83; Lo, *Small Property Versus Big Government*, 104.

26   Schulman, *The Seventies*, 211; Martin, *The Permanent Tax Revolt*, 105.

27   Schulman, *The Seventies*, 211; Sears and Citrin, *Tax Revolt*, 30; Kuttner, *Revolt of the Haves*, 74–77, 81–91.

28   "Maniac or Messiah."

29   Jarvis, *I'm Mad as Hell*, 178–79; "Sound and Fury over Taxes."

30   Martin, *The Permanent Tax Revolt*, 52, 55, 65, 66, 69, 70, 113–14.

31   For a good account of the movement's roots in postwar American conservatism see Lisa McGirr, *Suburban Warriors: The Origins of the New American Right* (Princeton, N.J.: Princeton University Press, 2001).

32   Martin, *The Permanent Tax Revolt*, 3; Lo, *Small Property Versus Big Government*, 79, 96.

33   Martin, *The Permanent Tax Revolt*, 55.

34   Jane Seagrave, "Conservative Group Takes on 'the Elite,'" *Albany (Oregon) Democrat-Herald*, 29 July 1982, 11 in WH WL Eph215, Wilcox Collection.

35   Robert O. Self, *American Babylon: Race and the Struggle for Postwar Oakland* (Princeton, N.J.: Princeton University Press, 2003), 306–7; ARC, Part 3, Black Panther Party, reel 123.

36   Martin, *The Permanent Tax Revolt*, 59; "About the Citizens Action League," MEJ Records, Box 18, Folder 3.

37   "Why the Citizens Action League," MEJ Records, Box 18, Folder 3; Martin, *The Permanent Tax Revolt*, 51.

38   CAL press release, 7 December 1977, 1, MEJ Records, Box 18, Folder 2. CAL activists also sang specially penned songs, including "Which Side Are You On?," "We Are the Citizens Action League" and "Take Us Up to the Capitol," CAL song sheet, MEJ Records, Box 18, Folder 3.

39   "Why the Citizens Action League" and "About the Citizens Action League."

40   Martin, *The Permanent Tax Revolt*, 62, 65; Derek Shearer, "CAP: New Breeze in the Windy City," *Ramparts*, 11 October 1973, 12–13.

41   Derek Shearer, "CAP: New Breeze in the Windy City," *Ramparts*, 11 October 1973, 13–15.

42   Martin, *The Permanent Tax Revolt*, 69, 70; Schulman, *The Seventies*, 207; Lo, *Small Property Versus Big Government*, 180; Kuttner, *Revolt of the Haves*, 310–11.

43   Schulman, *The Seventies*, 207–8.

44   Lo, *Small Property Versus Big Government*, 180–82; Martin, *The Permanent Tax Revolt*, 69–70.

45   Martin, *The Permanent Tax Revolt*, 94, 77.

46   Leaflet, "About the Movement for Economic Justice" and leaflet, "Tax Justice Project," in ARC, Part 4, Movement for Economic Justice, reel 221.

47 Martin, *The Permanent Tax Revolt*, 99.

48 Ronald Smothers, "Welfare Activist Plans New Group," *New York Times*, 17 December 1972, 49; "Dr. George Wiley Feared Drowned," *New York Times*, 10 August 1973, 13; Martin, *The Permanent Tax Revolt*, 75, 77, 99. For the welfare rights movement see, for example, Premilla Nadasen, *Welfare Warriors: The Welfare Rights Movement in the United States* (New York: Routledge, 2004).

49 Martin, *The Permanent Tax Revolt*, 77, 95, 99; "Dr George Wiley Feared Drowned"; Nick Kitz, "Remembering George Wiley," in ARC, Part 4, Movement for Economic Justice, reel 221; George A. Wiley, "The Need for a Taxpayer's Uprising," 1, 3, MEJ Records, Box 11, Folder 2, WHS. On tax clinics see Wiley, "The Need for a Taxpayer's Uprising," 3 and E. Edward Stephens, "Free and 'Impartial' Tax Clinics May Soon Dot the Countryside," *Evening Bulletin*, 14 January 1974 and Nick Lalli, "Free Tax Clinics Set for 46 Cities," *Federal Times*, 4 April 1973, MEJ Records, Box 22, Folder 11, WHS.

50 Lo, *Small Property Versus Big Government*, xi, xii, xiii.

51 Martin, *The Permanent Tax Revolt*, 59; Lo, *Small Property Versus Big Government*, 57–58, 60.

52 David Lowery and Lee Sigelman, "Understanding the Tax Revolt: Eight Explanations," *American Political Science Review* 75, 4 (December 1981): 969.

53 Lo, *Small Property Versus Big Government*, 72, 73.

54 Ibid., 75; Arthur O' Sullivan, Terri A. Saxton, and Steven M. Sheffrin, *Property Taxes and Tax Revolts: The Legacy of Proposition 13* (Cambridge: Cambridge University Press, 1995), 3.

55 Lo, *Small Property Versus Big Government*, 3.

56 Ibid., 79. In Culver City, 1966, tax protest leader Bruce Kay had addressed a rally of 700 and declared that "the voice of the people will be heard" (104).

57 Ibid., 164–66.

58 Letter, February 1972, from Donald A. Feder, National Chairman, New Right Coalition; "Boston Manifesto"; Helen E. Sullivan, "Pickets Protest State Tax," *Sunday Herald Traveler*, 27 June 1971; Gordon D. Hall, " "New Right" group has a little old, and a lot new," *Sunday Herald Traveler*, 26 March 1972, 20; NRC posters—all in New Right Coalition, Box 4-3, Folder 790/1/4, Hall-Hoag.

59 http://www.donfeder.com, accessed 1 August 2008; Martin, *The Permanent Tax Revolt*, 113–14.

60 Lo, *Small Property Versus Big Government*, 162, 160.

61 Jarvis, *I'm Mad as Hell*, 110–11.

62 "President Reagan Warns of the Dangers of the Welfare State, 1964," in Robert Griffith and Paula Baker, eds., *Major Problems in American History Since 1945* (Boston: Houghton Mifflin, 2001), 221–23.

63 Schulman, *The Seventies*, 209. For the role of public sector unions in the rise of New Right conservatism, see Joseph A. McCartin, "'A Wagner Act for Public Employees': Labor's Deferred Dream and the Rise of Conservatism, 1970–1976," *Journal of American History* 95, 1 (June 2008); Joseph A. McCartin, "Turnabout Years: Public Sector Unionism and the Fiscal Crisis," in Bruce J. Schulman and Julian E. Zelizer, eds., *Rightward Bound: Making American Conservative in the 1970s* (Cambridge, Mass.: Harvard University Press, 2008).

64 Letter—c. Nov 1978, from Howard Jarvis—"Dear Fellow Taxpayer," in American Tax Reduction Movement, RH WL Eph 354, Folder 1, Wilcox Collection.

65 Jarvis, *I'm Mad as Hell*, 113.

66 Lo, *Small Property Versus Big Government*, 36.

67   Ibid., 2, 36, 79.

68   Jarvis, *I'm Mad as Hell,* 52.

69   Lo, *Small Property Versus Big Government,* 76; Jarvis, *I'm Mad as Hell,* 29.

70   Jarvis, *I'm Mad as Hell,* 13.

71   Martin, *The Permanent Tax Revolt,* 114.

72   *Taxing Times: The Official Newsletter of the American Tax Reduction Movement,* c. 1978–1979, 2, in Box 60-1, Folder 2429, Hall-Hoag.

73   MEJ, "Tax Justice Project," leaflet, in ARC, Part 4, Movement for Economic Justice, reel 221.

74   Flyer, Massachusetts People's Bicentennial Coalition—"Citizens of Massachusetts! Taxpayers' Revolt!," MEJ Records, Box 22, Folder 17.

75   Martin, *The Permanent Tax Revolt,* 3; Lo, *Small Property Versus Big Government,* 70.

76   Lo, *Small Property Versus Big Government,* 104, 171–72. The cry "Taxation without representation" was widespread—see, for example, Alan Crawford, "The Taxfighters Are Coming!" *Conservative Digest,* November 1975, 13–14, reprinted in Ronald Story and Bruce Laurie, *The Rise of Conservatism in America, 1945–2000* (Boston: Bedford/St. Martin's, 2008), 100–103.

77   Crawford, "The Taxfighters Are Coming!" 102.

78   Joseph F. Sullivan, "Trenton Topics: Group Asks Repeal of State Income Tax," *New York Times,* 23 August 1976, 53; "Trenton Topics: Income Tax Opponents Plan Rally in Front of the State House Today," *New York Times,* 18 September 1976, 51; "Jersey "Tea Party" Planned for Byrne," *New York Times,* 19 September 1976, 30.

79   "Tax-Cut Group, Meeting in St. Louis, Plans Strategy," *New York Times,* 30 July 1978, 18.

80   "Dallas Rejects Bid for a 30 percent Tax Cut," *New York Times,* 19 January 1981, A18.

81   See Lo, *Small Property Versus Big Government,* xi, 36. For a broader discussion of this see Lizabeth Cohen, *A Consumers' Republic: The Politics of Mass Consumption in Postwar America* (New York: Knopf, 2003).

82   Jarvis, *I'm Mad as Hell,* 6–7.

83   Lo, *Small Property Versus Big Government,* 160.

84   Ibid., 56.

85   Ibid., 67.

86   Martin, *The Permanent Tax Revolt,* 126. See, for example, Thomas Byrne Edsall with Mary D. Edsall, *Chain Reaction: The Impact of Race, Rights, and Taxes on American Politics* (New York: Norton, 1991), 130–31; Kuttner, *Revolt of the Haves,* 17.

87   *Taxing Times: The Official Newsletter of the American Tax Reduction Movement,* c. Nov 1978, 1, 2, in Box 60-1, Folder 2429, Hall-Hoag; Adam Clymer, "California Vote Seen as Evidence of U.S. Tax Revolt," *New York Times,* 8 June 1978, A23; Jarvis, *I'm Mad as Hell,* 178–19; Lo, *Small Property Versus Big Government,* 1–2.

88   Lo, *Small Property Versus Big Government,* 183; O'Sullivan, Saxton, and Sheffrin, *Property Taxes and Tax Revolts,* 1; Jarvis, *I'm Mad as Hell,* 178–79; Edsall and Edsall, *Chain Reaction,* 131. For a brief history of tax limitation efforts across the U.S. in the aftermath of Proposition 13, see Kuttner, *Revolt of the Haves,* 275–306.

89   Schulman, *The Seventies,* 231.

90   John M. Lee, "The 70's: America Learns to Expect a Little Less," *New York Times,* 16 December 1979, F1, 11.

91 *Phyllis Schlafly Report* 7, 8 (March 1974): 2, in Box 45-1, Folder 557/2/1, Hall-Hoag.

92 Martin, *The Permanent Tax Revolt*, 1.

93 Jarvis, *I'm Mad as Hell*, 39, 102; Martin, *The Permanent Tax Revolt*, 128–30; John Micklethwait and Adrian Wooldridge, *The Right Nation: Conservative Power in America* (New York: Penguin, 2004), 89; Sean Wilentz, *The Age of Reagan: A History, 1974–2008* (New York: HarperCollins, 2008), 121.

94 Milton Friedman, "The Message from California," *Newsweek*, 19 June 1978, 26.

95 Steven V. Roberts, "House G. O. P. Freshman Are Speaking Up on Party Issues," *New York Times*, 29 October 1979, A16.

96 "Power *Back* to the People!" *Conservative Digest*, February 1976, in Conservative Caucus, Box 49-5, Folder 1750, Hall-Hoag.

97 Leaflet, "An Introduction to the Conservative Caucus," n.d., in Conservative Caucus, Box 49-5, Folder 1750, Hall-Hoag.

98 Ibid.

99 Letter, Meldrim Thomas, Jr., 1975, 1; "An Introduction to the Conservative Caucus."

100 Leslie Wayne, "The States Look at Supply Side," *New York Times*, 31 October 1982, F4.

101 Jarvis, *I'm Mad as Hell*, 55.

102 O'Sullivan, Saxton, and Sheffrin, *Property Taxes and Tax Revolts*, 3; Sears and Citrin, *Tax Revolt*, 31; John Herbers, "A Year After Proposition 13, Government Bodies Vie to Trim Taxes and Costs," *New York Times*, 4 June 1979, B33.

103 Jarvis, *I'm Mad as Hell*, 147; Kuttner, *Revolt of the Haves*, 81–91.

104 Adam Clymer, "Tax Revolt: An Idea Whose Time Has Come?" *New York Times*, 7 January 1979, AS3, 18.

105 Judith Miller, "Carter and Byrd Ask for Fiscal Restraint," *New York Times*, 11 June 1978, 33.

106 Martin, *The Permanent Tax Revolt*, 111.

107 Ibid., 109, 110.

108 Lo, *Small Property Versus Big Government*, 5, 47; Sears and Citrin, *Tax Revolt*, 235.

109 Micklethwait and Woolridge, *The Right Nation*, 88.

110 Jarvis, *I'm Mad as Hell*, 284; Martin, *The Permanent Tax Revolt*, 126.

111 Martin, *The Permanent Tax Revolt*, 16.

112 John Herbers, "After Jaws II, the Taxpayers Are Still Restless," *New York Times*, 8 June 1980, E5.

113 Sears and Citrin, *Tax Revolt*, 44, 47, 50; Lo, 65; O'Sullivan, Saxton, and Sheffrin, *Property Taxes and Tax Revolts*, 3; Kuttner, *Revolt of the Haves*, 18, 93–94. CAL was one progressive organization that urged elimination of "waste" and "fat" and introduction of efficiency savings. See CAL Tax Campaign Bulletin (September 3) and CAL Poster, MEJ Records, Box 18, Folder 3.

114 Sears and Citrin, *Tax Revolt*, 47; Lo, *Small Property Versus Big Government*, 65.

115 Jarvis, *I'm Mad as Hell*, 111; Edsall and Edsall, *Chain Reaction*, 130.

116 Sears and Citrin, *Tax Revolt*, 168, 185; see also Roger Wilkins, "California Tax Vote: Blacks Worry About Racism," *New York Times*, 23 June 1978, A12.

117 Martin, *The Permanent Tax Revolt*, 106. As Kevin Kruse has shown in his recent study of Atlanta, one consequence of desegregation in the "City Too Busy to Hate" during the 1950s was "white flight," whereby increasing numbers

of middle-class whites left the city to live in the suburbs. In the process they abandoned public spaces that had been desegregated—such as parks, golf courses, swimming pools and public transportation—and came increasingly to rely on "private" alternatives. As Kruse has demonstrated, they also "fought to take their finances with them," thereby staging an "early, though often overlooked, tax revolt, rebelling against the use of their taxes to support municipal spaces and services that they no longer used." In 1962 voters defeated a proposed bond issue designed to fund a series of public works and civic improvements. "Ultimately," argues Kruse, "the politics of privatization and the tax revolt" enjoyed strength and support in the largely white world of suburbia—where residents found it easy to "free themselves from what they regarded as an unfair tax system" by adopting localist arguments—"one that insisted on keeping tax revenues at home, not redistributing them across the metropolitan area." The color-blind discourse of the tax revolt and the suburban context in which it was often rooted, has thus obscured the fact that both the tax revolt and the broader conservative politics with which it became associated, were "in no small measure, a product of . . . urban struggles over race and class." Kevin M. Kruse, "The Politics of Race and Public Space: Desegregation, Privatization, and the Tax Revolt in Atlanta," *Journal of Urban History* 31, 5 (July 2005), esp. 610–13, 628–30.

118   Esdall and Edsall, *Chain Reaction*, 131.

119   Ellen Stern Harris, "An Alternative to Helpless Outrage," *Los Angeles Times*, 5 October 1975, MEJ Records, Box 18, Folder 3.

120   Sears and Citrin, *Tax Revolt*, 8. As Jarvis put it, "since Watergate, I suppose, the people don't believe a Goddamned word a politician says." Jarvis, *I'm Mad as Hell*, 50.

121   Carter quoted in Martin, *The Permanent Tax Revolt*, 126. See also Kuttner, *Revolt of the Haves*, 27.

122   Schulman, *The Seventies*, 216; Edsall and Edsall, *Chain Reaction*, 140.

Chapter 6. The Anti-Abortion Movement

1   "25,000 in Capital Call for Amendment to Outlaw Abortion," *New York Times*, 23 January 1975, 15.

2   James Risen and Judy L. Thomas, *Wrath of Angels: The American Abortion War* (New York: Basic Books, 1998), 23–31; *Roe v. Wade*, http://www.law.cornell.edu/supct/html/historics/ USSC_CR_0410_0113_ZO.html, accessed 6 January 2010.

3   Dallas A. Blanchard, *The Anti-Abortion Movement and the Rise of the Religious Right: From Polite to Fiery Protest* (New York: Twayne, 1994), 29.

4   Risen and Thomas, *Wrath of Angels*, 10–14.

5   Taken from ibid., 10–16.

6   Ibid., 16–17; Connie Page, *The Right to Lifers: Who They Are, How They Operate, Where They Get Their Money* (New York: Summit, 1983), 51.

7   Blanchard, *The Anti-Abortion Movement*, 52, 62; Page, *The Right to Lifers*, 85.

8   Risen and Thomas, *Wrath of Angels*, 39.

9   Blanchard, *The Anti-Abortion Movement*, 63, 69.

10   Ibid., 55, 59.

11   William Booth, "Doctor Killed During Abortion Protest," *Washington Post*, 11 March 1993, A01; Risen and Thomas, *Wrath of Angels*, 339–44.

12 Risen and Thomas, *Wrath of Angels*, 153–54; Adam Clymer, "Former Rep. Henry Hyde is Dead at 83," *New York Times*, 30 November 2007.

13 Blanchard, *The Anti-Abortion Movement*, 90, Risen and Thomas, *Wrath of Angels*, 131.

14 Bill Mears, "Justices Uphold Ban on Abortion Procedure," CNN.com law center, 18 April 2007; http://www.cnn.com/2007/LAW/04/18/scotus.abortion/, accessed 24 January 2010.

15 Richard L. Hughes, "Burning Birth Certificates and Atomic Tupperware Parties: Creating the Antiabortion Movement in the Shadow of the Vietnam War," *Historian* 68, 3 (Fall 2006): 542.

16 Ibid.; Richard L. Hughes, "'The Civil Rights Movement of the 1990s?': The Anti-Abortion Movement and the Struggle for Racial Justice," *Oral History Review* 33, 2 (2006): 5.

17 Hughes, "Burning Birth Certificates," 546.

18 Page, *The Right to Lifers*, 67–69.

19 Risen and Thomas, *Wrath of Angels*, 60–61; Hughes, "'The Civil Rights Movement of the 1990s?'," 5–6; Charles Fager, "Abortion and Civil War," 2, www.kimopress.com/ abortion.html, accessed 15 May 2007, 1–3.

20 Risen and Thomas, *Wrath of Angels*, 62.

21 Blanchard, *The Anti-Abortion Movement*, 63.

22 For a detailed discussion of O'Keefe's life and activist career see Risen and Thomas, *Wrath of Angels*, 43–77.

23 Hughes, "'The Civil Rights Movement of the 1990s?'," 14–15.

24 "Operation Rescue: *A Week of Victory!*," *May Pro-Life Newsbrief* (May 1988, publication of Project Life, 1–2, in Operation Rescue, Box 1-7, Folder 616, Hall-Hoag.

25 Randall Terry, "Operation Rescue: The Civil-Rights Movement of the Nineties," *Policy Review—Washington* 47 (Winter 1989): 82.

26 Ibid.

27 New International Version.

28 Terry, "Operation Rescue," 83. For Operation Rescue's imitation and adoption of civil rights movement tactics see, for example, Ronald Smothers, "Atlanta Protests Prove Magnet for Abortion Foes," *New York Times*, 13 August 1988, 6.

29 Terry, "Operation Rescue," 83.

30 Operation Rescue Newlsetter (September 1988), 2–3, in Operation Rescue, Box 1-7, Folder 616/1, Hall-Hoag.

31 Operation Rescue Newsbrief (March 1989), "Michigan Stages First All Black Rescue," 3, in Operation Rescue, Box 1-7, Folder 616/1/1, Hall-Hoag.

32 Blanchard, *The Anti-Abortion Movement*, 66.

33 Hughes, "'The Civil Rights Movement of the 1990s?'," 2.

34 Garry Wills, "Save the Babies," *Time*, 1 May 1989. We Shall Overcome was often sung by anti-abortion protesters. See, for example, "Protesters in Capital Clash over Abortion," *New York Times*, 23 June 1985, 18.

35 Quoted in Risen and Thomas, *Wrath of Angels*, 279.

36 Philip Green, "Abortion: The Abusable Past," *The Nation*, 7/14 August 1989, 177–79.

37 Wills, "Save the Babies."

38 Green, "Abortion: The Abusable Past," 177–79.

39   Charles R. DiSalvo, "What's Wrong with Operation Rescue?," *Commonweal,* December 1989, 666–67. On activists' refusal to give their names see, for example, "Abortion Foes Jailed in Atlanta," *New York Times,* 30 July 1988, 30.

40   Julian Bond, "Dr. King's Unwelcome Heirs," *New York Times,* 2 November 1988, 27.

41   DiSalvo, "What's Wrong with Operation Rescue?," 666–67.

42   Bond, "Dr. King's Unwelcome Heirs."

43   Karen De Witt, "Abortion Foes March in Capital on Anniversary of Legalization," *New York Times,* 23 January 1979, C10.

44   "Collegians Denounce Abortions," *Moral Majority Report,* 26 April 1982 in Moral Majority, Box 15-9X, Folder 535/1/3, Hall-Hoag.

45   Andrew Rosenthal, "President and GOP Take Aim at Abortion on Roe Anniversary," *New York Times,* 23 January 1992, 18.

46   Robin Toner, "Right to Abortion Draws Thousands to Capital Rally," *New York Times,* 10 April 1989.

47   Nancy Hicks, "Both Sides Press Abortion Views," *New York Times,* 23 January 1974, 38.

48   See Hughes, "Burning Birth Certificates."

49   Willy Thorn, "March for Life President Reflects on Past 30 Years," *Catholic Herald,* 16 January 2003; http://www.catholicherald.com/cns/march-gray.htm, accessed 30 June 2008.

50   Tom Wells, *The War Within: America's Battle over Vietnam* (Berkeley: University of California Press, 1994), 550.

51   Ibid., 391.

52   Hughes, "Burning Birth Certificates," 556.

53   An anti-abortion poster, c. 1990, featured an American flag with the casualty figures of America's wars—Revolutionary War, Civil War, World War I and II, Korea and Vietnam, represented with crosses. It then included the figure for the "war on the unborn"—which it claimed at more than 28 million lives. See "American War Casualties" Poster, Box 1-3, Folder 1421, Hall-Hoag.

54   Toner, "Right to Abortion Draws Thousands." A "cemetery of the innocent" was also created by anti-abortion activists in Cape Girardeau, Missouri, next to Interstate 55. See *Celebrate Life* (newsletter of American Life League), November–December 1997, 8 in Box 1-1, Folder 618, Hall-Hoag.

55   Kirk Johnson, "Connecticut Abortion Protesters Clog Jails," *New York Times,* 21 June 1989, B1; Charles DeBenedetti with Charles Chatfield, *An American Ordeal: The Antiwar Movement of the Vietnam Era* (Syracuse, N.Y.: Syracuse University Press, 1990), 199.

56   Rev. Jesse L. Jackson, "How We Respect Life Is Over-Riding Moral Issue," in Columbus Right to Life Society, Box 1-3, Folder 1935, Hall-Hoag.

57   Wells, *The War Within,* 48–49, 122–23; DeBenedetti, *An American Ordeal,* 185.

58   Hughes, "Burning Birth Certificates," 551–52; "Photo That Haunted the World," http://news.bbc.co.uk/1/hi/world/asia-pacific/718106.stm, accessed 1 July 2008.

59   Hughes, "Burning Birth Certificates," 550.

60   Ibid., 553; Toner, "Right to Abortion Draws Thousands"; Blanchard, *The Anti-Abortion Movement,* 98.

61   Hughes, "Burning Birth Certificates," 554.

62   "Questions from America," *Moral Majority Report,* June 1984, 18–19 in Moral Majority, Box 15-9X, Folder 535/1/4, Hall-Hoag.

63   Ronald Story and Bruce Laurie, *The Rise of Conservatism in America, 1945–2000: A Brief History with Documents* (New York: Bedford/St. Martin's, 2007), 18–19; Page, *The Right to Lifers*, 126.

64   Michael Knight, "Drive for Abortion Rights Begins," *New York Times*, 23 January 1980, 12.

65   "From the Director's Desk," *Christian American*, July/August 1992, 25 in Christian Coalition, Box 4-1, Folder 1483, Hall-Hoag.

66   Donald T. Critchlow, *Phyllis Schlafly and Grassroots Conservatism: A Woman's Crusade* (Princeton, N.J.: Princeton University Press, 2005), 224.

67   Newsletter, 7/3/89, 2, Operation Rescue, Box 1-7, Folder 616, Hall-Hoag.

68   "Building from the Bottom Up," *ALL About Issues*, June–July 1990, 40 in American Life League, Box 1-1, Folder 618, Hall-Hoag.

69   For a good example of how militant anti-abortion activism could alienate an entire community, irrespective of their stance on abortion, see Lisa W. Foderaro, "Town Is Caught, Shellshocked, in Abortion War," *New York Times*, 20 November 1990, B1.

70   Of course, Americanism was also invoked by those seeking to defend a woman's right to choose—many of whom portrayed the anti-abortion forces as anti-American. A cartoon in a 1977 edition of the Abortion Rights Council of Minnesota, for example, showed anti-abortion activists lighting the "fuses on sticks of dynamite . . . in a structure entitled, 'Constitution & Bill of Rights.'" See Marsha L. Vanderford, "Vilification and Social Movements: A Case Study of Pro-Life and Pro-Choice Rhetoric," *Quarterly Journal of Speech* 75, 2 (1989): 169.

71   James T. Patterson, *Restless Giant: The United States from Watergate to Bush v. Gore* (Oxford: Oxford University Press, 2005), 134; John Micklethwait and Adrian Wooldridge, *The Right Nation: Conservative Power in America* (New York: Penguin, 2004), 81; Critchlow, *Phyllis Schlafly*, 219, 221.

72   Eagle Forum flyer "The Alternative to Women's Lib," n.d.c. 1983, in Eagle Forum, Box 45-1, Folder 557/1/1, Hall-Hoag.

73   Ibid.

74   Phyllis Schlafly, "Bicentennial Outlook," *Phyllis Schlafly Report* 9, 8, sec.1 (March 1976): 4 in Eagle Forum, Box 45-1, Folder 557/2/4, Hall-Hoag.

75   Richard Alvarez, "'Silent Scream' Upsets Pro-Abortion Leaders," *Moral Majority Report*, April 1985, 17, in Moral Majority, Box 15-9X, Folder 535, Hall-Hoag.

76   For Reagan's challenge, http://www.ford.utexas.edu/grf/timeline.asp, accessed 26 June 2008.

77   Martin Tolchin, "Rally Demands Ban on Abortion," *New York Times*, 23 January 1976, 20. See also, Robin Toner, "Reagan Exhorts Foes of Abortion at Capital Rally," *New York Times*, 23 January 1986, D25.

78   Bruce J. Schulman, *The Seventies: The Great Shift in American Culture, Society, and Politics* (New York: Da Capo, 2002), 202; Micklethwait and Wooldridge, *The Right Nation*, 81-85, Patterson, *Restless Giant*, 138, 141; Page, *The Right to Lifers*, 135.

79   Jerry Falwell, "America Was Built on Seven Great Principles," *Moral Majority Report*, 18 May 1981, 8 in Moral Majority, Box 15-9X, Folder 535/1/2, Hall-Hoag.

80   Letter, Jerry Falwell, 1982, 2 in Moral Majority, Box 15-22, Folder 535/2/1, Hall-Hoag.

81   Blanchard, *The Anti-Abortion Movement*, 63.

82   *A.L.L. About Issues,* September–October 1987, 22, in Box 1-1, Folder 618, Hall-Hoag.

83   Fundraising letter, Senator Gordon J. Humphrey, c. March 1987, Box 1-1, Folder 618/1/1, Hall-Hoag.

84   *A.L.L. About Issues,* June–July 1988, 40–41 in Box 1-1, Folder 618, Hall-Hoag.

85   Nadine Brozan, "503 Held in Abortion Protest on E. 85th St.," *New York Times,* 3 May 1988, B1.

86   Operation Rescue Newsbrief (March 1989), 6, in Operation Rescue, Box 1-7, Folder 616/1/1, Hall-Hoag.

87   "What Is at Stake?," Flyer, "Operation Rescue: Atlanta Continues…October 3–8" (1988), 4, in Operation Rescue, Box 1-7, Folder 616, Hall-Hoag.

88   Operation Rescue, letter, 5 December 1989, p. 2; Flyer, "Repentance & Rescue" (December 1989), both in Box 1-7, Folder 616, Hall-Hoag.

89   Maurice Isserman and Michael Kazin, *America Divided: The Civil War of the 1960s* (New York: Oxford University Press, 2000), 205–20.

90   Jeffery Kahn, "Ronald Reagan Launched Political Career Using the Berkeley Campus as a Target," *UC Berkeley News,* 8 June 2004; http://berkeley.edu/news/media/releases/2004/06/ 08_reagan.shtml, accessed 5 July 2008.

91   Story and Laurie, *The Rise of Conservatism in America, 1945–2000,* 79.

92   Interview with Chuck Colson, *Christian American,* May/June 1993, 16–17 in Christian Coalition, Box 4-1, Folder 1483, Hall-Hoag; http://www.washingtonpost.com/wp-srv/ onpolitics/watergate/charles.html, accessed 7 July 2008.

93   Godfrey Hodgson, *The World Turned Right Side Up: A History of the Conservative Ascendancy in America* (Boston: Houghton Mifflin, 1996), 177–78.

94   Critchlow, *Phyllis Schlafly and Grassroots Conservatism,* 194, 197, 202.

95   Phyllis Schlafly, "The Problem of the Supreme Court," *Phyllis Schlafly Report* 9, 5, sec. 1 (December 1975):1, in Eagle Forum, Box 45-1, Folder 557/2/3, Hall-Hoag.

96   Thomas Byrne Edsall with Mary D. Edsall, *Chain Reaction: the Impact of Race, Rights, and Taxes on American Politics* (New York: Norton, 1991), 109. Similarly, addressing the 1980 March for Life, anti-gay rights campaigner Anita Bryant explained that she was "not just concerned about one issue. To me, abortion is a sin against almighty God. All these issues are just symptoms of the moral decadence in America." See Leslie Bennetts, "Thousands March in Capital, Seeking Abortion Ban," *New York Times,* 23 January 1980, 12.

97   Paul Weyrich, "Building the Moral Majority," *Conservative Digest,* August 1979, 18–19 in Story and Laurie, *The Rise of Conservatism in America,* 115–16.

98   Hodgson, *The World Turned Right Side Up,* 177.

99   Rick Perlstein, *Nixonland: The Rise of a President and the Fracturing of America* (New York: Scribner, 2008), 655–56.

100   Ibid., 615.

101   Page, *The Right to Lifers,* 117.

102   See John Herbers, "Ultraconservative Evangelicals a Surging New Force in Politics," *New York Times,* 17 August 1980, 1.

103   Hodgson, *The World Turned Right Side Up,* 182.

104   Critchlow, *Phyllis Schlafly and Grassroots Conservatism,* 265–67; Risen and Thomas, *Wrath of Angels,* 129–30.

105   Risen and Thomas, *Wrath of Angels,* 130–31, Story and Laurie, *The Rise of Conservatism in America,* 25; Hodgson, *The World Turned Right Side Up,* 251.

106 "Abortion Foes Meet with Reagan After March in Capital," *New York Times*, 23 January 1981, 14; Dudley Clendinen, "President Praises Foes of Abortion," *New York Times*, 23 January 1985, 1.

107 Story and Laurie, *The Rise of Conservatism in America*, 127.

108 Critchlow, *Phyllis Schlafly and Grassroots Conservatism*, 282.

109 "President Warned by Conservatives," *New York Times*, 22 January 1982, 20.

110 David E. Rosenbaum, "Poll Shows Few Votes Changed by Abortion Issue," *New York Times*, 8 October 1984, B8; Gallup Poll, 1980, cited in Risen and Thomas, *Wrath of Angles*, 107.

111 Risen and Thomas, *Wrath of Angels*, 130.

112 Ibid., 197–98. On the rise of anti-abortion violence during 1984 see, for example, James Barron, "Violence Increases Against Abortion Clinics in '84," *New York Times*, 5 November 1984, B15; Blanchard, *The Anti-Abortion Movement*, 53–60.

113 Risen and Thomas, *Wrath of Angels*, 377.

Conclusion

1 Scholar and former SDS president Todd Gitlin, a leading proponent of the "declension" interpretation, titled his history of the 1960s *The Sixties: Years of Hope, Days of Rage*.

2 Stephen Tuck, "'We Are Taking Up Where the Movement of the 1960s Left Off': The Proliferation and Power of African American Protest During the 1970s," *Journal of Contemporary History* 43, 4 (October 2008): 641, 653. There were numerous other movements, not explored in this book, that also appear to have been influenced strongly by the protests of the 1960s. See, for example, Felicia Kornbluh, *The Battle for Welfare Rights: Politics and Poverty in Modern America* (Philadelphia: University of Pennsylvania Press, 2007); Premilla Nadasen, *Welfare Warriors: The Welfare Rights Movement in the United States* (New York: Routledge, 2004); Roger Sanjek, *Gray Panthers* (Philadelphia: University of Pennsylvania Press, 2009); and Joseph P. Shapiro, *No Pity: People with Disabilities Forging a New Civil Rights Movement* (New York: Three Rivers Press, 1994).

3 At both the national and local levels the Bicentennial was used as an organizing focus by leftists. The most prominent group was the People's Bicentennial Commission, founded by Jeremy Rifkin and other New Leftists, which sought to use the example of eighteenth-century radicals such as Thomas Paine to challenge the power of corporate America. See John Bodnar, *Remaking America: Public Memory, Commemoration, and Patriotism in the Twentieth Century* (Princeton, N.J.: Princeton University Press, 1994), 234–37; Christopher Capozzola, "'It Makes You Want to Believe in the Country': Celebrating the Bicentennial in an Age of Limits," in Beth Bailey and David Farber, eds., *America in the Seventies* (Lawrence: University Press of Kansas, 2004), esp. 34–48; Andrew Feffer, "Show Down in Center City: Staging Redevelopment and Citizenship in Bicentennial Philadelphia, 1974–1977," *Journal of Urban History* 30, 6 (2004), esp. 809–11; Ted Howard, *The P.B.C.: A History: 1971–1976* (Washington, D.C.: People's Bicentennial Commission, 1976); Robert Reinhold, "Radical Group Presses New Bicentennial View," *New York Times*, 18 January 1976, 38—and see also the group's prominent advertisement on p. 160; Marylin Bender, "Staff Informers Offered Reward," *New York Times*, 12 August 1976, F1; "Ford Burned

in Effigy," *New York Times*, 8 February 1976, 44; John Kifner, "2 Counterrallies in Philadelphia," *New York Times*, 5 July 1976, 14. See also O. C. Bobby Daniels, "The Bicentennial: Contradictions in American Democracy," *Black Scholar* 7, 10 (1976).

4   See, for example, James T. Patterson, *Restless Giant: The United States from Watergate to Bush v. Gore* (Oxford: Oxford University Press, 2005), 81; Godfrey Hodgson, *More Equal Than Others: America from Nixon to the New Century* (Princeton, N.J.: Princeton University Press, 2004), 34. Writing in the fall of 2006, *Salon* columnist Andrew O'Hehir noted that "sometimes it seems as if the dichotomy in American cultural and political life has itself become the only subject of public discourse. It's contained in every Supreme Court nomination, every death in Iraq and every Gulf Coast hurricane." See Andrew O'Hehir, "Is the Homeland Where America's Heart Is?" *Salon*, 28 September 2006 (www.salon.com), 1.

5   32 percent favored small government in 1973, 56 percent in 1998. Godfrey Hodgson, *The World Turned Right Side Up: A History of the Conservative Ascendancy in America* (Boston: Houghton Mifflin, 1996), 281, 284; Hodgson, *More Equal Than Others*, 2.

6   Steve Fraser and Gary Gerstle, "Epilogue" in Fraser and Gerstle, eds., *The Rise and Fall of the New Deal Order, 1930–1980* (Princeton, N.J.: Princeton University Press, 1989), 297.

7   Joan Walsh, "Party Like It's 1995!," www.salon.com, 15 April 2009.

8   Alex Koppelman, "Tea-Baggers Hit Lafayette Park," www.salon.com, 15 April 2009; Liz Robbins, "Tax Day Is Met with Tea Parties," *New York Times*, 16 April 2009.

9   Joan Walsh, "Tea-Baggers Hit San Francisco Civic Center," www.salon.com, 15 April 2009.

10   Robbins, "Tax Day Is Met with Tea Parties."

11   Ibid.; Kirsten Berg, "Gay Rights Activists Protest Inequalities on Tax-Filing day," *Daily Free Press*, 16 April 2009; http://www.dailyfreepress.com/gay-rights-activists-protest-inequalities-on-tax-filing-day-1.1718340, accessed 6 August 2009.

Bibliography

Archival Sources, United Kingdom

British Library of Political and Economic Science, London School of Economics

The Gay Rights Movement: Mattachine Society of New York, Inc.; from the International Gay Information Center, New York Public Library. Microfilm. New York: Research Publications International, 1998. (MSNY)

The Gay Rights Movement: Gay Activists Alliance; from the International Gay Information Center, The New York Public Library. Microfilm. New York: Research Publications International, 1998. (GAA)

ACT UP/NY: the AIDS Coalition to Unleash Power / New York records from the New York Public Library Manuscripts and Archives Division. Woodbridge, Conn.: Primary Source Microfilm, 1999.

Brotherton Library, University of Leeds

Radicalism and Reactionary Politics in America. Series 1, the American Radicalism Collection. From the American Radicalism Collection, Special Collections, Michigan State University Libraries (ARC), Part 1: Leftist Politics and Anti-War Movements; Part 3: Race, Gender, and the Struggle for Justice and Equal Rights; Part 4: Twentieth-Century Social, Economic, and Environmental Movements. Woodbridge, Conn.: Primary Source Microfilm, 2003.

Women and Social Movements in the United States, 1600–2000. Alexandria, Va.: Alexander Street Press.

University Library, Cambridge University

Bracey, John H., Jr., and Sharon Harley, eds., *Papers of the NAACP, Part 29, Branch Department, Series B: Branch Newsletters, Annual Branch Reports, and Selected Branch Department Subject Files, 1966–1972; Series C: Branch Newsletters and Regional Field Office Files, 1966–1971.* Black Studies Research Sources, UPA (*NAACP Papers, B; C*)

University Library, University of Sheffield

The Bayard Rustin Papers, Introduction by John H. Bracey and August Meier, Guide Compiled by Nanette Dobrosky. Frederick, Md.: University Publications of America, 1988.

Archival Sources, United States

John Hay Library, Brown University

Gordon Hall and Grace Hoag Collection of Dissenting and Extremist Printed Propaganda (Hall-Hoag)

Rare Book and Manuscript Library, Columbia University

Robert L. Wilbur Protest Literature Collection (Wilbur Collection)

Oral History Research Office, Columbia University

Student Movements of the 1960s Oral History Project
Gay Officers Action League Oral History Project

Kenneth Spencer Research Library, University of Kansas

Wilcox Collection of Contemporary Political Movements (Wilcox Collection)
University Daily Kansan
Queers and Allies. also Lawrence Gay Liberation Front; Gay and Lesbian Services of Kansas; LesBiGay Services (Queers and Allies) University of Kansas Archives (UKA)

Library of Congress (LC)

National Association for the Advancement of Colored People Records. (NAACP Records).

Wisconsin Historical Society, Madison (WHS)

Movement for Economic Justice Records, 1972–1980 (MEJ Records)
Kathleen Nichols and Barbara Constans Papers, 1975–1979
The United Records, 1977–1981 (UR)

Newspapers and Magazines

Atlanta Daily World
The Black Panther
Baltimore Afro-American
Capital Times (Madison)
Chicago Defender

Los Angeles Sentinel
New Pittsburgh Courier
New York Amsterdam News
New York Times
Norfolk Journal and Guide
Philadelphia Tribune
Time
Wisconsin State Journal (Madison)
Yale Daily News

Published Primary Sources

Blasius, Mark and Shane Phelan, eds. *We Are Everywhere: A Historical Sourcebook of Gay and Lesbian Politics*. New York: Routledge, 1997.
Bloom, Alexander and Wini Breines, eds. *"Takin' it to the streets": A Sixties Reader.* New York: Oxford University Press, 1995.
Carson, Clayborne et al., eds. *The Eyes on the Prize Civil Rights Reader: Documents, Speeches, and Firsthand Accounts from the Black Freedom Struggle.* New York: Penguin, 1991.
Douglas, Davison M., ed. *School Busing: Constitutional and Political Developments.* Vol. 2, *The Public Debate over Busing and Attempts to Restrict Its Use.* New York: Garland, 1994.
Gross, Larry and James D. Woods. *The Columbia Reader on Lesbian and Gay Men in Media, Society, and Politics.* New York: Columbia University Press, 1999.
Keetley, Dawn and John Pettigrew, eds. *Public Women, Public Words: A Documentary History of American Feminism.* Vol. 2, *1900 to 1960*; Vol. 3, *1960 to the Present.* Lanham, Md.: Rowman and Littlefield, 2005.
Scheer, Robert, ed. *Eldridge Cleaver: Post-Prison Writings and Speeches.* New York: Vintage, 1969.
Teodori, Massimo, ed. *The New Left: A Documentary History.* Indianapolis: Bobbs-Merrill, 1969.
Washington, James Melvin. *A Testament of Hope: The Essential Writings and Speeches of Martin Luther King, Jr.* New York: HarperOne, 1990.
Williams, Walter L. and Yolanda Retter, eds. *Gay and Lesbian Rights in the United States: A Documentary History.* Westport, Conn.: Greenwood Press, 2003.
National Commission on the Observance of International Women's Year. *The Spirit of Houston: The First National Women's Conference: An Official Report to the President, the Congress and the People of the United States, March, 1978.* Washington, D.C.: the Commission and U.S. GPO.
Reporting Civil Rights. Part 2, *American Journalism 1963–1973.* New York: Library of America, 2003.

Autobiography and Oral Testimony

Curry, Constance et al. *Deep in Our Hearts: Nine White Women in the Freedom Movement.* Athens: University of Georgia Press, 2002.
Duberman, Martin L. *Stonewall.* New York: Dutton, 1993.
Hampton, Henry, and Steve Fayer, eds. *Voices of Freedom: An Oral History of the Civil Rights Movement from the 1950s Through the 1980s.* New York: Bantam, 1990.

Jarvis, Howard, with Robert Pack. *I'm Mad as Hell: The Exclusive Story of the Tax Revolt and Its Leader.* New York: Times Books, 1979.

Kisseloff, Jeff. *Generation on Fire: Voices of Protest from the 1960s.* Lexington: University Press of Kentucky, 2007.

Marcus, Eric. *Making Gay History: The Half Century Fight for Lesbian and Gay Equal Rights.* New York: Harper Paperbacks, 2002.

Seale, Bobby. *Seize The Time: The Story of the Black Panther Party and Huey P. Newton.* New York: Vintage, 1970.

Books

Aptheker, Bettina. *Intimate Politics: How I Grew Up Red, Fought for Free Speech, and Became a Feminist Rebel.* Emeryville, Calif.: Seal Press, 2006.

Bailey, Beth. *Sex in the Heartland.* Cambridge, Mass.: Harvard University Press, 2002.

Bailey, Beth, and David Farber, eds. *America in the Seventies.* Lawrence: University Press of Kansas, 2004.

Barber, David. *A Hard Rain Fell: SDS and Why It Failed.* Jackson: University Press of Mississippi, 2008.

Berkeley, Kathleen C. *The Women's Liberation Movement in America.* Westport, Conn.: Greenwood Press, 1999.

Berry, Mary Frances. *Why ERA Failed: Politics, Women's Rights, and the Amending Process of the Constitution.* Bloomington: Indiana University Press, 1986.

Black, Earl and Merle Black. *The Rise of Southern Republicans.* Cambridge, Mass.: Belknap Press of Harvard University Press, 2002.

Blanchard, Dallas A. *The Anti-Abortion Movement and the Rise of the Religious Right: From Polite to Fiery Protest.* New York: Twayne, 1994.

Bloom, Alexander, ed. *Long Time Gone: Sixties America Then and Now.* Oxford: Oxford University Press, 2001.

Bodnar, John. *Remaking America: Public Memory, Commemoration, and Patriotism in the Twentieth Century.* Princeton, N.J.: Princeton University Press, 1994.

Bolner, James, and Robert Shanley. *Busing: The Political and Judicial Process.* New York: Praeger, 1974.

Brennan, Mary. *Turning Right in the Sixties: The Conservative Capture of the GOP.* Chapel Hill: University of North Carolina Press, 2007.

Bronski, Michael, ed. *Taking Liberties: Gay Men's Essays on Politics, Culture and Sex.* New York: Richard Kasak, 1996.

Brown, David S. *Beyond the Frontier: The Midwestern Voice in American Historical Writing.* Chicago: University of Chicago Press, 2009.

Bull, Chris, and John Gallagher. *Perfect Enemies: The Religious Right, the Gay Movement, and the Politics of the 1990s.* New York: Crown, 1996.

Burner, David. *Making Peace with the 60s.* Princeton, N.J.: Princeton University Press, 1996.

Carroll, Peter N. *It Seemed like Nothing Happened: America in the 1970s.* New Brunswick, N.J.: Rutgers University Press, 1990.

Carter, Dan T. *The Politics of Rage: George Wallace, the Origins of the New Conservatism, and the Transformation of American Politics.* Baton Rouge: Louisiana State University Press, 2000.

Carter, David. *Stonewall: The Riots That Sparked the Gay Revolution.* New York: St Martin's Griffin, 2005.

Chafe, William H. *The Unfinished Journey: America Since World War II.* Oxford: Oxford University Press, 2006.

Cleaver, Kathleen, and George Katsiaficas, eds. *Liberation, Imagination, and the Black Panther Party: A New Look at the Panthers and Their Legacy.* New York: Routledge, 2001.

Clendinen, Dudley, and Adam Nagourney. *Out for Good: The Struggle to Build a Gay Rights Movement in America.* New York: Touchstone, 1999.

Colburn, David R., and Jeffrey S. Adler, eds. *African-American Mayors: Race, Politics, and the American City.* Urbana: University of Illinois Press, 2001.

Costain, Anne N. and Andrew S. McFarland, eds. *Social Movements and American Political Institutions.* Lanham, Md.: Rowman and Littlefield, 1998.

Critchlow, Donald T. *Phyllis Schlafly and Grassroots Conservatism: A Woman's Crusade.* Princeton, N.J.: Princeton University Press, 2005.

Cruickshank, Margaret. *The Gay and Lesbian Liberation Movement* New York: Routledge, 1992.

Cullen, Jim. *The American Dream: A Short History of an Idea That Shaped a Nation.* Oxford: Oxford University Press, 2003.

Dahlerup, Drude, ed. *The New Women's Movement: Feminism and Political Power in Europe and the USA.* London: Sage, 1986.

Darsey, James. *The Prophetic Tradition and Radical Rhetoric in America.* New York: New York University Press, 1997.

Davies, Gareth. *From Opportunity to Entitlement: The Transformation and Decline of Great Society Liberalism.* Lawrence: University Press of Kansas, 1999.

———. *See Government Grow: Education Politics from Johnson to Reagan.* Lawrence: University Press of Kansas, 2007.

Davis, Jack E. *The Civil Rights Movement.* New York: Wiley-Blackwell, 2000.

DeBenedetti, Charles, with Charles Chatfield. *An American Ordeal: The Antiwar Movement of the Vietnam Era.* Syracuse, N.Y.: Syracuse University Press, 1990.

D'Emilio, John. *Making Trouble: Essays on Gay History, Politics, and the University.* New York: Routledge, 1992.

———. *Sexual Politics, Sexual Communities: The Making of a Homosexual Minority in the United States, 1940–1970.* Chicago: University of Chicago Press, 1983.

D'Emilio, John, William B. Turner, and Urvashi Vaid, eds. *Creating Change: Sexuality, Public Policy, and Civil Rights.* New York: St. Martin's, 2000.

Denning, Michael. *The Cultural Front: The Laboring of American Culture in the Twentieth Century.* London: Verso, 1998.

Diggins, John Patrick., *The Rise and Fall of the American Left.* New York: Norton, 1992.

Dudziak, Mary. *Cold War Civil Rights: Race and the Image of American Democracy.* Princeton, N.J.: Princeton University Press, 2000.

Durham, Martin. *The Christian Right, the Far Right and the Boundaries of American Conservatism.* Manchester: Manchester University Press, 2000.

Echols, Alice. *Daring to Be Bad: Radical Feminism in America, 1967–1975.* Minneapolis: University of Minnesota Press, 1989, 2003.

Edsall, Thomas Byrne with Mary D. Edsall. *Chain Reaction: The Impact of Race, Rights, and Taxes on American Politics.* New York: Norton, 1991.

Epstein, Barbara. *Political Protest and Cultural Revolution: Nonviolent Direct Action in the 1970s and 1980s.* Berkeley: University of California Press, 1991.

Eisenbach, David. *Gay Power: An American Revolution.* New York: Carroll and Graf, 2006.

Evans, Sara M. *Personal Politics: The Roots of Women's Liberation in the Civil Rights Movement and the New Left.* New York: Vintage, 1980.

———. *Tidal Wave: How Women Changed America at Century's End.* New York: Free Press, 2003.

Faderman, Lillian, and Stuart Timmons. *Gay L.A.: A History of Sexual Outlaws, Power Politics, and Lipstick Lesbians.* New York: Basic Books, 2006.

Fairclough, Adam. *Better Day Coming: Blacks and Equality, 1890–2000.* New York: Penguin, 2002.

Farber, David, ed. *The Sixties: From Memory to History.* Chapel Hill: University of North Carolina Press, 1994.

Farber, David, and Jeff Roche, eds. *The Conservative Sixties.* New York: Peter Lang, 2003.

Fiorina, Morris P. with Samuel J. Abrams and Jeremy C. Pope. *Culture War? The Myth of a Polarized America.* New York: Pearson Longman, 2005.

Foner, Eric. *The Story of American Freedom.* New York: Norton, 1999.

Formisano, Ronald P. *Boston Against Busing: Race, Class, and Ethnicity in the 1960s and 1970s.* Chapel Hill: University of North Carolina Press, 1991.

Fraser, Steve, and Gary Gerstle, eds. *The Rise and Fall of the New Deal Order, 1930–1980.* Princeton, N.J.: Princeton University Press, 1989.

Frost, Jennifer. *An Interracial Movement of the Poor: Community Organizing and the New Left in the 1960s.* New York: New York University Press, 2005.

Gans, Herbert. *Deciding What's News: A Study of CBS Evening News, NBC Nightly News, Newsweek and Time.* London: Constable, 1980.

Garrow, David J. *Bearing the Cross: Martin Luther King, Jr., and the Southern Christian Leadership Conference.* 1986. London: Vintage, 1993.

Gitlin, Todd. *The Sixties: Years of Hope, Days of Rage.* New York: Bantam, 1993.

Gosse, Van. *The Movements of the New Left, 1950–1975: A Brief History with Documents.* Boston: Bedford/St. Martins, 2005.

Gosse, Van, and Richard Moser, eds. *The World the Sixties Made: Politics and Culture in Recent America.* Philadelphia: Temple University Press, 2003.

Griffith, Robert and Paula Baker, eds. *Major Problems in American History Since 1945.* 2nd ed. Boston: Houghton Mifflin, 2001.

Hall, Simon. *Peace and Freedom: The Civil Rights and Antiwar Movements in the 1960s.* Philadelphia: University of Pennsylvania Press, 2005.

Hendriks, Aart, Rob Tielman, and Evert van der Veer, eds. *The Third Pink Book: A Global View of Lesbian and Gay Liberation and Oppression.* New York: Prometheus, 1993.

Hodgson, Godfrey. *More Equal Than Others: America from Nixon to the New Century.* Princeton, N.J.: Princeton University Press, 2004.

———. *The World Turned Right Side Up: A History of the Conservative Ascendancy in America.* Boston: Houghton Mifflin, 1996.

Hoff, Joan. *Nixon Reconsidered.* New York: Basic Books, 1995.

Hofstadter, Richard. *The American Political Tradition and the Men Who Made It.* New York: Vintage, 1974.

Howard, Ted. *The P.B.C.: A History, 1971–1976.* Washington, D.C.: People's Bicentennial Commission, 1976.

Hunt, Andrew. *The Turning: A History of Vietnam Veterans Against the War.* New York: New York University Press, 1999.

Isserman, Maurice. *If I Had a Hammer...The Death of the Old Left and the Birth of the New Left.* New York: Basic Books, 1987.

Isserman, Maurice, and Michael Kazin. *America Divided: The Civil War of the 1960s.* New York: Oxford University Press, 2000.

Jacobson, Matthew Frye. *Roots Too: White Ethnic Revival in Post-Civil Rights America.* Cambridge, Mass.: Harvard University Press, 2006.

Jackson, Julian. *Living in Arcadia: Homosexuality, Politics, and Morality in France from the Liberation to AIDS.* Chicago: University of Chicago Press, 2010.

Jeffries, Judson L., ed. *Black Power in the Belly of the Beast.* Urbana: University of Illinois Press, 2006.

Joseph, Peniel E., ed. *The Black Power Movement: Rethinking the Civil Rights-Black Power Era.* New York: Routledge, 2006..

———. *Waiting 'Til The Midnight Hour: A Narrative History of Black Power in America.* New York: Holt, 2006.

Judt, Tony. *Postwar: A History of Europe Since 1945.* London: Heinemann, 2005.

Kazin, Michael, and Joseph A. McCartin, eds. *Americanism: New Perspectives on the History of an Ideal.* Chapel Hill: University of North Carolina Press, 2006.

Kenny, Michael. *The First New Left: British Intellectuals After Stalin.* London: Lawrence and Wishart, 1995.

Klatch, Rebecca. *A Generation Divided: The New Left, the New Right, and the 1960s.* Berkeley: University of California Press, 1999.

Klimke, Martin, and Joachim Scarloth, eds. *1968 in Europe: A History of Protest and Activism, 1956–1977.* New York: Palgrave Macmillan, 2008.

Kotlowski, Dean. *Nixon's Civil Rights: Politics, Principle, and Policy.* Cambridge, Mass.: Harvard University Press, 2002.

Kornbluh, Felicia. *The Battle for Welfare Rights: Politics and Poverty in Modern America.* Philadelphia: University of Pennsylvania Press, 2007.

Kuttner, Robert. *Revolt of the Haves: Tax Rebellions and Hard Times.* New York: Simon and Schuster, 1980.

Lassiter, Matthew D. *The Silent Majority: Suburban Politics in the Sunbelt South.* Princeton, N.J.: Princeton University Press, 2006.

Lo, Clarence Y. H. *Small Property Versus Big Government: Social Origins of the Property Tax Revolt.* Berkeley: University of California Press, 1990.

Lupo, Alan. *Liberty's Chosen Home: The Politics of Violence in Boston.* Boston: Little, Brown, 1977.

Mansbridge, Jane J. *Why We Lost the ERA.* Chicago: University of Chicago Press, 1986.

Martin, Isaac William. *The Permanent Tax Revolt: How the Property Tax Transformed American Politics.* Stanford, Calif.: Stanford University Press, 2008.

Marwick, Arthur. *The Sixties: Cultural Revolution in Britain, France, Italy, and the United States, c. 1958–c. 1974.* Oxford: Oxford University Press, 1998.

Masur, Louis P. *The Soiling of Old Glory: The Story of a Photograph That Shocked America.* New York: Bloomsbury Press, 2008.

Mathews, Donald and Jane De Hart. *Sex, Gender and the Politics of ERA: A State and the Nation.* New York: Oxford University Press, 1990.

Matusow, Allan J. *The Unraveling of America: A History of Liberalism in the 1960s.* New York: Harper and Row, 1984.

McGirr, Lisa. *Suburban Warriors: The Origins of the New American Right.* Princeton, N.J.: Princeton University Press, 2001.

McMillan, John, and Paul Buhle, eds. *The New Left Revisited.* Philadelphia: Temple University Press, 2003.

Micklethwait, John, and Adrian Wooldridge. *The Right Nation: Conservative Power in America.* New York: Penguin, 2004.

Miller, James. *Democracy Is in the Streets: From Port Huron to the Siege of Chicago.* Cambridge, Mass.: Harvard University Press, 1994.

Miller, Neil. *Out of the Past: Gay and Lesbian History from 1869 to the Present.* New York: alyson books, 2006.

Mills, Kay. *This Little Light of Mine: The Life of Fannie Lou Hamer.* Lexington: University Press of Kentucky, 2007.

Morgan, Robin, ed. *Sisterhood Is Global: The International Women's Movement Anthology.* New York: Anchor, 1984.

Nadasen, Premilla. *Welfare Warriors: The Welfare Rights Movement in the United States.* New York: Routledge, 2004.

Naison, Mark. *Communists in Harlem During the Depression.* Urbana: University of Illinois Press, 2005.

Nava, Michael, and Robert Dawidoff. *Created Equal: Why Gay Rights Matter to America.* New York: St. Martin's, 1994.

Ness, Immanuel, ed. *Encyclopedia of American Social Movements.* Vol. 4. Armonk, N.Y.: Sharpe, 2004.

Newman, Mark. *Divine Agitators: The Delta Ministry and Civil Rights in Mississippi.* Athens: University of Georgia Press, 2004.

Norton, Mary Beth, and Ruth Alexander, eds. *Major Problems in American Women's History.* 3rd ed. Boston: Houghton Mifflin, 2002.

O'Sullivan, Arthur, Terri A. Saxton and Steven M. Sheffrin, *Property Taxes and Tax Revolts: The Legacy of Proposition 13.* Cambridge: Cambridge University Press, 1995.

Packer, George, ed. *The Fight Is for Democracy: Winning the War of Ideas in America and the World.* New York: Perennial, 2003.

Page, Connie. *The Right to Lifers: Who They Are, How They Operate, Where They Get Their Money.* New York: Summit, 1983.

Patterson, James T. *Restless Giant: The United States from Watergate to Bush v. Gore.* Oxford: Oxford University Press, 2005.

Perlstein, Nick. *Nixonland: The Rise of a President and the Fracturing of America.* New York: Scribner, 2008.

Power, Lisa. *No Bath But Plenty of Bubbles: Stories from the London Gay Liberation Front, 1970–73.* London: Continuum International, 1995.

Pride, Richard A. *The Political Use of Racial Narratives: School Desegregation in Mobile, Alabama, 1954–97.* Urbana: University of Illinois Press, 2002.

Pride, Richard A., and J. David Woodard. *The Burden of Busing: The Politics of Desegregation in Nashville, Tennessee.* Knoxville: University of Tennessee Press, 1985.

Rieder, Jonathan. *Canarsie: The Jews and Italians of Brooklyn Against Liberalism.* Cambridge, Mass.: Harvard University Press, 1985.

Risen, James, and Judy L. Thomas, *Wrath of Angels: The American Abortion War.* New York: Basic Books, 1998.

Robbins, Mary Susannah, ed. *Against the Vietnam War: Writings by Activists.* Rev. ed. Lanham, Md.: Rowman and Littlefield, 2007.

Rosen, Ruth. *The World Split Open: How the Modern Women's Movement Changed America.* New York: Viking, 2000.

Rossinow, Doug. *The Politics of Authenticity: Liberalism, Christianity, and the New Left in America.* New York: Columbia University Press, 1998.

———. *Visions of Progress: The Left-Liberal Tradition in America.* Philadelphia: University of Pennsylvania Press, 2008.

Rorty, Richard. *Achieving Our Country: Leftist Thought in Twentieth-Century America.* Cambridge, Mass.: Harvard University Press, 1998.

Rubin, Lillian B. *Busing and Backlash: White Against White in a California School District.* Berkeley: University of California Press, 1972.

Rupp, Leila. *Worlds of Women: The Making of an International Women's Movement.* Princeton, N.J.: Princeton University Press, 1997.

Sandbrook, Dominic. *White Heat: A History of Britain in the Swinging Sixties.* London: Little, Brown, 2006.

Sanjek, Roger. *Gray Panthers.* Philadelphia: University of Pennsylvania Press, 2009.

Schulman, Bruce J. *The Seventies: The Great Shift in American Culture, Society, and Politics.* New York: Da Capo, 2002.

Schulman, Bruce J., and Julian E. Zelizer, eds. *Rightward Bound: Making America Conservative in the 1970s.* Cambridge, Mass.: Harvard University Press, 2008.

Sears, David O. and Jack Citrin, *Tax Revolt: Something for Nothing in California.* Cambridge, Mass.: Harvard University Press, 1982.

Schlesinger, Arthur M., Jr. *The Disuniting of America: Reflections on a Multicultural Society.* New York: Norton, 1992.

Self, Robert O. *American Babylon: Race and the Struggle for Postwar Oakland.* Princeton, N.J.: Princeton University Press, 2003.

Shapiro, Joseph P. *No Pity: People with Disabilities Forging a New Civil Rights Movement.* New York: Three Rivers Press, 1994.

Sklar, Kathryn Kish, and Thomas Dublin. *Women and Social Movements in the United States, 1600–2000.* Alexandria, Va.: Alexander Street Press, 1967–. Database.

Small, Melvin. *Covering Dissent: The Media and the Anti-Vietnam War Movement.* New Brunswick, N.J.: Rutgers University Press, 1994.

Smith, Bonnie G., ed. *Global Feminisms Since 1945.* London: Routledge, 2000.

Sitkoff, Harvard, ed. *Perspectives on Modern America: Making Sense of the Twentieth Century.* New York: Oxford University Press, 2001.

Stacewicz, Richard. *Winter Soldiers: An Oral History of the Vietnam Veterans Against the War.* Chicago: Haymarket Books, 2008.

Stein, Marc. *City of Sisterly and Brotherly Loves: Lesbian and Gay Philadelphia, 1945–1972.* Chicago: University of Chicago Press, 2000.

———, ed. *Encyclopedia of Lesbian, Gay, Bisexual, and Transgender History in America.* New York: Scribner, 2004.

Stephan, Walter G., and Joe R. Feagin, eds. *School Desegregation: Past, Present, and Future.* New York: Plenum Press, 1980.

Story, Robert, and Bruce Laurie, *The Rise of Conservatism in America, 1945–2000: A Brief History with Documents.* New York: Bedford/St. Martins, 2007.

Teachout, Woden. *Capture the Flag: A Political History of American Patriotism.* New York: Basic Books, 2009.

Tuck, Stephen. *We Ain't What We Ought To Be: The Black Freedom Struggle from Emancipation to Obama.* Cambridge, Mass.: Belknap Press of Harvard University Press, 2010.

Valk, Anne M. *Radical Sisters: Second-Wave Feminism and Black Liberation in Washington, D.C.* Urbana: University of Illinois Press, 2008.

Van Deburg, William L. *New Day in Babylon: The Black Power Movement and American Culture, 1965–1975.* Chicago: University of Chicago Press, 1993.

VVAW. *The Winter Soldier Investigation: An Inquiry into American War Crimes.* Boston: Beacon Press, 1972.

Walter, Aubrey. *Come Together: The Years of Gay Liberation, 1970–1973.* London: Heretic Books, 1981.

Wells, Tom. *The War Within: America's Battle over Vietnam.* Berkeley: University of California Press, 1994.

Wilentz, Sean. *The Age of Reagan: A History, 1974–2008.* New York: HarperCollins, 2008.

Wilkinson, J. Harvie, III. *From* Brown *to* Bakke*: The Supreme Court and School Integration, 1954–1978.* New York: Oxford University Press, 1978.

Willie, Charles V. and Susan L. Greenblatt, eds. *Community Politics and Educational Change: Ten School Systems Under Court Order.* New York: Longman, 1981.

Woods, Randall B., ed. *Vietnam and the American Political Tradition: The Politics of Dissent.* Cambridge: Cambridge University Press, 2003.

Articles and Essays

Bailey, Beth. "She 'Can Bring Home the Bacon': Negotiating Gender in Seventies America." In Beth Bailey and David Farber, eds., *America in the Seventies.* Lawrence: University Press of Kansas, 2004.

Baldwin, Bridgette. "In the Shadow of the Gun: The Black Panther Party, the Ninth Amendment, and Discourses of Self-Defense." in June Lazerow and Yohuru Williams, eds., *In Search of the Black Panther Party: New Perspectives on a Revolutionary Movement.* Durham, N.C.: Duke University Press, 2006.

Bawer, Bruce. "Integration vs. Liberation." *Lambda Book Report*; www.brucebawer.com/ bronski.htm, 25 September 2006.

———. "Notes on Stonewall." *New Republic,* 13 June 1994.

———. "The Road to Utopia." *The Advocate,* 20 September 1994

———. "Truth in Advertising." *The Advocate,* 11 July 1995; www.brucebawer.com/ truth.htm, 25 September 2006.

Beale, Frances. "Double Jeopardy: To be Black and Female." In Bloom and Breienes, eds., *"Takin' it to the streets."*

Beemyn, Brett. "The Silence Is Broken: A History of the First Lesbian, Gay, and Bisexual College Student Groups." *Journal of the History of Sexuality* 12, 1 (April 2003).

Bender, Thomas. "Wholes and Parts: The Need for Synthesis in American History," *JAH* 73, 1 (June 1986).

Bloom, Alexander. "Why Read About the 1960s at the Turn of the Twenty-First Century?" In Bloom, ed., *Long Time Gone.*

Brown, Sarah S. "Popular Opinion of Homosexuality: The Shared Moral Language of Opposing Views." *Sociological Inquiry* 70, no. 4 (Fall 2000).

Capozzola, Christopher. "'It Makes You Want to Believe in the Country': Celebrating the Bicentennial in an Age of Limits." In Bailey and Farber, eds., *America in the Seventies.*

———. "A Very American Epidemic: Memory, Politics and Identity Politics in the AIDS Memorial Quilt, 1985–1993." *Radical History Review* 82 (Winter 2002): 91–109.

Cassara, Ernest. "The Development of America's Sense of Mission." In Louis Parkinson Zamora, ed., *The Apocalyptic Vision in America: Interdisciplinary Essays on Myth and Culture.* Bowling Green, Ohio: Bowling Green University Popular Press, 1982.

Chappell, Marisa, Jenny Hutchinson, and Brian Ward, "'Dress modestly, neatly . . . as if you were going to church': Respectability, Class and Gender in the Montgomery Bus Boycott and the Early Civil Rights Movement." In Peter

J. Ling and Sharon Monteith, eds., *Gender in the Civil Rights Movement.* New York: Garland, 1999.

Ciabattari, Jane. "To Be a Woman: How Other Women Gave Me the Courage to Change." *Redbook,* November 1973. In Griffith and Baker, eds., *Major Problems in American History Since 1945*

Cirilo-Medina, Amelia, and Ross Purdy. "The South and Southwest: Corpus Christi, Texas: A Tri-Ethnic Approach." In Willie and Greenblatt, eds., *Community Politics and Educational Change.*

Combahee River Collective. "A Black Feminist Statement" (1977). In Keetley and Pettigrew, eds., *Public Women, Public Words*

Critchlow, Donald. "Conservatism Reconsidered: Phyllis Schlafly and Grassroots Conservatism." In Farber and Roche, eds., *The Conservative Sixties.*

Daniels, O. C. Bobby. "The Bicentennial: Contradictions in American Democracy." *Black Scholar* 7, 10 (1976)

D'Emilio, John. "Placing Gay in the Sixties." In Bloom, ed., *Long Time Gone.*

DiSalvo, Charles R. "What's Wrong with Operation Rescue." *Commonweal,* December 1989.

Dufour, Claude. "Mobilizing Gay Activists." in Costain and McFarland, eds., *Social Movements and American Political Institutions..*

Echols, Alice. "Nothing Distant About It: Women's Liberation and Sixties Radicalism." In Farber, ed., *The Sixties.*

———. "Women's Liberation and Sixties Radicalism." In Griffith and Baker, eds., *Major Problems in American History Since 1945.*

Evans, Sara M. "American Women in the Twentieth Century." In Sitkoff, ed., *Perspectives on Modern America.*

Fairclough, Adam. "What Makes Jesse Run?" *Journal of American Studies* 22, no. 1 (1988).

Feffer, Andrew. "Show Down in Center City: Staging Redevelopment and Citizenship in Bicentennial Philadelphia, 1974–1977." *Journal of Urban History* 30, 6 (2004).

Flamm, Michael W. "The Politics of 'Law and Order'." In Farber and Roche, eds., *The Conservative Sixties.*

Foss, Karen A. "Harvey Milk: 'You Have to Give Them Hope'." *Journal of the West* 27, 2 (1988).

Fout, Ellen Pratt. "'A Miracle Occurred!': The Houston Committee of International Women's Year, Houston, 1977." *Houston Review of History and Culture* 1, Part 1 (2003).

Freeman, Jo. "The Origins of the Women's Liberation Movement." *American Journal of Sociology* 78, 4 (January 1973): 792–811.

Gilmore, Stephanie. "The Dynamics of Second-Wave Feminist Activism in Memphis, 1971–1982: Rethinking the Liberal/Radical Divide." *NWSA Journal* 15, 1 (Spring 2003): 94–117.

Ginsburg, Faye. "Rescuing the Nation: Operation Rescue and the Rise of Anti-Abortion Militance." In Rickie Solinger, ed., *Abortion Wars: A Half Century of Struggle, 1950–2000.* Berkeley: University of California Press, 1998.

———. "Saving America's Souls: Operation Rescue's Crusade Against Abortion." In Martin E. Marty and R. Scott Appleby, eds., *Fundamentalisms and the State: Remaking Polities, Economies, and Militance.* Chicago: University of Chicago Press, 1993.

Gitlin, Todd. "Varieties of Patriotic Experience." In Packer, ed., *The Fight Is for Democracy.*

Gosse, Van. "Postmodern America: A New Democratic Order in the Second Gilded Age." In Gosse and Moser, eds., *The World the Sixties Made.*

Green, Donald Philip and Jonathan A. Cowden, "Who Protests: Self-Interest and White Opposition to Busing." *Journal of Politics* 54, 2 (May 1992).

Hall, Simon. "The NAACP, Black Power, and the African American Freedom Struggle, 1966–1969." *Historian* 69, no. 1 (March 2007).

———. "Marching on Washington: The Civil Rights and Anti-War Movements of the 1960s." In Matthias Reiss, ed., *The Street as Stage: Public Demonstrations and Protest Marches Since the Nineteenth Century.* Oxford: Oxford University Press, 2007.

———. "On the Tail of the Panther: Black Power and the 1967 Convention of the National Conference for New Politics," *Journal of American Studies* 37, 1 (April 2003).

———. "Protest Movements in the 1970s: The Long 1960s." *Journal of Contemporary History* 43, 4 (October 2008).

Heale, M. J. "The Sixties as History: A Review of the Political Historiography." *Reviews in American History* 33 (2005).

Herman, Ellen. "Good Gays and Bad: The Respectability Question in Gay and Lesbian History." *Radical History Review* 56 (1993).

Higham, John. "Beyond Consensus: The Historian as Moral Critic," *American Historical Review* 67, 3 (April 1962)

Hughes, Richard L. "Burning Birth Certificates and Atomic Tupperware Parties: Creating the Antiabortion Movement in the Shadow of the Vietnam War." *Historian* 68, 3 (Fall 2006).

———. "'The Civil Rights Movement of the 1990s?': The Anti-Abortion Movement and the Struggle for Racial Justice." *Oral History Review* 33, 2 (2006).

Hunt, Andrew. "How New Was the New Left?" In McMillan and Buhle, eds., *The New Left Revisited.*

Hunter, Charlayne. "Many Blacks Wary of 'Women's Liberation' Movement." In Keetley and Pettigrew, eds., *Public Women, Public Words.*

Isaacson, Walter. "The Battle over Abortion." *Time* 6 April 1981

Isserman, Maurice and Michael Kazin, "The Contradictory Legacy of the Sixties." In Griffith and Baker, eds., *Major Problems in American History Since 1945.*

Kazin, Michael. "A Patriotic Left." *Dissent* (Fall 2002).

Kesselman, Amy. "Women's Liberation and the Left in New Haven, Connecticut, 1968–1972." *Radical History Review* 81 (Fall 2001).

Kissack, Terence. "Freaking Fag Revolutionaries: New York's Gay Liberation Front, 1969–1971." *Radical History Review* 62 (Spring 1995).

Koedt, Anne. "Women and the Radical Movement." In *Notes from the First Year,* June 1968. In Keetley and Pettigrew, eds., *Public Women, Public Words.*

Kruse, Kevin M. "The Politics of Race and Public Space: Desegregation, Privatization, and the Tax Revolt in Atlanta." *Journal of Urban History* 31, 5 (July 2005).

Lassiter, Matthew D. "The Suburban Origins of 'Color-Blind' Conservatism: Middle-Class Consciousness in the Charlotte Busing Crisis." *Journal of Urban History* 30, 4 (May 2004).

Lowery, David and Lee Sigelman. "Understanding the Tax Revolt: Eight Explanations." *American Political Science Review* 75, 4 (December 1981).

Lutcovich, Joyce Miller and Elaine Clyburn, "Erie, Pennsylvania: The Effect of State Initiative." In Willie and Greenblatt, eds., *Community Politics and Educational Change.*

Manley, John F. "American Liberalism and the Democratic Dream: Transcending the American Dream." *Policy Studies Review* 10, 1 (Fall 1990).

Martin, Donald R. and Vicky Gordon Martin. "Barbara Jordan's Symbolic Use of Language in the Keynote Address to the National Women's Conference." *Southern Speech Communication Journal* 49, 3 (Spring 1984).

McAndrews, Lawrence. "The Politics of Principle: Richard Nixon and School Desegregation." *Journal of Negro History* 8, 3 (Summer 1998).

McCartin, Joseph A. "Turnabout Years: Public Sector Unionism and the Fiscal Crisis." In Schulman and Zelizer, eds., *Rightward Bound.*

Mckee, J. McClendon. "Racism, Rational Choice, and White Opposition to Racial Change: A Case Study of Busing." *Public Opinion Quarterly* 49 (1985).

Meeker, Martin. "Behind the Mask of Respectability: Reconsidering the Mattachine Society and Male Homophile Practice, 1950s and 1960s." *Journal of the History of Sexuality* 10, 1 (January 2001).

Meier, August. "On the Role of Martin Luther King." In Meier and Elliott M. Rudwick, *Along the Color Line: Explorations in the Black Experience.* Urbana: University of Illinois Press, 1976.

Miller, Stephen H. "Who Stole the Gay Movement?" *Christopher Street Magazine,* October 1994; www.indegayforum.org/news/show/26829.html, 25 September 2006.

Minchin, Timothy J. "'Don't Sleep with Stevens!': The J. P. Stevens Boycott and Social Activism in the 1970s." *Journal of American Studies* 39, 3 (2005).

Morrison, Toni. "What the Black Woman Thinks About Women's Lib" (1971). In Keetley and Pettigrew, eds., *Public Women, Public Words.*

Moser, Richard. "Was It the End or Just a Beginning? American Storytelling and the History of the Sixties." In Gosse and Moser, eds., *The World the Sixties Made.*

Nixon, Richard. "School Desegregation: A Free and Open Society." 24 March 1970. In Douglas, ed., *School Busing.*

Oglesby, Carl. "Notes on a Decade Ready for the Dustbin." *Liberation* 14, 5–6 (August–September 1969): 5–19.

Perlstein, Rick. "Who Owns the Sixties?" In Griffith and Baker, eds., *Major Problems in American History Since 1945.*

Raffel, Jeffrey A. and Barry R. Morstain. "Wilmington, Delaware: Merging City and Suburban School Systems." In Charles V. Willie and Susan L. Greenblatt, eds., *Community Politics and Educational Change: Ten School Systems Under Court Order* New York: Longman, 1981.

Robinson, Patricia. "Poor Black Women" (1968). In Keetley and Pettigrew, eds., *Public Women, Public Words*

Schulz, Kristina. "The Women's Movement." In Klimke and Scarloth, eds., *1968 in Europe.*

Schuparr, Kurt. "'A Great White Light': The Political Emergence of Ronald Reagan." In Farber and Roche, eds., *The Conservative Sixties.*

Sears, David O., Carl P. Hensler and Leslie K. Speer. "Whites' Opposition to 'Busing': Self-Interest or Symbolic Politics?" *American Political Science Review* 73, 2 (June 1979).

Severn, Jill. "Women and Draft Resistance: Revolution in the Revolution" (April 1968). In Keetley and Pettegrew, eds., *Public Women, Public Words.*

Shearer, Derek. "CAP: New Breeze in the Windy City." *Ramparts,* 11 October 1973.

Shelley, Martha. "Gay Is Good." 1970. In Blasius and Phelan, eds., *We Are Everywhere.*

Sibalis, Michael. "The Spirit of May '68 and the Origins of the Gay Liberation

Movement in France." In Leslie Joe Frazier and Deborah Cohen, eds., *Gender and Sexuality in 1968: Transformative Politics in the Cultural Imagination.* New York: Palgrave Macmillan, 2009.

Sklar, Kathryn Kish and Thomas Dublin, "How Did the National Women's Conference in Houston in 1977 Shape an Agenda for the Future?" In Sklar and Dublin, *Women and Social Movements in the United States, 1600–2000.*

Smith, Joshua. "Boston: Cradle of Liberty or Separate But Equal?" *Theory into Practice* 17, 1 (February 1978).

Spruill, Marjorie J. "Gender and America's Right Turn." In Schulman and Zelizer, eds., *Rightward Bound.*

Teaford, Jon C." 'King Richard' Hatcher: Mayor of Gary." *Journal of Negro History* 77, 3 (1992).

Tuck, Stephen. "Introduction: Reconsidering the 1970s—The 1960s to a Disco Beat?" *Journal of Contemporary History* 43, 4 (October 2008).

———. " 'We Are Taking Up Where the Movement of the 1960s Left Off': The Proliferation and Power of African American Protest During the 1970s." *Journal of Contemporary History* 43, 4 (October 2008).

Useem, Bert. "Trust in Government and the Boston Anti-Busing Movement." *Western Political Quarterly* 35, 1 (1982).

Vanderford, Marsha L. "Vilification and Social Movements: A Case Study of Pro-Life and Pro-Choice Rhetoric." *Quarterly Journal of Speech* 75, 2 (1989).

Wittman, Carl. "A Gay Manifesto." In Blasius and Phelan, eds., *We Are Everywhere.*

Woliver, Laura R. "Social Movements and Abortion Law." in Costain and McFarland, eds., *Social Movements and American Political Institutions.*

Zeitz, Josh. "Rejecting the Center: Radical Grassroots Politics in the 1970s—Second-Wave Feminism as a Case Study." *Journal of Contemporary History* 43, 4 (October 2008).

Index

Acknowledgments

Since beginning work on *American Patriotism, American Protest* I have run up an assortment of debts—financial, intellectual, and emotional—and it is a particular pleasure to have the opportunity to acknowledge those who have offered help, encouragement and other forms of assistance.

First: the money. Vital research trips to Brown University, Columbia University, and the University of Kansas were made possible thanks to a British Academy Small Grant, while my own department generously provided funds that enabled me to carry out archival work in Cambridge, London, and Madison, Wisconsin. A year's leave during 2006-2007 (funded by the School of History and the Faculty of Arts at the University of Leeds) provided me with the time needed to think, read, research, and begin writing. Peter Agree, editor-in-chief at the University of Pennsylvania Press, has been an enthusiastic champion of this project and I am extremely grateful to him for giving me the opportunity to publish again with Penn, and to his excellent staff for making the process as smooth as possible.

In the course of researching and writing this book I have benefited enormously from the professionalism and expertise of numerous librarians and archivists. At the Brotherton Library, University of Leeds, Jane Saunders has helped me to locate rare books, journals, and other materials. She also secured electronic access to a range of American newspapers and played a critical role in persuading the library to purchase, at some considerable cost, the *Radicalism and Reactionary Politics* microfilm collection—a source that has proved invaluable for this project. Staff at the British Library of Political and Economic Science at the London School of Economics, and the Cambridge University Library, were friendly and helpful (especially Ann Toseland in the UL microform reading room). Tim Engels and his fantastic team at the John Hay Library, Brown University, made researching in the Hall-Hoag collection a genuine pleasure. Similarly, Becky Schulte and her staff at the Kenneth Spencer Research Library, University of Kansas, were exceptionally helpful and welcoming. Becky also arranged for me to meet Laird Wilcox, founder of the Wilcox Collection, which was a real treat. Working at the Wisconsin Historical Society is always a dream, and once again I must thank Harry Miller and Dee Grismund for their assistance. The staff of Columbia University's Rare Book and Manuscript Library and Oral History Research Office answered my many queries, showed enormous patience, and sent materials to me after I had returned to England. The enthusiasm of the graduate students who took Hist5842M (Patriotic Protest: Social Movements and Political Dissent in the United States of America) during 2009 was particularly welcome.

During my visits to the United States I have relied (yet again) on the generous hospitality of friends. In my old stomping ground of Madison, Eric Tadsen and Patrick and Martha Michelson let me stay with them, chauffeured me around, and kept me entertained. John Cornelius and Kerry Taniguchi are fab. Jordi Getman and Frances Mejia have put me up in New York on numerous occasions, shown me the highlights of life in the Big Apple, and been generally wonderful (although that ride on the Cyclone at Coney Island did almost finish me off).

Since the idea behind *American Patriotism, American Protest* emerged during the course of a long and increasingly incoherent conversation with Dominic Sandbrook, I suppose that he deserves some credit, although—since another of the ideas that we discussed (and about which he enthused) involved a comparative study of the leadership qualities of Walt Disney and Oprah Winfrey— perhaps not too much. Dominic has, though, been genuinely interested in this project throughout, and kindly read drafts of chapters and offered valuable suggestions and encouragement. In trips to Cambridge, Andrew and Fran Preston have been excellent hosts and remain good friends.

Tony Badger has been supportive since my time at the University of Cambridge. He helped me secure funding for this project, and in March 2007 gave me the opportunity to present some of my findings at the Boston University-Cambridge University Colloquium on American Politics during the 1970s, which was a thoroughly stimulating event. Jon Bell and Kendrick Oliver also invited me to speak at the Institute for Historical Research in London, where I received useful comments on my work. Robert Cook helped inspire me to become an American historian when I was a student at the University of Sheffield, and has continued to offer valuable advice and encouragement in the years since. Robert very kindly read a complete draft of the manuscript and, in characteristic fashion, offered numerous detailed and critical suggestions that improved the final book no end. I hope that his long-anticipated biography of William Pitt Fessenden makes it to the Silver Screen. Stephen Tuck also took time out from finishing his own book to read through an entire draft of mine, offering welcome encouragement and helpful ideas in just the right measure. Kate Dossett, Katrina Honeyman, Patrick Michelson, and Joe Street also read chapters and discussed their thoughts with me, which was greatly appreciated. Moritz Föllmer provided useful bibliographic advice at a critical time. I'd also like to thank Hugh Wilford for a reader's report that contained generous comments and constructive suggestions for improvements. Rather regrettably, professional convention dictates that, while the credit is shared, I must take sole responsibility for any mistakes.

I'm fortunate in having some great friends who've offered support and encouragement and, much more important, numerous and exciting distractions. Emma Coombs and Shane Doyle, Kate Dossett and Robert Jones, William and Olivia Gould, and Katrina Honeyman all deserve a big shout out, but will have to settle for a mention instead. And word also to Kevin Watson and Tracey Wire, Joe and Ruth Street, Katharine Aylett, John and Michelle Canning, and Nigel Sutcliffe. Most important, I'd like to thank my parents, Brian and Marilyn; my Gran; my sister Emma and brother-in-law Ian; and Angela and David for being fantastic. János, meanwhile, makes my whole world rock.

CPSIA information can be obtained
at www.ICGtesting.com
Printed in the USA
LVHW09*2300040918
589181LV00001B/4/P